Man Enough

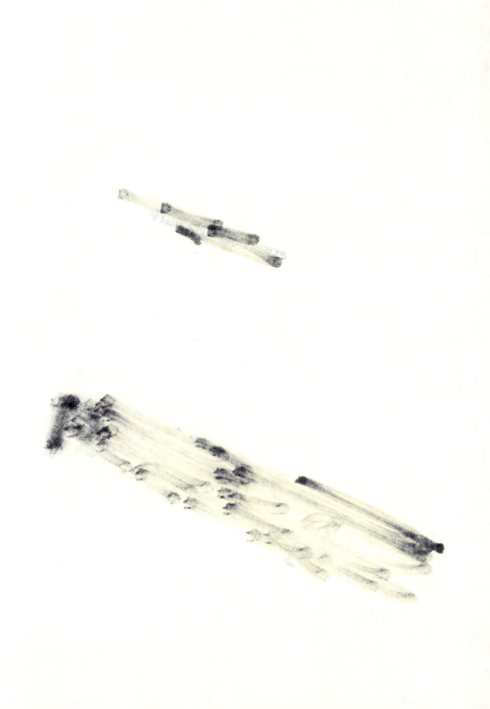

Man Enough

Embodying Masculinities

Victor Jeleniewski Seidler

SAGE Publications
London · Thousand Oaks · New Delhi

First published 1997

 SAGE Publications Ltd
6 Bonhill Street
London EC2A 4PU

SAGE Publications Inc
2455 Teller Road
Thousand Oaks, California 91320

SAGE Publications India Pvt Ltd
32, M-Block Market
Greater Kailash - I
New Delhi 110 048

British Library Cataloguing in Publication data

A catalogue record for this book is available
from the British Library

ISBN 0 7619 5407 4
ISBN 0 7619 5408 2 (pbk)

Library of Congress catalog card number 97-068533

Typeset by Typestudy, Scarborough
Printed in Great Britain by Redwood Books, Trowbridge,
Wiltshire

*For David Boadella, Terry Cooper and
Bob Moore who have each, in their own way,
helped me explore my own path.
With love and appreciation.*

Do not threaten a child. Either punish or forgive them.

Semachot

A father complained to the Besht that his son had forsaken God.
  'What, Rabbi, shall I do?'
  'Love him more than ever,' was the Besht's reply.

Some are born humanized, and others have to humanize themselves slowly.

Czeslaw Milosz

The path to one's own heaven always leads through the voluptuousness of one's own hell.

Nietzsche (1974) The Gay Science, p. 269

If Nietzsche and psychoanalysis have shown that instinctuality, especially in the form of sexuality, extends its reaches up to the highest pinnacles of human spirituality, then we have attempted to show the degree to which spirituality extends its reaches down to the deepest valleys of 'vitality'.

Ludwig Binswanger (1932) Being-in-the-World, p. 2

At stake, was knowing to what extent the effort to think about one's own history can emancipate thought from what it silently thinks, and permit it to think differently.

Michel Foucault (1985) The Use of Pleasure, p. 15

Contents

Preface		xi
Introduction: Hopes, Dreams and Uncertainties		1
1	Identities	15
2	Authorities	32
3	Aspects of Self	41
4	Myths of Manhood	49
5	Wounds	60
6	Initiations	79
7	Transitions	103
8	Experience	119
9	Language	135
10	Emotions and Feelings	153
11	Relationships	165
12	Sexualities	184
13	Responsibilities	197
14	Spiritual Groundings	209
	References	224
	Index	232

Preface

Do such efforts actually lead to a different way of thinking?

Michel Foucault (1985) *The Use of Pleasure*, p. 17

The preface brings the writer face to face with the reader. It comes at the beginning as a way of introducing the work but is often the last thing written. Thinking about the preface takes you back to the beginning, to the early inspirations that inform the writing. Often there is a question that is rarely far from consciousness but cannot readily be put into words. It takes the process of writing sometimes to discover the questions that have been disturbing you. The question 'am I man enough?' is often a question that remains unasked though it hovers at the edge of so many men's conscious minds. Sometimes it is too threatening to put it into words. But it has remained a defining concern for dominant masculinities in the modern West.

Within an Enlightenment vision of modernity masculinity can rarely be taken for granted. It is something that always has to be proved. This creates an uneasy intensity in many men's lives as they can feel haunted by a sense of inadequacy, a sense that they are not good enough, but have to prove that they are 'man enough'. This can force many men into compulsive activity and can make it difficult for men to feel at ease and accepting of themselves. In contemporary Western society this has developed into a crisis of masculinities where traditional forms of affirming male identities are no longer readily available to many men. Robert Bly in *Iron John* saw this in terms of the West having lost a sense of how boys can be initiated into manhood and he was tempted to return to traditional notions of masculinity. I was excited about much of his work and was ready to support it in the face of the disdain that it so often met with. There was a fear of the emotional depths he was revealing.

Often as men we grow up fearful of the revelations of our inner natures, for emotions are deemed to be 'feminine' and so threatening to male identities. But this blocks men in developing an inner connection with themselves and often creates a gap between the ways men might be feeling inside and the ways they present themselves even to those closest to them. This fear of intimacy can make it difficult for men with diverse class, 'race' and ethnic identities to establish open and loving relationships. But I was also uneasy with the directions working with men was taking under the influence of Bly. It could easily set up new ways for men to feel inadequate and not 'man enough'. It also threatened to minimize what men could learn from feminism and from gay men. I thought that we needed different visions of masculinity and a different sense of how boys could grow up to be men.

I started writing this work when my son Daniel was eleven and daughter Lily was six. I was concerned with the ways he was to be initiated into manhood but I was also concerned with my place as a father in Lily's development into womanhood. Initiation seemed within the modern world to have less to do with an event, though Daniel's Barmitzvah at 13 did mark an important entrance into the public world and his assuming particular responsibilities for himself. It meant an important step in becoming his own person, in being able to take moral decisions for himself. But as he acknowledged, it was part of a process into manhood. As a father it was a matter of sustaining a meaningful relationship with him which could validate the changes he was going through. It is a relational vision of initiation which does not separate out the psychological from the social and political. It opens up new ground, which helps to connect the personal with the theoretical. Too often accounts of men and masculinities have insisted upon separating the personal from the structural, so finding it difficult to illuminate the lived contradictions of men's experiences.

I am writing this preface on Daniel's fifteenth birthday, 15 years after some of the experiences around his birth which I share. It is difficult to reflect upon experiences without unwittingly generalizing from a particular experience. Some of the anguish, frustration and difficulty so easily gets lost and you can feel the inadequacies of memory and the ease with which stories come to assume a life of their own. I wanted to find a voice in which I could share more of my own learning whilst also opening up ways of thinking about the predicament of contemporary masculinities. Since an Enlightenment vision of modernity has been set within the terms of dominant masculinity, this involved unsettling rationalist forms of social theory and philosophy. It called for different ways of thinking and feeling. Somehow we need to link new psychologies, informed by psychotherapy but not limited by its disembodied visions of mental life, with social theories that have learned from feminism and ecology to reinstate emotions and feelings as sources of knowledge. Discontented with some of the paths opened up within postmodern thinking, I wanted to learn from its more complex notions of the fluidity and fragmentation of identities while refusing the erasure of emotional and spiritual depth and experience.

I have had the love and support of many men and women who are also struggling with the issues in this book. Many of the ideas have been developed with others in the context of different groups. In the 1980s the diverse responses of men to feminism were sharpened in the collective practice that developed around the magazine *Achilles' Heel* that served as an important catalyst for men's writing and politics. There was an important conversation between politics and therapy as well as between straight and gay men. More recently I know how much I have learnt from being part of the Men for Men group at Spectrum, London. It has been a constant source of insight and support through the difficult process of writing. It constantly helps to ground my experience and values.

I appreciate the support that I have had in completing the manuscript. Anna, my partner for 20 years, has watched it grow from its inception. She has constantly challenged me to be more honest and critical in my thinking and to appreciate the significance of a sensitivity and intuition so often devalued within the academy. The Gender Studies group in the Department of Sociology at Goldsmiths, Ross Gill, Caroline Ramazanoglu and Fran Tonkiss have provided crucial support. The many students who have taken my course Knowledge, Science and Nature have been a constant source of inspiration in their search for more meaningful forms of social theory. Steven Frosh and Mary Maynard provided helpful remarks for the rewriting of the manuscript and Chris Rojek believed in the project at a moment when it really mattered. I also remember crucial conversations with David Boadella, Larry Blum, Terry Cooper, Mike Dalton, Sheila Ernst, Carol Gilligan, Lucy Goodison, Michael Ignatieff, Michael Kimmel, Paul Morrison, Piers Partridge, Sally Potter, Janet Ransom, Joanna Ryan, Janet Sayers, Dennis Scott, Carol and Hilmar Schonauer, Tony Seidler, Rob Senior and Angelika Strickner.

Over the years I have also learnt a great deal from the English Group that has worked with Bob Moore in Denmark. It has enriched my understandings of processes of growth and development and helped me recognize what was involved in establishing a deeper connection with aspects of ourselves. It taught me a great deal about the emotional and spiritual life of the body and about the connections between psychotherapy and healing. Specifically it has helped me rethink the relationship between beliefs, emotions and the heart connection established through feeling. These groups provided me with the support of a spiritual community that has sustained me in my thinking and relationships. They have challenged me to rethink the Eurocentrism of much social theory, through giving me ways of taking seriously different Eastern and Western spiritual traditions. In their different ways they have shown in practice what is involved in treating the body and feelings as sources of knowledge.

I have also learnt from alternative forms of psychotherapy the importance of open and honest communication with partners and with children. The place of honesty and truthfulness is rarely acknowledged within social theory, which has yet to focus upon the difficulties of living a just life within unjust social relations. This is also part of the challenge of feminism and sexual politics. In terms of psychotherapy the work of Virginia Satir (1989) reminds us of the importance of honest communication. This was not easy for me to learn since I had so little of it in my own childhood. But if changes are to be made we have to make them for ourselves, for otherwise we will unwittingly relate to our children in the ways we were related to. This is something Anna has constantly challenged me with. Daniel and Lily have grown up in this process and have shown an equal patience as I struggled to complete this work. Sometimes it feels as if they have learnt a great deal more for they both have a wisdom and a clarity that I did not know at their age. In many ways they have been teachers too, for their experience also finds its way into these pages.

In the months that I was bringing the manuscript to completion three men died who had in different ways been encouraging and supportive to me, though sometimes they did not even know it. Lily and Bee Davis had been helpful in their enthusiasm for some of the themes, and they suggested a title *Of Boys and Men*. Sadly Bee died in August 1996. He had been there as a supportive older man from my earliest boyhood days. Rabbi Arthur Katz had also been there as a source of advice and as a link with a generation before the Second World War. He constantly warned against a narrow materialism. Along with the death of Bee Davis I was also to hear of the death of Rabbi Hugo Grynn who had in countless ways, as a survivor of Auschwitz and as a man with an enduring sense of ethics, been an inspiration to so many in Anglo-Jewry. In very different ways these men served as mentors, as guides in a difficult world. This book is also dedicated to them.

As we open up a dialogue between different generations of men, so we can begin to learn from each other. We can respect differences and know that we are struggling with diverse masculinities, locked in relationships of power and dominance with men and women. As different men explore their inherited masculinities and discover their own voices, they can begin to share their pains as well as joys, their sufferings as well as blessings. As Tony Bayfield (1996) recalls, 'Hugo's prophetic picture was a globe composed of numerous beautiful gardens, cultivated by the many faith, ethnic, and cultural groups of which the world is made up. Each person should be able to wander peacefully and admire the other gardens, whilst always returning, enriched, to their own.' As men living in relation to diverse masculinities we also know where the garden is in which we can find peace and nourishment. We also need to learn that reaching out to others for support is not a sign of weakness, but rather a source of strength, love and solidarity.

Victor Jeleniewski Seidler
Dalston, London

Introduction: Hopes, Dreams and Uncertainties

Nobody can build you the bridge over which you must cross the river of life, nobody but you alone.

Nietzsche (1983) *Untimely Meditations*, p. 165

Hidden Anxieties

In the West heterosexual men have responded to the challenges of feminism and gay liberation in different ways, but they have left many men feeling uncertain and confused about what it means 'to be a man' as we approach the millennium. There seems to be a crisis of masculinities initiated through the feminist questioning of traditional forms of male power and superiority that have been structured into the very terms of an Enlightenment vision of modernity. Often as white middle class heterosexual men we have grown up to feel self-assured, at least on the surface, for the modern world has been very much made in our image. Men often expected to be the centre of their social worlds. It can be hard to accept a period of uncertainty and change. The 1980s witnessed a backlash against feminism in the United States and Europe and the reassertion of traditional forms of masculinity. For younger men this has shown itself in a laddish culture which takes refuge in irony whilst glorifying sexist behaviour.

A dominant Western vision of modernity identified a white, heterosexual masculinity with a notion of reason, radically separated from nature. As men learnt to identify with their reason so they were expected to legislate what is best for others as well as for themselves. Men were supposed to know what they wanted and needed. Not only were they the rulers of their own lives but they had the power to rule the lives of women and children. But often this has meant that, as heterosexual men, we had to *hide* our own anxieties and uncertainties, which we might only dare to whisper to our sexual partners in the dark of the night. At some level we recognized that we were less honest with ourselves than we could be. But the culture did not value truth and honesty and often we grew up to hide what we were feeling, for emotions could so easily threaten male identities. As men we can feel trapped into living out ideals that are not of our own making. It can be as if we have betrayed an inner knowledge of ourselves, in order to prove when we were still young boys that we could be 'man enough'.

The restructuring of democratic capitalist societies in the West in the 1980s and 1990s has often worked to undermine traditional sources of male identity. There are far fewer traditional working class jobs that could sustain men in their positions as breadwinners. Fathers cannot sustain their authority within working class families through being able to pass on a job in, for instance, shipbuilding or mining. Their sons can feel resentful at being left at the mercy of the educational system which itself cannot promise future employment. There are no longer the job opportunities around that can sustain a sense of ambition and self-worth. Not only as a wage earner but also as a father or family provider, young men can feel lost with the break-up of family relationships and the undermining of traditional sources of masculine identities. This has left many young men feeling vulnerable and threatened.

There is a widespread and growing feeling that as men we are living in a radically different world from our fathers. There is a feeling of cultural dislocation as young men can no longer rely upon what their fathers might have taught them. There are no longer the same certainties about what it means for a boy to make a transition to manhood. Often there is silence and unspoken resentment in the relationships between fathers and sons, as young men with different class, 'racial' and ethnic backgrounds feel that their fathers were not there for them emotionally and that now it is too late to establish a relationship. At the same time young men can feel strangely tied to their fathers, wanting at some level to feel closer to them but unable to reach out because of their hidden resentments. There is also a widespread feeling that as heterosexual and gay men we want to be able to relate more equally and openly to our partners and that we want to have different relationships with children than those we knew with our fathers.

Positioning Men

The first generation of heterosexual men who responded to the women's movement in the early 1970s often felt uneasy about a dominant heterosexual masculinity which had served to oppress and subordinate women and gay men. They were concerned with the injustices and the sufferings that were caused by men. They felt that masculinity had to be deconstructed because it was part of the problem and it seemed as if it could not be part of any solution. The focus on the development of an anti-sexist men's politics where it was clear that men needed to take a clear stand against male violence, rape and sexual harassment of women. The misery and sufferings that were created by a dominant masculinity had to be undone if there was to be any chance of greater gender equality. It seemed only right for men to give primary attention to the sufferings of women, for there was the major injustice and oppression. This has been a strong tendency, especially where men have been working with violence against women.

From the beginning there has also been a tendency towards men's liberation, which has felt easier thinking about ways that men can change. In liberal terms it thought of gender as role and it was ready to argue that as women were limited by the expectations of their role, so also were men limited by their roles. As women should be free to work in the public sphere, so men should be free to be more involved in the private sphere of domestic work and childcare. Helpful in being able to focus upon the experience of men, notions of men's liberation were unable to illuminate the structured character of gender relations of power. They tended to slip into a false parallelism between men and women and tended to avoid the power and violence that was often structured into gender relations.

In England the journal *Achilles' Heel* sought some kind of compromise between these positions, developing a third position that could recognize the structured relations of power whilst at the same time talk about the importance of redefining masculinities. It refused to theorize masculinity as exclusively a relationship of power and insisted on being able to illuminate the contradictions that men often felt in relation to dominant masculinities. Men were not to be identified with their masculinities, but we also needed to think about the contradictions in men's lived experience. We needed to take seriously what men felt and thought about themselves, rather than assuming that we had to confront them immediately with the power that a patriarchal society had provided them. This involved listening to men and allowing them to *voice* their experience in their own terms. It brought a recognition that men were not supposed to have emotions and feelings, for these were deemed to be 'feminine' and so a threat to dominant heterosexual male identities.

Achilles' Heel contained a diversity of different writings from a variety of different positions It illuminated the contradictions that many men felt between the powerless feelings they might have in their personal lives and the power they might have in the larger society. It also showed the hidden injuries of diverse masculinities, as men were struggling to live up to images of themselves, partly out of fear of being put down or rejected. Drawing upon the experience of different masculinities, it soon recognized that there was no single homogenized vision of masculinity that all men felt they had to aspire to. At the same time with modernity there was a dominant masculinity that very much set the terms for the relationships of power between different men and different masculinities. We needed to analyse the power relations between different men, not just between men and women.

Personal/Theoretical/Political

As with early feminist work there was often a tension between the richness of these first person accounts and the terms in which they were to be theorized. The notion that 'the personal is political' was inspiring but it was difficult to think carefully about the ways it transformed classical forms of social

theory and philosophy. At one level it challenged an assumption shared by
Marx, Weber and Durkheim that for oppression and injustice to be 'real' it
must take place within the public realm of politics. It was in the public
sphere that we had the play of power. Sufferings that took place within the
personal realm were taken to be 'private' and a matter of personal relations.
It was in this way that feminists provided a crucial challenge to the
masculinist terms of modernity, though this has often been missed when the
discussions around postmodernity have focused upon whether feminism
assumes a unified notion of 'woman' and so of a subject who is oppressed
and can be liberated. Sadly some postmodern feminism misses the point in
its rejection of a discourse of oppression.

In the 1990s we have witnessed a fear of the personal and this has gone
hand in hand with the rejection of experience as a theoretical category. Too
often this is dismissed as a form of humanism and essentialism, before we
have effectively grasped what these positions involve. As theoretical feminism has taken its place within the academy it has often lost connection with
its activist and political roots. At some level there seems to be a tension
between the 'personal' and the 'theoretical', as if to think in personal terms,
rather than grounding what we have to say, somehow proves a lack of theoretical sophistication. Hopefully there are some signs of a shift and a recognition that we need ways of taking seriously both the text and the voice.
Within the dominant terms of discourse theory there was a clear privileging
of the text and a sense that we can only know experience through the terms
in which it is articulated in a text. The later Wittgenstein helped me to
appreciate the importance of voice and relation, and this helps provide a
different reading of feminism from the emphasis on text and discourse
which was influenced by the turn to Saussure.

In terms of the development of men's politics in the 1990s these tendencies expressed themselves in different terms. There was an attempt to marginalize the complexity of the *Achilles' Heel* work through arguing that it
presented an attempt to reduce the political to the personal. This was a
theme in Lynne Segal's *Slow Motion* (1990) as well as in R.W. Connell's
Gender and Power (1987) which it tended to follow theoretically. There was
an attempt to treat masculinity as a set of social practices and to theorize a
hegemonic masculinity. Both these works were important contributions that
did a great deal to open up the discussion of different masculinities and to
contextualize them institutionally and practically. The emphasis was upon
masculinities but it was not open to the contradictory nature of men's lives
and their complex relationships *with* diverse masculinities. Rather it casti-
gated these concerns as 'personal' or, as in Connell's later work *Masculinities* (1996), as 'therapeutic'. Somehow we had ended up with reinstating a
distinction between the 'personal' and the 'political'.

This also meant that we could not think about how boys had grown up
into manhood and the transitions that had taken place in the process. We
might be able to study a diversity of different masculinities in the present,
but we would find it difficult to grasp how these men had become the men

that they are. This also reflects another difference between this kind of theoretical work and my *Rediscovering Masculinity* (1989), where I drew upon the *Achilles' Heel* work. The idea was that though men had power they were also limited and in some ways oppressed by dominant masculinities. The lives of men were impoverished through the disconnections they had to make with their bodies and emotions. Within an Enlightenment vision of modernity, men were expected to be independent and self-sufficient. Emotional needs were a sign of weakness and therefore were often suppressed as a threat to male identities.

It was in the context of consciousness-raising groups that men discovered a space in which they could share more of their lives with each other. Rather than feel threatened by the closeness of other men who might take advantage of any sign of vulnerability, they could learn to draw support from each other. In their exploration of differences between them they could also discover what they shared in their experience as men. Sometimes these were not easy contexts for men, who often found it easier to talk about and intellectualize their experience rather than share it. At some level men often felt locked out of their own experience, trapped as observers of what was going on for them. In part this is what encouraged an interest in experiential forms of psychotherapy which could help some men break through their isolation and loneliness which too often they kept to themselves.

The argument against attempts to connect the 'personal' with the 'political' was that this has to be an attempt to reduce the political to the personal. What is more, masculinities were not impoverished or limited but rather were varied and offered men opportunities and possibilities that were denied to women. But these structural accounts of masculinity often retained traces of an orthodox Marxism which found it difficult to illuminate the identification of a dominant masculinity with self-denial, with a Protestant moral culture. There were difficulties in exploring contradictions in men's lives and the ways that men *could* change. While there was a recognition that men could change, there was little sympathy and understanding of the ways this could happen or the kinds of confrontations it would involve men in with themselves. Rather there was a disdain for therapy and a dismissal of emotional work as 'therapeutic'. Too often if sustained some of the weakness of the sexual politics of the 1970s, which otherwise it wanted to question in its moralism and its sense that people could change through will and determination alone.

Some of these differences show in notions of how to work with men who are violent. Some men deeply identified with anti-sexist men's politics think that the first step is to confront men with consequences of their violence towards women. The idea is that it is often through guilt that men will change. Other men have also recognized that it is important to establish links with the men themselves through an understanding of what experiences in their own boyhoods have made them into the violent men they are. Men have also to come to terms with their own experience as men and the ways they were treated in their families. If a boy has been treated violently

this is often the way he will go on to relate to others. The links between violence and masculinities are crucial to explore here. Of course it is absolutely
crucial that men stop their violent behaviours towards women. It is also
important that men come to terms with their own experiences as part of a
process of change. This is emotional work that men have to do for themselves since others cannot do it for them.

Men have to come to terms with their power in relation to women and
children. They have to question notions of male superiority that they have
grown up to take very much for granted. But as I argued in *Recreating
Sexual Politics* (1991a) it is also important for men to question the practice
of self-denial they have grown into within a Protestant moral culture. The
notion that men are 'bad' and that male sexuality is 'animal' are part of the
dominant culture. Rather than help to question this, feminism unwittingly
tended to reinforce these notions. It left many heterosexual men feeling bad
about themselves, as if the impossible task they had to attempt was to
abandon or forsake their masculinities. This was a further process of *denial*
that could leave men feeling that women always had morality on their side
because they were oppressed as a gender. Feeling guilty, men often withdrew into a sullen silence, unable to voice their own needs and wants. This
reinforced the notion that men should not have needs and that to give time
and attention to themselves as men is a form of self-indulgence.

Men and Masculinities

This was a weakness in some of the anti-sexist men's responses to feminism.
Men were often left feeling uneasy and confused about their masculinities.
They found it hard to define themselves as men. Sometimes they identified
too closely with the sufferings and pain of women, feeling angry at their
fathers and with men in general. It is as if they did not want to be men at
all. This coincided in the culture with a widespread feeling that men were
useless and that women could live their lives well without them. Women had
found their diverse voices and had a clarity and self-definition that many
men silently envied. But there was also resentment and a feeling of guilt, at
some level, for the ways that men, including fathers, were being portrayed
within the larger culture.

The publication of Robert Bly's *Iron John* (1990) resonated with this
moment, both in its exploration of the ways some men seemed to have forsaken and lost a sense of themselves as men in their identification with
feminism, and also in its expressions of anger at the ways that men were
increasingly being demeaned in media portrayals. It reached towards a
much broader spectrum of men than any previous men's book. It was taken
up by many men who felt themselves to be unrecognized in the portrayals
of feminism. It was also taken up as part of a backlash to feminism by many
men who had identified with men's rights movements, especially in the
United States. They were angry at the power they had lost to feminism and

they were concerned to reinstate their rights as men. They often argued that gender divisions were based in nature. In some of the latest expressions in the 1990s, such as the Promise Keepers, allied to the Christian right, it was argued that if men recognized they had forsaken their responsibilities and so also the promises they had made as husbands and fathers, then women could return to their traditional duties as wives and mothers. If men were to be encouraged to become more emotionally involved with their children, they were also to be clear in their position as authorities within the family.

In many ways it was Bly's discussion of fathers, and his sense that American men carried a silent hunger for their fathers, that touched men most deeply. He articulated in the clearest terms what men had lost because their fathers had been too involved in the 1950s and 1960s in the public sphere of work where male identities are sustained. Men felt that not only were their fathers not there to initiate them into manhood, but at some level they were *not* entitled to their anger about this absence because it was unreasonable when their fathers were working hard, not for themselves, but for their families. In this way Bly challenged the traditional form of the family as he also questioned the ways men had lost their spontaneity in their identification with corporate America. In the generations since the industrial revolution, according to Bly, there had been a weakening of contact between fathers and sons. In some ways boys were left to grow up on their own, at the mercy of the TV and popular culture.

In contrast to the anti-sexist men's movement Bly's work, along with the work of James Hillman and Michael Meade, set the terms for a mythopoetic men's movement. They shared a vivid sense that men needed the love and support of each other and that if your father was not there to hold and contain you, then this nourishment could be given by other men who would be there for you emotionally. It recognizes, as some of the writing in *Achilles' Heel* in England had done before, that it was crucial to respect and honour the needs that men have and which they have learnt to deny within modernity. Sometimes we can be locked into an expectation that our fathers might change and eventually give us the nourishment and support that we have wanted all along. But often it is more important to recognize that we can change, even if our fathers do not. Bly shares a sense with others in the mythopoetic movement that Western societies have failed in their initiation of young men into manhood. We have failed to contain and to support young men in their growth and development.

To do this we need to challenge the dominant conceptions of masculinity that have helped to shape an Enlightenment vision of modernity. We have to question the dominant ideal that men have to be independent and self-sufficient if we are to establish more equal gender relations. I share a sense that masculinities need to be redefined so that men can recognize their own emotional needs and learn to communicate more equally and openly within their intimate relationships. But I think that the traditional conception of masculinity that Bly often seems to offer needs to be *revisioned* so that we can *also* recognize how our masculinities are learnt in relations with women and children too. I want to help to open up a conversation between an anti-sexist men's movement and the mythopoetic movement, which so often seem to talk past each other. I want to open up a different path which, whilst learning from these different traditions, establishes a different form of psychopolitics. Rather than find ourselves locked into separate camps I think it is important to envision a different sense of direction.

In the 1990s we have seen a general withdrawal from the media conception of the 'new man' who was in many ways driven by the discovery of a new market. Young men wanted to be more involved with their children and were concerned to negotiate a more equal relationship with their partners. This media construction was quickly denigrated as 'wimpish', so bringing to the surface the fear of emotions and their identification with softness and femininity. It was difficult to break the cultural homophobia which argued that to be emotional was to be 'feminine'. In the context of the economic crisis that had hit the West in the 1980s there was an intensification of work for those who were employed and there was a reassertion of a work ethic that could be applied to men and also to women who had newly joined these workplaces. In some offices you could not admit to having a cold because this only proved that you could not 'take the pace'. Rather there was a recovery of a traditional work ethic that left young men and women in their twenties and thirties competing with each other for the few jobs available. If this meant an equality in relationships it was often at the expense of putting off having children till a time that never seemed to come.

Often middle class men who had expressed an intention to be more involved with their children as fathers found that they did not have the time or energy left after work. It was in this context that a reassertion of a traditional masculinity, also in part offered by Bly, seemed to be appealing. It seemed to offer a way of assuaging some of the guilt and broken promises. Sometimes men even felt the need to leave their heterosexual partners in order to spend time recovering a 'lost masculinity'. Within the context of the mythopoetic movement there was talk of a deep masculinity to which men needed to reconnect if they were to have a chance of being initiated into manhood. We need to explore the appeal that some of these myths have for men. There seems to be a resonance for many men from diverse backgrounds with the idea of being initiated into manhood, or rather a sense that this has not happened for them in the West. This seems to be experienced as some kind of loss that seems different from the traditional masculinist idea that as a man you are always having to prove your masculinity and always open to the feeling of not being 'man enough'.

Traditionally it was through war that men affirmed their masculinities, and it is striking that people like Robert Bly in the United States and Robin Skynner in England can talk more unproblematically about masculinity, being the generation that fought in the Second World War. It has made a difference to the ways they have felt challenged by feminism. In some ways it gives them a security in their male identities that a younger generation of men might not be able to have. In other ways it can also make them less sensitive to the challenges of feminism and the kind of revisions of manhood that it calls for. This is not simply to meet the demands of feminism but it is what men in their diverse masculinities need for their own growth and development.

Initiating Men

Bly makes men wonder if they can properly father their children if they have not been fathered themselves. Rather than simply blaming the mother, as Freud does, Bly is also prepared to bring older men to account. He has been able to touch men's lives through the recognition he gives to their unmet needs. But *Iron John* is too ready to assume that feminism has had a negative impact upon men through 'feminizing' them, as if the task is to return men to a 'lost' masculinity. In many ways this remains a traditional account, though it is very insightful and moving in its reading of the Grimm's fairy story about the boy who has to steal the key from underneath his mother's pillow before being carried off into the forest to go through a process of initiation into manhood. The different stages are engaged with in a revealing way, showing that young men have to confront themselves and their emotional histories as part of the process of growing into manhood. In many ways it is a striking challenge to an Enlightenment vision of modernity that suggests, as I shall argue, that young men should learn, in Kant's terms, to 'rise above' their animal natures so that they can prove themselves to be independent and self-sufficient rational selves.

But the story carries its own limitations, as I shall show, for it sees the process of initiation in traditional terms as the moving of the boy from the mother's house to the father's house. Though it is crucial to recognize what older men can pass on to younger men and the needs that can be fulfilled in this relationship, it is important not to sustain Freud's notion that masculinity remains a negative notion, defined against the mother's femininity. The structure of Bly's work, even though this is not his explicit intention, serves to reinforce this traditional notion which makes love, caring and compassion seemingly 'feminine' qualities. It reinforces the notion that to be a man is not to be a woman. This is what sustains homophobia as an integral part of heterosexual masculinities. It creates a fear of intimacy and contact, for men so easily feel that their male identities will disintegrate. So it is that men feel threatened in their relationship with themselves for they fear the revelations of their natures. I do not want to know my sadness, let alone my fear, if it is going to threaten my sense of male identity. So it is that men learn to suppress so much of their emotional lives.

In the 1990s when there is so much uncertainty in relation to work and when so many of the traditional supports of a masculine identity have been eroded across different social classes, 'race' and ethnic identities, it is hardly surprising if there is so much fear of emotions and personal life. Rather, feeling threatened, many men have to tough it out, and the hard body and the hours spent in the gym have become the proving ground of so many contemporary masculinities. If men cannot prove themselves as breadwinners, and if the breakdown of sexual relationships means that men cannot prove themselves as fathers when so many women are choosing to have children on their own, there is a crisis of masculinities. Men take refuge in their own bodies. They become impatient with any talk of emotional life for they need to protect themselves against accusations of being 'wimps'. When men feel so generally under threat, it is often difficult for them to be open emotionally and ready to change. They more easily withdraw into themselves.

A younger generation of men who have grown up in the 1970s are less concerned with working out a relationship with feminism. They know the difficulties of these concerns and want to explore their inherited forms of masculinity in relation to their experience as men. For men in their early thirties there seems to be a desire to avoid being too self-absorbed which they identify with women. They do not want to be obsessed, as they see it, with how they look and how they dress and with how they should behave. Yet this is part of a postmodern uncertainty where style has assumed a new significance for men and where it often seems all-important to be up with the latest styles and music. In part as a reaction to this we also have the reassertion of a 'new lad' culture which allows young men to return to the traditional pursuits of alcohol, sex and football. As first formulated by Sean O'Hagan in *Arena* in 1991, the new lad was 'a hybrid: a would-be New Man who can't quite shake off his outmoded but snug-fitting laddishness'. Back then he saw it as 'a tentatively positive reaction to three decades of feminism'. But it has developed differently, as O'Hagan readily admitted in 1996: 'the philosophy of Lad is pretty sad: the same old beer-stained, sexist, macho posturing by men who should know better' (p. 21).

If we are to revision men then we have to recognize the importance of opening up a conversation between different generations of men. It is not enough simply to rediscover old myths, however telling they might be of conflicts we face in the present; we also have to create stories of our own as we share what we have learnt with each other. Unable to appreciate what men could learn from feminism, Bly was also silent on what men could learn about their masculinities from their relationships with women and children. If there is a time when men need to be together on their own, there is also a time when we can learn from women, from gay men and from children. We also have to recognize and respect the different paths that different men will want to take in relation to their different histories and different masculinities. I know that as a Jewish man I have had to come to terms with the horrors of the Shoa and the post-war stories that said that Jews went 'like lambs to the slaughter'. These stories hurt and they marked us as we grew up. African-American men and black British men have had their own histories to come to terms with. We can learn some important lessons from the path that Bly shares with us, but we have to learn our own lessons, recognizing that this is one path amongst many. While learning from *Iron John* I will also point out false directions that the text can tempt us into. Bly has to take responsibility for some of the misreadings, especially in the ease with which the book can be interpreted to sustain the anti-feminist arguments of men's rights.

It is too easy and tempting for men to think of themselves as warriors. This language can so easily be misconstrued and taken out of context. It is much harder for men to stay grounded in the conflicts of their everyday relationships to do with who is to put the children to bed and who is to do the washing up. Bly understands so well the ease with which men seek to escape and withdraw, or as he puts it so well, 'ascend' away from themselves. It is also true that if we have a particular responsibility as fathers towards our sons, we have an equal responsibility towards our daughters. We need to discover myths that can also help to illuminate the relationships fathers can have with their daughters. This is also part of what it means to grow into our responsibilities as fathers.

The mythical language which the mythopoetic movement draws up can help men from diverse backgrounds into a deeper connection with themselves. It helps to challenge the rationalism of late modernity and the notion that men should be able to guide their lives through reason alone. As I argued in *Unreasonable Men* (1994), it is the identification of a dominant white heterosexual masculinity with a conception of reason radically separated from nature which serves to sustain an 'unreasonable' form of reason. It serves to disconnect men from their bodies and emotional lives which are deemed to be part of nature. It also fosters an emotional suppression as men learn to split from their emotions and feelings as subjective and irrational forms of unreason which can only threaten their male identities. A dominant masculinity learns to identify with reason as a mark of its superiority. So it is that men often have to know best. But this tends to foster an ungrounded and disembodied conception of knowledge which is blind to its own very emotional attachment to reason.

Learning to disdain emotions and feelings as sources of knowledge, men often distance themselves from their own emotional lives. This produces its own forms of dishonesty as men learn to deny what is going on for them emotionally and to recognize only what they 'should' feel in the situation. Since men are left with an externalized relationship to self, it can be hardly surprising that rationalist forms of social theory often dominate, even within postmodern theory. As identities are treated as the effects of discourse, we find that the suppression of interiority, of an inner relationship to self, that has characterized an Enlightenment vision of modernity, continues within much postmodern theory. There is a disdain for the personal and for the emotional, as necessarily being traces of an untheorized essentialism.

Postmodern Masculinities

Postmodern theories have often focused upon the decentring of the Cartesian subject. We learn to think that where modernity was characterized by a unified conception of self with a given nature, within postmodernity the self has been fragmented and exists in pieces. Freedom lies in being able to create identities out of whatever discourses are culturally available to us. So it is that we 'are' what we present ourselves to be. There is no inner nature that we are seeking to give expression to. There is no truth about ourselves that is waiting to be discovered beneath the surface of appearances. There is no longer a sense in which we can be false to ourselves, for there is no truth that can be waiting to be expressed. Within a postmodern world we have to celebrate the realm of appearances, for we 'are' what we choose to show to others. This is the importance of style and image. We do not have to worry about betraying some inner knowledge we have of ourselves, for this was a fiction, like any other, that happened to characterize modernity. In this context truth is whatever is articulated within prevailing discourses. Honesty too often becomes a form of self-presentation.

As I argue it, feminism and ecology provide their own critiques of an Enlightenment vision of modernity and so promise a different vision of the postmodern. I hope to show that modernity is *already* cast within the terms of a dominant white heterosexual masculinity and this is reflected in the splits between reason and nature, mind and body, thought and emotions, matter and spirit. A disenchanted vision of modernity goes together with an objectivist conception of personal identity which is also reflected in dominant schools of psychology and social theory. A disembodied conception of reason and knowledge goes hand in hand with a disembodied conception of the person. As the later Wittgenstein understood, these disconnections shape inherited forms of thinking and feeling so that it is only through grasping how our experiences are shaped through these dualities that we can begin a process of change and transformation. This is the intention of the early parts of the *Philosophical Investigations* (1958), to show us how within modernity we live these Cartesian disconnections. I try to take this further through showing the links with a dominant white heterosexual masculinity.

Recovering a language of myth can help us connect to different levels of experience. This is one of the promises of Robert Bly's *Iron John*. It is not an easy text and it works at different levels but it does have a stunning awareness of how men can also suffer through these disconnections. At the same time it is easy to disdain this kind of work, for we are not used to linking the personal with the theoretical. Within the academy we can feel uneasy and embarrassed by the personal which is too easy derided as subjective and anecdotal. But if we are to challenge the false universalism that allows men to legislate for others, before they have learnt to speak more personally for themselves, we have to explore ways in which dominant masculinities can begin to recognize themselves within their own experience. We have to be ready to question a dominant masculinity's relationship to language and we have to recognize language as an important source of male power.

If we are to make space for different voices, as Carol Gilligan (1982) has argued in relationship to women's moral voice of care and concern, we have to be ready to confront a masculine fear of the personal and the emotional. As we seek embodied forms of psychology and social theory we have to learn to speak and write in different ways. This is a risky task and I am very aware of the difficulties in using 'we' in the text. This is not in the hope of drawing upon some shared commonalities, but in the full respect for differences that we can also sometimes speak across. In many ways this remains a personal text in which I share more of my own experience and process. This is partly because this is the way I have been able to make some of these theoretical connections and because I want to explore different ways of theorizing. It shares part of what I have had to go through in order to discover my own voice.

I have shared a particular middle class, heterosexual, Jewish masculinity and the tensions and contradictions that this has created for me. Bly's work shares a very different kind of masculinity. I think there is a shared sense that if we are to feel more defined in our identities, then in a postmodern world we have to conceive of freedom and responsibility in different terms. We need to revision the postmodern as we learn to revision masculinities, for otherwise we remain trapped unwittingly within the rationalist terms of a dominant masculinity. Rather than feeling trapped into proving ourselves in terms not of our own making, we have to give voice to a whole range of different masculinities. This is a process that is beginning to happen, though it has taken years to break the silence of men in the face of feminist challenges.

Rather than escape into identities that we are constantly recreating, freedom involves learning how to confront where we have come from, both historically and emotionally. This involves sometimes challenging the terms of psychoanalysis and psychotherapy which can insist on treating identities within the context of childhood experience alone. In revisioning the transition from boyhood to manhood, we will also be recognizing the need to rethink childhood. As we learn to treat the body and emotions as forms of knowledge, so we begin to question the rationalist terms of modernity. Bly can help us to reinstate an embodied language of myth, though I question the terms in which he does this. He shares a sense that, as men, we cannot avoid our histories and seek refuge in a future but also have to descend into the darkness of grief and pain. But Bly is far less clear about relationships of class, ethnic and sexual power which continue to separate men from each other, let alone the power that so often disfigures men's relationships with women and children. However, we can still learn from the depth of some of his psychological insight.

But if we are to face some of these issues in creating more equal relationships with women and children as well as celebrating gay and lesbian identities, we have to be ready to tell a different story. We have to be prepared to make revisions in the story that Bly presents and the terms in which he tells it, as part of a process of revisioning men. If heterosexual men are to learn from the challenges of feminism and gay liberation then they must be ready to explore their inherited masculinities and the relations of power they embody. Being ready to question the impartial, objective and universal voice of reason which a dominant masculinity so readily identifies with, we have to learn to discover our own more personal and emotionally connected voices. As we learn to listen to ourselves in different ways, so we can learn to be more responsive to others.

Over the years many men have been uneasy with feminism, feeling that they have so often been reduced to silence, watchful about what they could say or do. Rather than explore their inherited masculinities, men have often withdrawn into a sullen and resentful silence. When this breaks through the surface it expresses itself as anti-feminism and as a claim for men's rights. We need to be able to engage critically with some of these movements, learning what draws men into their ranks. To do this we have to grasp the contradictions in men's experience and be ready to challenge feminist notions which would identify masculinity exclusively as a relationship of power. We have to be ready to listen to what men have to say about themselves so that we do not discount their feelings of anxiety, frustration and powerlessness. This needs to be part of a critical engagement with men in their relationships with diverse masculinities. It has taken time for heterosexual men to appreciate that sexism and gender politics are not simply issues for women and gay men.

1
Identities

A Time of Change

Since the 1960s there has been a growing realization that traditional forms of sexual relationships based upon an unequal division of labour and responsibilities cannot be legitimated. This has been sustained by a central challenge of feminism which has meant that women with diverse identities of class, 'race' and ethnicity, even when they refuse to identify with feminism, are not prepared 'to take the shit' that they used to. There was a refusal by growing numbers of women to live in relation to husbands and children, as they insisted that they needed to exist as persons in their own right.[1] Women have demanded their freedom and liberation and have often refused to conceive of these in terms of a liberal language of rights. Women wanted more than equal access to the public world of work, for they sensed from the beginning of the women's movement that this could not happen unless men were ready to change. Men could no longer assume that they would be at the centre of a woman's life as women learnt to value their own friendships and, collectively with other women, began a process of redefining their own meanings and values. There was no way of turning the clock back.

Men often felt uneasy and confused by these changes for they could no longer appease with the notion that they were working long hours for their partners and families.[2] Women insisted that men had also to be more emotionally involved in relationships and take greater responsibility for domestic work and childcare. There have been many compromises in renegotiating more equal gender contracts, especially where men have had professional careers so that if women have entered the workplace, it has been through being able to employ the labour of other, less fortunate women. But there is a very widespread aspiration towards greater equality and shared decision making in relationships, especially in North America and Western Europe. Though it is important not to overstate the changes that men have made, since relatively little has changed in domestic work patterns, some significant shifts have taken place.

But men have had great difficulties in accepting the loss of power and status that has gone along with these changes. This has shown itself in a high divorce rate and in a greater incidence of domestic violence and even child sexual abuse. Often men withdraw into a sullen silence, refusing to talk about what is happening to them, and at other moments this breaks into violence and rage that is difficult to contain within the relationship. At a time when men from diverse class and ethnic identities feel threatened at work in terms of high unemployment and recession, it is easy for them to experience domestic challenges as betrayal, for they want to feel they are at least secure on the 'home front'. *Iron John* (Bly, 1990) has been important because it has reached a far broader group of men who would not have identified with any men's movement. It provided a context in which they could begin to explore the emotions and unresolved feelings they were carrying. Being able to learn from the experience of other men, they could begin to forge an emotional language and learn how to draw support. Most significantly, perhaps, they were helped to *accept* their masculinity rather than to feel there was something wrong and shameful in being a man. Men could also learn to take pride in their experience as men.

At the same time there was an edge for many men who sought to blame feminism for the ways they had come to feel about themselves as men. It was as if resentment that had accumulated over the years could break surface and find expression. This rage against women has deep sources in our experience as men but it has to be carefully handled because it also has sources in the power that men have often assumed to treat women as their property. It is not just that patriarchy has also hurt men as well as women, as Bly sometimes argues. It is not so simple, as some men's rights movements suggest, as identifying a common enemy because we also have to explore how our dominant notions of masculinity are intimately tied up with the power we traditionally exercise in relation to women. There is a relationship of superiority and inferiority that has to be carefully tracked down. Within modernity, as I have tried to explore in *Unreasonable Men* (1994), this has been given a particular form: men's power has been normalized as legitimate, as somehow working in the interests of all, and so has been deemed 'rational'.

Though Bly says a great deal about the importance of facing our shadow he says relatively little about male sexualities. The reliance upon myths can make it difficult to explore the difference between sexual fantasies and the reality we live in our relationships. Within a Protestant moral culture we have grown up feeling guilty about our sexual fantasies because we assume they indicate our 'evil' natures. So we learn to suppress our fantasies and feel ashamed and embarrassed to share them because we fear giving grounds to others to reject us. But unless we are ready to *acknowledge* our fantasies it becomes impossible to work on them emotionally. There is no sense, within a Protestant moral culture, that we might be able to act them out and explore the meanings they hold in a safe and supportive environment. Rather we tighten against them as we learn to suppress them and live as if we do not have them at all. This helps to close up any space that might otherwise exist between our fantasies and how we relate to women, say. Often as heterosexual men we feel burdened by these fantasies because we feel ashamed of them. Sometimes we feel that it is obvious to others, as if our fantasies are written on our foreheads for everyone else to see.

Men might come to feel as men that it is wrong to treat women as sexual objects, but know of no other ways of relating. This was part of the moralism that was integral to the sexual politics of the 1970s. We imagined that we could change the ways we felt through an exercise of will and determination. This was to reproduce the rationalist notion of how people change. It involved an ethics of self-suppression. Rather than take the risk of learning more about how our own sexualities as men work, we learnt to police our emotions and feelings around women. We often learnt to behave in acceptable ways while all the time resenting that we felt false about ourselves. The resentments that men felt towards feminism went underground as women claimed virtue was all on their side, and did not break the surface till the 1980s when men began to feel that they had to explore their own sexualities as men, rather than simply accommodate to the expectations of women. Bly's work is part of this movement but it needs to be carefully placed in relation to men's responses to feminism.

Men and Feminism

Within a Protestant moral culture men often grow up feeling bad about themselves. Boys are animals who need to be trained so that from a very early age we are harshly treated. As boys we learn to live without emotional needs, which mean that it is a threat to feel connection to people or things. At the same time we learn to *split* from our emotions which are interpreted as signs of weakness. This is why it can be so threatening when as men we are challenged to share more of our emotions within relationships. It is easy to feel we have enough to deal with to prove our masculinity in the public realm of work without having it threatened by those we are closest to. This can touch the critical self-image we often carry as men and turn out to be just something else that we are not 'good enough' at. So it can easily seem that feminism is yet another way of making men feel bad about themselves.

   Talk about the power that men have within the larger culture in relation to women can seem odd to many men who feel powerless in their own personal lives and intimate relationships. Feminism has certainly begun to change the ways that many younger men and women learn to relate to each other. Often it leaves a trail of confusion for men who learn to do 'the right thing' but who might feel quite different inside. They fear rejection and have learnt to behave differently, but at another level little has changed. When men accept the feminist idea that the institutional power of patriarchy defines the terms for women's access to the public realm, this can leave them feeling guilty about their own masculinity which exists exclusively as a relationship of power. This self-rejection of masculinity is the response to feminism which Bly's *Iron John* targets. Sometimes it has left men feeling unsettled and confused about their own sexuality, especially when they have also absorbed the idea that penetrative sex is essentially oppressive. But if this response to feminism has sharpened men's moral rejection of patriarchal power, their refusal to collude with the forces of patriarchy, it has been only one response amongst many.

There has always been a tension between an emphasis on anti-sexism in which men have more readily defined themselves in terms of the goals of struggling against sexism and institutional patriarchy, and notions of men's liberation which have sought to free men from the restrictive nature of men's roles. Anti-sexist men were concerned to ally with the women's movement in the struggles against sexism and pornography. This was crucial work which a men's liberation vision might not have fully appreciated, tending to see a too easy parallel between women's oppression and the ways men are also supposedly oppressed by their gender roles as men. A men's liberation view tends to see sexual politics in more *personal* terms and tends to think that equality can be realized within personal relationships if men and women learn to see the tasks they face as shared. Both genders have been limited, it is argued, by the expectations that have been culturally placed and both should be equally free to participate in both the public and the private realms. The emphasis here, which can get lost in an anti-sexist politics, is possibly more on the changes that men can make in their own lives.[3]

But there were always movements that refused any sharp distinction between these different perspectives and insisted upon learning from both. In England *Achilles' Heel* presented an attempt to struggle against the realities of patriarchal power, so supporting in different ways the women's movement while at the same time accepting that men had to redefine their masculinities. We argued that this was not a matter of restrictive roles and personal relationships alone. It also had to do with facing the power that men had within the larger society. The writing that developed was open and exploratory, for we appreciated that the language of politics had to be transformed if we were to take to heart the idea that the personal is political. In many ways we felt not only challenged but also liberated by feminism, for relationships could be more open and honest. As men we no longer had to play games we did not believe in. Some of this early writing has been made available in *The Achilles' Heel Reader* and *Men, Sex and Relationships* (Seidler, 1991c; 1992). We recognized that as love could not be separated from power, so reason could not be separated from emotion. As men we could not change through will alone but had to learn how to support each other emotionally. These were early years of exploration and excitement.

Men have responded to feminism ever since the women's movement was born in the very early 1970s. But it was easy for many men to feel that feminism had to do with women and that women should be left alone to get on with it. Since women were often suspicious of men getting together in consciousness-raising groups, thinking this was yet another way of regaining power, men could easily distance themselves. But sadly it means that men were slow to recognize the need to change themselves. It is striking that when feminism was relatively weak, fragmented and under attack in the backlash of the 1980s, there was such a massive response to the publication of Bly's *Iron John*. It certainly struck a chord as no other book had managed to do, though it is by no means an easy and accessible read. Possibly this was because it touched the issue of the grief that many men felt in their unresolved relationship with their fathers. It gave a voice to a hidden yearning that men felt across differences of culture, 'race' and ethnicity. But it was also expressed in the language of myth that allowed a certain emotional distance and safety to be created. Crucially, as I have argued, it allowed men to feel that they could reclaim a masculinity while giving them a way of avoiding the charge of being 'macho'.

The mythopoetic movement has helped to restore a knowledge of the transitions from boyhood to manhood that has been lost within contemporary cultures.[4] By fostering a respect for myth it offers men a different way of relating to themselves and so of sidestepping the traps of a rationalism that makes it so hard to share ourselves emotionally as men. It is unhelpful to think of the movement as 'essentialist' or simply as nostalgic for a conception of masculinity that has passed, though these dangers are present. It seeks a new path for men to explore their inherited traditions of manhood, while also appreciating that these cannot simply be grafted onto a contemporary reality. The fact that we might appreciate the need for boys to be initiated does not mean it will be easy to work out viable rituals. But at least we can appreciate the *need* for such rituals and traditions that we have largely lost within modernity.

Bly has distanced himself from some of the wildman groups, sometimes saying that he would never get his flowing white hair dirty in the mud. His groups seem more concerned with men learning how to speak directly from the heart. But he is a complicated figure and it is easy to feel that he sometimes pulls in different directions at once. Some of his remarks can so easily encourage a backlash against feminism, even if this is not his intention. He is quoted, for instance, as saying: 'Men are really tired of being told they should be women. Someone said that in the last 30 years, a woman can be anything she wants, but a man has to be a woman. Now a lot of women are unhappy with this, but they should have thought of that before they asked men to get rid of their aggression and their maleness' (quoted in *I-D*, 'Identity' issue, November 1991).

This kind of loose talk blames women and leaves you with a bad taste in the mouth about Bly's feelings on feminism. It is important for men to engage critically with feminism, especially in relation to what it says about men. It is too easy to be left by Bly with an impression that maleness is to be identified with aggression and to fail to appreciate that feminism has challenged the ways this aggression is used in the objectification of women. If there are confusions about how men should relate to the challenges of feminism it does not help to blame feminism in blanket terms, and it is plainly provocative to suggest that feminism has to be arguing that men 'should be women'. It might have proved difficult for men to discern the difference between anger and aggression, having learnt to suppress both as oppressive to women. This might have been damaging for many men who

were honestly attempting to respond to feminism. But it does not help at all
to confuse the issue by saying that feminism is arguing that 'a man has to be
a woman.' This is a travesty of an argument. It tempts men to feel that they
should reassert their traditional masculinity, aggression and all, for this is
what it means to be a man and to argue otherwise is somehow to 'go against
nature'. Bly knows a lot better than this but he sometimes allows himself to
become a hostage to fortune when he fails to clarify his position.

Fear and Difference

Bly has some striking things to say about men's 'tameness' which he connects to a loss of spontaneity. He recognizes ways that men in recent generations have learnt to adapt to the expectations of others both at work in
corporations and offices and also in their relationships. It is also true that if
men assume that women somehow have virtue on their side, so that men as
the possessors of power must always be in the wrong, they cease to exist for
themselves. So it is that men often seem less clear about themselves, and
less defined individually, than do women who have been influenced by
feminism. Often this hides a level of resentment that men rarely express,
though in the 1980s we have seen a number of clearly anti-feminist men's
movements.

It is in this context of men seeming to have lost a sense of their own vitality, individuality and direction that Bly's talk of men recovering their inner
ground makes most sense. A 'warrior' for Bly is a person who is able to
defend his inner ground, though it carries many quite other implications
within the larger culture. Bly talks about the issue in terms of men being
ready to defend their 'psychic house', graphically suggesting that it is like a
man looking on as his best possessions are being burgled. It is the fear of
identifying what is precious to us, what we value and would defend. A
failure to define ourselves in intimate and sexual relationships, so that we
can negotiate clearly from a position of knowing ourselves, is the fear Bly
touches.

This loss of vitality does not only affect men, though it might affect men
in particular ways. It is part of a critique of a conformist culture in which
people fear to be different. This is especially strong in American youth
culture where the one thing boys aspire too is to be 'popular'. It is a conformism cloaked in a language of individualism that J.S. Mill discerned in
On Liberty. We can grow up fearing to establish strong individual beliefs
and values lest this makes us different from others and so gives others the
grounds to reject us. It is certainly wrong to blame feminism which is in
many ways, at least as far as women have been concerned, a significant
protest against such tendencies. The anxieties of commentators about talk
of postfeminism is partly related to a desire to return to the mainstream of
consumerist culture and to forget about the difficult and stubborn challenges of feminism.

The 'inner warrior' has to face his own shadow and come to terms with the 'ashes work' that cannot be avoided. Bly reminds us of how easy it is to float up and away from our experiences of pain, hardship, disappointment and grief. We learn to put the past behind us, before we have 'taken in' what has happened to us. It is wonderful how Bly identifies the move to ascend which is so culturally endemic. Unless we are prepared to contact our own dark side we can never be free of it. This challenges the optimism of so much contemporary culture, the idea that we can simply 'move on' or create a different identity for ourselves. It is in Baudrillard's (1995) glorification of the culture of appearances that we are tempted to think that we can constantly remake ourselves in the images available through the media and mass communications.[5] Bly punctures this dream and brings us back to ourselves. He learns from Jung that a deeper contact with ourselves is possible, but that we have to work for it. There is no instant enlightenment waiting for us just round the corner. It is a matter of learning how to work on ourselves. It means accepting our pains as much as our joys.

Though Bly seeks to free himself from some of the Jungian inheritance, he also remains trapped by it. Jung (1986) sustained a vision of male superiority and dominance whilst at the same time finding ways of acknowledging the workings of the feminine principle, the anima. He helps men to face their feminine aspect and appreciate how this is an essential part of growing in their individuality. Learning to make space for our different aspects helps us to think of balance and harmony within the self. But it also helps sustain notions of the 'essentially masculine', as if this is a principle that is constantly informing and shaping our empirical lives, even if we remain unaware of this influence. Yet masculinity is also shaped by forces of culture and history and, though Bly moves back and forward between these different accounts, he remains trapped into thinking that male initiation takes place in the public realm which is the 'father's house' alone. This minimizes what we can learn about our masculinity from our relationships with our partners and children. Women, like feminism, are often left behind in Bly's account.

Bly fails to appreciate what the early men's movements learnt from their relationships with feminism. He fails to honour this history and experience and dismisses it too easily as a 'feminization' of men. He loses touch with the insights that were gained into men's emotional lives and relationships. He prepares new ground in which men do not have to learn from their own history. In this way he is responsible if his work can so easily be used by the masculinist tendency which sets itself the task of reclaiming the power which it believes women have taken. It is quite misleading to see the sexual politics of the 1970s as having been entirely motivated by guilt and self-hatred. Heterosexual men responded to feminism and the gay and lesbian movements in diverse ways. There was also a great deal of support, love and joy in our relationships with each other as men and in discovering new ways of relating to women.

If we do not learn from our history we will tend to repeat its mistakes. Often we misconstrue the past in order to show the present in a new light.

This is what Terry Daly has done in his defence of masculinism in the 1990s: 'I would define the New Man as an invention of feminism. He lived by denying his masculinity and consequently failed to satisfy both men and women. I think it was a real phenomenon, not just an advertising one, which has confused and damaged many men' (*I-D*, 'Identity' issue, November 1991). This is confusing and self-serving language which so easily encourages 'men to be men' and so ignore the challenges of feminism. Sometimes the fact of the media looking round for the anti-feminist position sustains the masculinist ego. This is the language of the backlash that is quite unprepared to learn from different feminisms or to engage critically. As Terry Daly goes on to say: 'Masculinism is a term I invented and it is basically about men feeling good about themselves, and having a good time, feeling proud and strong. It's about taking a close look at men and masculinity, from a male perspective. It's about bringing out the power of men . . . Power and pride are words that the feminist and gay struggle have appropriated. That's something that we would like to get our hands on, as men, as masculinists.'

There is lip-service to feminism and gay liberation, but also an undertone that they have had it their own way for too long and now it is time for heterosexual men to get their own back. It is as if the time has come to 'stand up to feminism' which for too long has dictated to men who they ought to be. If this finds some resonance even amongst men who are sympathetic to feminism, it is partly because men often fail to recognize themselves in the images portrayed within feminist writings. It is also because of a growing frustration that fosters a belief that at last men have to take responsibility for their own lives. This can be positive, if it is not set within the terms of a masculinist perspective. It is important also for heterosexual men to feel good about themselves as men, for the dominant culture is full of critical self-images that often encourage men to be too hard on themselves. This has to do at the very least with accepting our experience as men and learning from it rather than assuming that our partners must always be right. It is a matter of finding a balance between love and power. Within heterosexual relationships men and women can draw upon different sources of power, and within individual relationships it is important to recognize that not always are men powerful and women powerless.

It must be possible for men to increasingly find their own voices so that they can negotiate more openly and honestly within relationships, without having to deny the oppression of women and the institutionalized power of men. Possibly the pendulum has to swing in the other direction before we can discover more balance. There are also years of suppressed resentment to deal with on the part of many men who felt silenced when feminism felt powerful. But it is also crucially important for men to engage critically with those men who seek to deny the challenges of feminism to dominant forms of masculinity and to the ways we have learnt to be as men. It isn't good enough to feel proud of how we are as white middle class heterosexual men unless we *also* appreciate how women have felt devalued, unrecognized and diminished within traditional relationships of patriarchal power. So often as men we can only feel good about ourselves at the expense of others, for we are tied into competitive relations. It would be a welcome change if our acceptance of ourselves did not have to be through putting others down.

Manhood and Power

Since traditional Western notions of masculinity have been tied up with feelings of superiority in relation to women, it is hardly surprising that heterosexual men feel uneasy and confused about what it means to be a man after the challenges of feminism. It might be easier to deny the validity of these challenges and to reassert a return to traditional forms of male power. This is not something that Bly offers but many have read him as supporting such a view, as he seems at least to be offering a way of avoiding the dual difficulties of a macho masculinity on the one hand and a feminized masculinity on the other. But he is not consistent, and the notion of manhood he sometimes seems to be offering can feel like a return to a traditional notion of heterosexual masculinity that has never had to negotiate in the private and public spheres on equal terms with women. Nor is the vision Bly offers a masculinity that is at ease with its own sexuality and able also to acknowledge the autonomous sexuality of women. Somehow Bly does not really help us focus upon the issues we face in establishing open, loving and equal sexual relationships. This might not have been the task that he set himself and he might well argue that the initiation of men into their manhood is a prior issue. But I do not think that even this can be adequately presented in the terms that Bly offers.

Rather Bly also has to take responsibility for the ways his views have been invoked by others, for at the very least this says something about the ambivalence of the language he invokes. Some masculinists who are also Vietnam revisionists insist that the US lost the war in South East Asia because feminists helped to break the nation's 'warrior spirit'. One campaigner, John Wheeler (1991), has claimed that 'New York feminists poured the country's testosterone out the windows in the 60s.' Others, such as the National Coalition of Free Men (NCFM), campaign for men's rights, claiming that men are now more discriminated against than women. In the NCFM's journal *Transitions* we hear similar arguments to those presented by Neil Lyndon (1992) in England. The particular issues that are raised, especially around separation and divorce, have to be carefully assessed rather than dismissed out of hand. It is important for men who are more sympathetic to the claims of feminism to engage with these writings and to be ready to uncover the hurt and lack of recognition that is often concealed.

Heterosexual men have often been confused and demoralized in their responses to the challenges of feminism. They have lost a sense of a vision of masculinity and manhood they could believe in. It is far better that this discussion has broken out rather than be left festering underneath the surface. There is anger and rage that needs to be addressed. Men can recognize the need for greater iron, the clarity and definition in themselves they have so often lacked, without wanting to dominate in relationships in traditional ways. There is little doubt that Bly has made an important contribution in opening out this discussion, even if we contest the terms he sets. For at some level By remains basically nostalgic for some of the warrior and hunter identities men so long occupied. He believes that we are quite wrong if we think that men can change after so few generations. At some level he remains suspicious of the possibilities of men changing. The danger is that we deny an aggression that remains untamed beneath the surface. But this can feel like a return to arguments from nature which hold that men are naturally aggressive and that their sexual needs are pressing. Experience teaches us different, though we also recognize that these have long stood as legitimations for men's power and control.

These notions cloud rather than illuminate the issues that heterosexual men face in their sexual relationships with women and the difficulties that men have often felt with intimacy and commitment. If men have withdrawn in the face of the inner power that women have discovered through feminism and therapy, this has partly been because of the fear men have felt about closer contact with other men. Women have learnt to define themselves more clearly as they have differentiated their own meanings and values from those offered to them by the dominant patriarchal culture. They have also begun a process of identifying the sources of their spiritual power. Men still have much of this ahead of them and *Iron John* is a text that can be of enormous help if it is engaged with critically, rather than glorified as somehow having all the answers. As men we often want to know that we have the answers *before* we are ready to set off on the path. This gives us confidence and control. It is scary to set out without a clear map in our hand.

In many ways *Iron John* provides us with one path and the different stages we need to go through. It might not be a path which will suit everyone, but at least we learn that it is a process that takes time and cannot be rushed, for we have to be ready before we can move on. Again this is hard to take in because within modernity we often learn that it is not the process but the goal successfully achieved that matters. It becomes hard to acknowledge that we need different spaces at the different stages in the journey through our lives as men. Sometimes we need to find our way in the forest, while at other times we need to sit quietly by the lake watching the reflection of the full moon in the water. At other times we need to take time in the garden. Bly helps us appreciate these different moments. He helps us honour spiritual traditions we have lost contact with. He touches a spiritual hunger that modernity has largely neglected. For all these gifts we should be truly grateful. His book remains a central contribution and needs to be defended against the small-minded reviews, uncomfortable with its emotional honesty, that did it down in different parts of the world.

As women with different backgrounds discovered that they needed to explore their own space and time, to imagine their meanings and values, so men also need to explore their relationship to the patriarchal values and practices they have grown up to take very much for granted. This involves both an inner exploration and an outer transformation in ways that we relate to others. As we redefine our masculinities so we begin to think of our lives in different terms. We learn to appreciate the form and quality of our relationships with both women and men as we learn to take greater responsibility for our emotional and spiritual lives.

This involves a break with the idea that dominant male identities are always established at the expense of others, so that we can only feel good about ourselves if we put others down. It means facing our fears including our fear of closeness and love from other men.[6] So much of our transition from boyhood to manhood is clouded in fears of gayness that we often learn as heterosexual men to harden ourselves against our own sensitivity and tenderness. We learn to rely upon ourselves alone, but this leaves us feeling *more* isolated and alone than we like to acknowledge. We become suspicious of the support others might be offering us because we assume that at some level they want to put us down, or else prove themselves at our expense. It feels easier not to reach out for the help we need.

Sexual Identities

Bly's *Iron John* says little to support the struggles of gay men to sustain their identities in the face of a homophobic culture. Rather it is easy to feel that they have somehow allowed their masculinities to be 'feminized' and so they have failed in their initiation into manhood. Again this is not necessarily an explicit intention of Bly's but it is a danger that flows from the way the text is organized. It isn't enough to say that issues of gayness are not the focus for the work because, as in the sections which deal with men's relationships to feminism, gayness tacitly serves as a direction we need to be watchful about if we want to recover a lost manhood. Bly fails to come to terms with the power of heterosexuality in establishing relations of power between different groups of men. Not only has homophobia been traditionally invoked to police the boundaries of traditional masculinities but it has served as a way of sustaining fear and distance between different men.

In reality it was the gay liberation movement in the 1970s that initially opened up questions about the oppressive character of traditional forms of masculinity.[7] In finding the courage to come out both to themselves and also to others, gay men had to do significant emotional work in redefining their sexual identities. They learnt to feel pride in an identity that has been diminished and abused within contemporary culture. This involves a personal and political process of change and transformation that was never easy and involved taking risks, for it was never possible to know how others you are close to might respond. This is a form of truth telling that white heterosexual men have not had to engage with but it is something that we can learn from a great deal. The process of 'coming out' marks a very real initiation for it involves meeting one's self and taking stock and responsibility for one's sexual history and identity. So it is that gay men with diverse class and ethnic backgrounds have had to learn to define themselves and stand their ground. This has taken a great deal of iron for it has involved a crucial process of self-definition.

There have been long discussions about the relationship of gay men's identities to masculinity in its different forms which go back to the writings of Edward Carpenter (1906).[8] But in the context of the gay men's movement men could no longer stay in the 'copper realm' where they could pretend to be 'all things to all men'. They felt they had to define themselves and to defend the integrity of their sexual feelings and desires. They had to declare themselves and so take a stand, whatever the reactions of others. So it was that gay men and lesbian women in different ways began to explore their own histories and cultures, *refusing* to be evaluated in terms of traditional sex roles. Though people might choose to define themselves in different ways over time, the moment of 'coming out' seems to remain a powerful moment. Even if people refuse to be defined by their sexual orientation alone, recognizing that this is just one aspect of their identities, there is something significant in the process of coming out that can be difficult to appreciate theoretically.[9] Often it remains a landmark in self-awareness, for it involves making a personal commitment to one's feelings and sexuality, which heterosexual men rarely have to make.

Taking pride in one's gay identity has been no easy matter, especially with the onslaught of AIDS in the 1980s. But still there is a sustained aliveness and spontaneity that Bly talks about as 'wildness' and opposes to the tameness of the corporation man who simply adapts to what others expect of him. Often men carry an unrecognized sense of guilt for the ways we learnt to forsake our own emotions and desires to win the love and respect of parents and teachers. We learnt that love had to be earned, especially in the white middle classes. So we often learnt to compromise what we knew about ourselves, to win the love and approval of parents. We learnt to be 'good boys' through adapting to what others expected of us, rather than being able to stand up for what we needed for ourselves. We are then surprised to be haunted by a sense that others cannot really understand 'who' we are, even when we present ourselves to others in ways that feel compromised. So it is that we often lose an inner connection to the self as boys, as we learn to see ourselves from an early age very much in the terms that others see us. We lose any relationship to our inner lives without recognizing what we have lost.

Gay and lesbian politics helped to challenge the distinction at the core of liberal moral and political theory between the private and the public spheres. It insisted that sexuality was *too* significant for it to remain a purely private matter, for unless it was recognized and validated in public forms of expression it would remain hidden and shameful. Because how others see us matters to how we can feel about ourselves, it is important for there to be public recognition for different sexual orientations. This is why it was important for gay pride to take to the streets, for homophobia was an issue for the heterosexual communities to confront. Heterosexual men could learn that here this was a matter not of proving oneself to others but of somehow being true to oneself in the way that one lived. It is a refusal to live a lie. This is part of a different kind of humanist vision which is not reductive or essentialist but allows us all – gay or straight – to reclaim the sources of our spontaneity and aliveness which so easily wither and dry up if we only exist through the eyes of others. Such existence serves unwittingly to give others power over our lives but somehow to be disempowered ourselves, to fail to discover and explore what it means for us to live for ourselves.

We can think for a moment of an example, drawn from a white middle class life, about a doctor who has 'made it' but who falls asleep in front of the TV every night. He has done what others expected of him and he has lived out the dream of his father who was also a doctor. He has become a 'success' in their terms but he has never had to explore his *own* dreams or wonder what it might have been like for him to become a success in his own terms. We might say that he has never learnt how to develop a more individuated and defined sense of self. Sometimes he is left wondering whether this is all there is to life, for he can feel that he is on a treadmill not of his own making. He has lived out the dreams of others but never taken the time to discover what his own dreams for himself would be. This is so easy to do, for from a very early age we feel we have to prove ourselves as 'adequate' in the eyes of others. Life is rarely offered to us as a blessing and a gift, but more often in the Protestant terms of a task to win salvation from our original sin. Often we remain haunted, even within a secularized culture, and especially as men, by a sense that we have to be continually proving we are 'good enough'. At some level we fear the truth might be otherwise.

Gay Men/Straight Men

Gay men have a lot to teach heterosexual men, for they have had to face themselves and also face the negative and destructive anti-gay feelings in the larger society. They have been involved in an intensive process of self-exploration since the early 1970s that is only now transforming the terms of mainstream culture. In dark times they have also had to face chronic illness and death, finding ways to give support to those who are living with HIV and AIDS and exploring new ways of caring and loving each other. Bly could have gone further in welcoming the experience of gay men. He counts them as men like any other but in this way discounts a politics of difference and the particularities of their experience and sexualities. Not only does he do this but he tends to build a wall of 'naive' men, so-called feminized men who have responded to feminism, and then reassures heterosexual men that if they are to involve themselves in the 'third way' that he offers, they will *not* have to deal with the homosexual feelings that they may have long suppressed. But there can be no guarantees, and some men might discover their unresolved gay feelings as they open themselves up to a path of emotional exploration.

I cannot help feeling that some of the popular appeal of *Iron John* to white middle class heterosexual men was in its implicit guarantee that allows straight men to explore their masculinities and long-hidden emotional lives while making sure that this particular door that opens out to a gay experience is firmly closed. In truth no such guarantees can be given, and what will matter much more is the exploration that many more men begin for themselves. There is no single path and *Iron John* offers us a meditation on a single journey which might resonate at distinct points with the experience of other paths. The path shared in *Iron John* certainly reminds us of some dark stages that we might have hoped we could avoid. Bly reassures us otherwise, for there are no quick routes and really no guarantees about what we might discover about ourselves. But if we have to face our fears and resentments that we have for so long locked away, we can also break with the loneliness and isolation that we so often feel as men. Our fears as heterosexual men of becoming closer and drawing love and support from other men begin to dissolve as we learn to share more of ourselves.

Part of what we fear as heterosexual white middle class men in closer contact with other men is their judgements and the fear that they will *use* knowledge of our vulnerability to put us down. But it is often liberating to recognize how many of our hesitations and fears are silently shared by other men. We recognize how as middle class men they are struggling with similar critical voices in themselves and how they also seem to be pushing themselves too hard. As we begin to acknowledge a variety of different needs which are often conflated into a desire for sex, we can feel a little easier with ourselves. We begin to feel a little less embarrassed as heterosexual men in acknowledging our desires and needs. We begin a process of becoming more honest with ourselves and with others without so much fear about what they might think about us. As we begin to face our own fears of rejection, so we begin to be a little less judgemental of ourselves and a little easier in comparing ourselves with others. For we also begin to recognize difference, that others have made different decisions about their lives. As we slowly define ourselves more clearly so we begin to differentiate between our wants and needs. We become more focused as we learn to recognize and respect difference, to see that what others want for themselves does not bring us satisfaction and fulfilment.

Within the competitive cultures of white middle class masculinities men constantly compare themselves with others. Other men always seem to have their lives more together than us. Often we are so locked into comparisons that we give ourselves very little time to explore what we need for ourselves. Within a consumerist culture it is easy to fall into thinking that it is the power to purchase new commodities that will bring satisfaction. This also becomes the way in which we assert ourselves in relation to other men. If we are driving a new car, then within the terms of a consumerist culture we cannot be doing all that bad. If it is a faster car than others seem to be driving then it stands as some kind of proof that we must be doing better than them. Sometimes this can be a way of avoiding ourselves and curbing the low self-esteem we feel inside. Often as men we are fearful of spending much time with ourselves because we have so little relationship to our inner emotional lives. We distrust our emotions because they can so easily threaten the image we have of ourselves.

Learning to feel that whatever we do is not 'good enough' because someone else might have done it better is, within middle class masculinities, undermining to our sense of self. As Max Weber (1930) grasped it, the workings of the Protestant ethic help to shape contemporary masculinities. The notion that our natures are shameful has a deep impact upon the experience of gay men who often grow up feeling that there is something 'wrong' with them because of their sexual orientation. It makes it hard for gay men to accept their sexualities, let alone to celebrate them. AIDS has cast a long shadow over the early hopes of the gay liberation movements. As Simon Callow, the actor and director, has said:

> Homosexuality has, in the past 10 years, become synonymous with illness and early death to the extent that it seems impossible not to allude to these things in the depiction of gay men. At the point where gay men and women were slowly beginning to be perceived as part of life's rich pattern, different but essentially formed from the same common clay as the rest of humankind, suddenly we become A Problem again. (*The Observer*, 26 September 1993: 8)

So many early hopes were being dashed. Callow remembers when he first heard about the virus from Martin Sherman, the playwright, at a supper a little more than 10 years ago when Martin has just returned from New York:

> 'There's a terrible disease sweeping through New York, it's a sort of cancer that only gay men get.' Rupert and I laughed. Nervously. It seemed absurd; a paranoid reflex of the puritan conscience, or else something medieval, some echo from a savage past . . . As Martin spoke, giving more and more disturbing details, a great weariness overcame us. For the first time in living memory, gay women and men were beginning to stop apologising, stop hiding, stop lying about themselves. That would now all be spoiled; we were not going to be able to explore our new freedom, slowly mature from licentiousness into liberty. And so it proved. (1993: 8)

Callow like many others is haunted by a sense of apocalypse: 'Were the God of Love not well and truly dead, buried at the Somme, Katyn, and Dachau, AIDS would surely have finished him off' (1993: 8).

Despite the presence of AIDS there seems in the 1990s to be a fluidity in sexual identities and much easier contact between gay and straight men, especially for a younger generation. Young men seem more tolerant and able to learn from each other, though there is some confusion. But also many anti-gay and homophobic feelings have broken through the surface with AIDS. There has been an unwillingness to recognize how AIDS is an illness that affects us all and a desire to project it on to the gay community alone. This is part of a continuing discussion. As Callow writes:

AIDS, unlike cancer or multiple sclerosis, has an intensely political dimension in that it predominantly affects – in the West, certainly – a section of the community unloved by the establishment. Why was so little done to find a cure? Why is so little still being done? Is it a plot to let the gay population die off, or at the very least be exploited financially? More sinisterly, is it a form of chemical warfare deliberately engineered to wipe us out? All or none of these scenarios may be true. They are fuelled by the desperate, heartbreaking rage of individuals inexplicably struck down at young ages for no other reason than ignorance of the workings of their bodies and the workings of a universe inhabited by inexhaustibly mutating viruses, bent on annihilation. (1993: 8)

There are different kinds of ignorances and often as heterosexual men we do not want to know what is happening to our brothers. It is too painful or just too threatening. We turn our heads away, though at some level we remain shamed. We need a vision of brotherhood that can respect and celebrate difference, that allows men to learn from each other and to give support to each other at times of need. Men can learn much from each other about how to live as well as how to die with dignity and self-respect. Often it is our fear of our own sexualities that keeps heterosexual men apart, as well as an understandable fear of illness and death. But if we are to discover new visions which allow men with diverse sexualities to accept their emotions and feelings without compromising their masculinities, there is much to learn from gay men.

Notes

1 A helpful introduction to some of the ideas and aspirations that informed the emergence of the women's liberation movement is given in Sheila Rowbotham's *Woman's Consciousness, Man's World* (1973) and in her collected essays *Dreams and Dilemmas* (1983). An anthology that gives some of the feeling of these early years is *The Body Politic: Women's Liberation in Britain 1969–1972* compiled by Michelene Wandor (1972).

2 Some sense of the diverse responses of men to the development of feminism in the early 1970s is given in *The Achilles' Heel Reader: Men, Sexual Politics and Socialism*, edited by Victor J. Seidler (1991c).

3 Men's responses to feminism in the early years were roughly divided between those anti-sexist men who tended to put the emphasis upon the contributions that men could make to challenging the terms of women's oppression, so supporting the women's movement, and those who felt that men had also to focus upon challenging and redefining the terms of their own masculinities. Some of the men's liberation writing was weakened by its emphasis upon role theory which could slip into thinking that women and men are somehow equally restricted by the roles they are forced to adopt in patriarchal societies. It is significant that Warren Farrell, who wrote an early text entitled *The Liberated Man* (1974), went on in the 1980s to develop a men's rights position that was critical of feminism in his *The Myth of Male Power* (1986).

4 Robert Bly's *Iron John* (1990) has proved a central text in establishing the popular terms of the mythopoetic movement. His work draws upon diverse traditions and has developed in a lively exchange with other thinkers, such as James Hillman and Robert Moore. There is a shared sense that myths can help restore a lost initiation into manhood within contemporary industrial societies.

5 A helpful situating of Jean Baudrillard's intellectual development is provided by Mike Gane's *Baudrillard: Critical and Fatal Theory* (1991a) as well as his *Baudrillard's Bestiary* (1991b). For an overview provided through selected interviews see *Baudrillard Live*, edited by Mike Gane (1993).

6 The ways that contemporary heterosexualities are tied in with a fear of feeling and intimacy towards other men show the centrality of homophobia. It is as if boys can only feel secure in their own male identities if they can prove to themselves that they are not gay. This seems particularly strong in school sexual cultures where macho cultures still rule. Some helpful work in this area is M. Mac An Ghail's *The Making of Men* (1994) which explores some of these processes in the making; and David Jackson and Jonathan Salisbury, *Challenging Macho Values* (1996).

7 Some sense of the ideas and aspirations that informed the gay liberation movement in the 1970s is provided by Jeffrey Weeks's *Coming Out: Homosexual Politics in Britain* (1977) and in his *Sexuality and its Discontents* (1985). A sense of the development of lesbian theory and politics is given through Adrienne Rich's *Compulsory Heterosexuality and Lesbian Existence*.

8 The ways the relationship between gay men's identities and masculinities have been explored since Edward Carpenter are introduced in Sheila Rowbotham, *Socialism and the New Life: Edward Carpenter and Havelock Ellis* (1976). See Edward Carpenter's *Love's Coming of Age* (1906) and the collection of his writings prepared by the Gay Men's Press (Carpenter, 1990). For more recent explorations see *Heterosexuality*, edited by Gillian Hanscombe and Martin Humphries (1986).

9 For a sense of the ways gay indentities have been redefined over time see, for instance, *Growing Up before Stonewall*, edited by P. Nardi, David Sanders and Judd Marmon (1994); K. Porter and J. Weeks, *Between the Acts* (1990); *Mapping Desire: Geographies of Sexuality*, edited by David Bell and Gill Valentine (1995); and *What a Lesbian Looks Like*, National Lesbian and Gay Survey (1992).

2
Authorities

Postmodern Identities

Within modern Western culture many men with diverse class, racial and ethical identities seem to have lost a sense of what it means 'to be a man'. We are uncertain, especially as white middle class heterosexual men, about what others can expect of us and what we can expect of ourselves. This unease touches many men who have been brought up into quite different conceptions of masculinities, of what it means to be a man. This is part of a much wider spiritual malaise which exists in postmodern Western culture, no longer so certain of its values and place in the world. There is a sense that in certain areas of life, particularly to do with love, intimacy and relationships, we have lost our way and do not know where to look for guidance.

For men this crisis has become acute with the challenges and questionings of feminism and gay liberation. Since the early 1970s the women's movement has sought to encourage men to rethink the ways we are as white heterosexual men and the power that we have so long taken for granted within relationships.[1] This has only added to a sense of disconnection between the dominant intellectual and moral culture and the inner crisis that as heterosexual men we increasingly experience in our lives. At some level it is possible to feel that the broader intellectual culture of modernity has lost its way, for it no longer resonates with the anxieties and fears of everyday life.

Within the past decade there have been numerous attempts to identify the discontinuities which separate the postmodern world from the world and experience of our fathers and mothers. These help us realize that we cannot simply draw upon the models of relationships that have been passed down to us, for there is a broadly felt aspiration amongst diverse men to relate *differently* to our partners, friends and children. This makes it easy to feel that we are living in new times, having to deal with new patterns of gender and sexual relationships for which we are not emotionally prepared. In our anxieties it is easy, especially as dominant middle class men, to fall back into established patterns, only to regret the way we have behaved soon afterwards.

Every generation faces its own problems and probably feels that the issues it faces have never been faced before. At some level it is easy to feel that nothing really new happens under the sun and this can serve as an important reminder lest we get carried away by our own conceits. But, theories of postmodernism recognize that the 1960s provided some kind of watershed, reinforced with the developments of new technologies and the globalization of economic and political relations, to echo changes we experience in our everyday lives. At the same time the claims of postmodernity, which would tempt us into celebrating the realm of appearances that we witness on our television screens, easily disconnect us from a sense of the past. They can work to disconnect us from the patterns of modernity before we have taken space and time to acknowledge the ways we embody and live out aspirations and relationships drawn from modernity. We can be left feeling dizzy and unsettled trying to find a place for ourselves within a world that is changing too quickly.[2]

An Enlightenment vision of modernity has always fostered a distrust of the past, for it presents a realm of custom and tradition as something we have to be ready to break with if we are to live as free and equal rational agents. This has a particular meaning in the lives of men, for within modernity a dominant Eurocentric masculinity has been identified with reason. Within modernity we live in a man's world. A vision of change and transformation, whereby as men we are constantly striving for future goals and achievements, is part of the dream of modernity. Little of this changes in the movement towards a postmodern world where the present is often celebrated as being radically disconnected from the past. It can feel as if we are in a boat without a rudder, being offered so many possibilities and different 'ways of being' that along with a sense of excitement about the identities we can create for ourselves goes a *fear* of disintegration in the face of so many options. Life seems to be talked about as if it were a massive supermarket where identities and lifestyles can be chosen off the shelf, if only we have enough money to afford our desires.[3]

For a dominant white, Christian, heterosexual masculinity there is something familiar in the notion that the past can be left behind so that we can 'turn over a new leaf' and 'start over'. In part this has to do with the intimate relationship between masculinity and an Enlightenment vision of modernity. It links to the ways that in recent times men often separate and leave relationships to find new ones, sustaining little contact with their children. The capacity to 'disconnect' and 'withdraw' controls the way we relate to our emotional lives as men. Often there is an unconscious fear of rejection so that we learn to *reject* others before they have a chance to reject us. We can insist as middle class heterosexual men that we don't care and that we aren't touched by what happens to us, as a way of protecting our male identities. We inherit a fear of intimacy and contact because these threaten our male identities, because to have emotions or to need others is a sign of 'weakness' and 'femininity'. So it is that we learn to fear our vulnerability, especially in front of other men. We learn to 'keep up appearances' and to 'put on a good show' so that others might not suspect what we are feeling. We do not want to be put down in the eyes of others, for this threatens male identities which are affirmed within the public realm of work.

To what extent have our visions of a postmodern world been framed within dominant masculine terms as a way of softening the challenges of feminism and ecology? With Baudrillard (1995) we are often left with a celebration of appearances and with a denial that there is any 'reality' which underlies them and which somehow explains the shape they take.[4] We have to forsake any belief in truths that are waiting to be discovered since 'truth' is taken to be an effect of a particular discourse and so cannot be separated from the languages through which we know it. But this way of understanding the relation between language, truth and meanings can serve to disempower us for it can render us incapable of questioning the terms of contemporary culture and relationships. There seems to be nothing beyond what we are being offered within the realm of appearances. Consumerism is free to create its own meanings and the market becomes the legislator of values, for we are bereft of ways of judging the false values it can offer us.

Modernity and Reason

Within an Enlightenment vision of modernity we have learnt to live without myth, for myth is supposed to belong to a 'childish' state of being that we have left behind as part of premodern societies. Identities within modernity aspire towards being 'free and equal' rational agents who are able to live by the light of reason alone. We have supposedly outgrown a need for myths which protected us from dealing with reality in scientific terms. So it was that modernity was marked by a transition from myth towards science, from faith towards reason.

As Foucault helps us grasp within *Madness and Civilization* (1971), this vision of reason that was to bring order into the world involved a crucial exercise in exclusion. Within modernity reason came to be defined in fundamental opposition to nature.[5] Reason was discerned as an independent and autonomous faculty which alone was a source of impartiality, objectivity and knowledge. Dreams, fantasies and visions that had all in different ways been recognized as sources of knowledge came to be denigrated and redefined as sources of 'unreason' and irrationality. So it was that within modernity we were to learn to reject these aspects of our experience for they could *not* be acknowledged without somehow threatening our sense of ourselves as rational agents. This was particularly intense for European white men who had to separate from these aspects of their experience if they did not want to bring their masculine identities into question.

In their different ways our dreams, fantasies and desires were deemed to be 'childish' and we could only consider ourselves to be individuals in our own right if we had separated ourselves from childishness. This also meant separating ourselves from the 'inner child' who had to be silenced and denied. So our inner connection with ourselves was broken as our relationship with our early experiences of childhood was severed. The linear vision which characterized modernity's conception of progress meant that we had to leave our 'childish emotions' behind as we learnt to guide our lives by the pure light of reason alone. Modernity can be considered as an attack on 'childishness' and so on the child within, for it was held that the child has an 'animal' nature that had to be trained out if children were ever to make a move towards existing as 'rational selves'.

The identification of the child with animal nature has had such a powerful influence on the shaping of modernity. Dreams, fantasies and visions were all to be denigrated as forms of unreason and as expressions of an animal nature that had not succumbed to the controls of reason. They reflected a lack of self-control and so a threat to any aspirations towards a 'humanity' conceived in rational terms. For within modernity we have learnt to define the 'human' as what *separated us* from the 'animal'. So it was that the faculty of reason came to play such a decisive role. Men in particular had to learn to curb their 'animal natures' for there was always an abiding tension within modernity between masculinity in its identification with reason and a sense of male sexuality as unreconstructed 'animality'. It was part of the pervasive threat of male violence that, once disturbed, men could not consider themselves as 'being in control'.

The revelations of the inner child had to be feared for they threatened to show that we did not have the 'self-control' that was deemed so necessary for men. Emotions and feelings could so easily expose us in front of others, so humiliating us in the eyes of others. We had to suppress our inner emotions for they could question our status as 'rational selves'. So it was that the 'inner child' had to be curbed and controlled for it could threaten the sovereignty of reason. As men we learnt to take pride in the control that we could exercise over our emotional lives. We hid the slightest hint of emotions, lest they remind us of a self that we did not want to know. We came to fear the revelations of our own inner child.

The rule of reason came to be identified with the power of the father, for it was the father who made reason his own. It was through reason that the father learnt to legislate for others and to feel confident that he 'knew best' what was good for others. This gave the father power to decide what was right for others. As reason has to have authority over nature, so fathers within a traditional vision had sovereignty over the family. The father as the voice of reason became the source of authority. So it was that fathering within modernity involved sustaining a certain *distance* in the family, for otherwise the independence of his authority would be questioned. A father was not supposed to be too familiar or intimate with his family for otherwise they would lose the necessary respect for him. As reason existed independently of nature, so the father also had to be a source of external authority within the family.[6] In the traditional family you had to wait for father to come home to exercise his authority and bring order into familial relationships. Of course the shape of paternal authority takes different forms in different class, racial and ethnic contexts.

In the dominant form of male authority within modernity the father learnt to rule in the name of reason. He was respected because of the position that he held, but increasingly he was to earn this respect through the wisdom of his judgements. The father's word was so powerful because it was supposedly impartial and objective. Fathers could claim to speak in the universal voice of reason while women and children were locked into the 'subjectivity' of experience, for being closer to nature they were more susceptible to the influence of emotions and desires. As Kant (1960) has it, it is only through a relationship with a man that a woman or a child can be sure of the guidance of reason. This is the only way they can escape from the influence of their experience which is 'subjective' and 'personal'. That white Christian men could take their reason for granted while 'others' had to prove their rationality was the way that modernity secured the power and authority of men. It rendered invisible many of the sources of male power which were written into the terms of modernity. No longer was it an issue of men's personal qualities alone.

Within an Enlightenment vision of modernity experience became diminished as a source of knowledge as it came to be reformulated within an empiricist tradition as having its source outside ourselves. In different ways we learnt to deride and devalue our experience as being 'merely' subjective and so as being 'unreal' when compared with the impartiality of reason. In Kant's terms we had to learn to silence our 'inclinations' – our emotions, feelings and desires – if we were to be able to heed the pure voice of reason. What is crucial is the way Kant establishes that we can only enjoy an 'inner' relationship with reason which thus becomes the source of 'freedom' and 'autonomy' because we have an 'external' relationship with emotions, feelings and desires which are part of 'nature'. This dualistic conception of the self gives moral expression to Descartes's idea that we exist as rational selves through our minds while we have an external relationship with our bodies, which are part of the empirical realm of nature governed by its own laws.

So it is that modernity establishes the autonomy of knowledge as separated from experience and so existing independently of our everyday lives. This helps legitimate the authority of professional knowledge. So, for example, when we visit the doctor it is easy to feel that our bodies exist as objects of medical knowledge alone. It is easy to devalue whatever experience we have of our bodies as somehow irrelevant to what is going on, for it is 'subjective' and 'personal'. Often even to ask a question is to be made to feel you are challenging the authority and expertise of the doctor, who implicitly says, 'don't worry yourself since this is my profession.' So it is that as women and men we learn how not to listen to ourselves, not to honour and appreciate what our bodies are trying to tell us. For the body has been disenchanted, portrayed as a machine which can be understood in mechanical terms alone. We learn to discount what we know as 'mere experience' and we do not learn *how* to listen to ourselves. Rather we learn that to listen to our inner selves is 'childish' and can only get in the way of the external voice of reason and science. So it was that science produced its own mythologies. It became the exclusive arbiter of knowledge and so discounted other sources of knowledge and wisdom.

Within an Enlightenment vision of modernity we were educated into for-saking the myths that supposedly 'primitive' peoples lived by and so proving ourselves superior through being able to live by reason alone. We un-wittingly absorbed the notion that to recognize the power of myth was to admit to a condition of dependency and to live in a state of childishness. We were to prove our freedom and independence by showing that we could live without the consolations of myth. We learnt that myths were fictions and so were 'unreal' and 'unscientific', that we were to be guided in our freedom by reason and science alone. The dominant West claimed 'civilization' and 'modernity' in its own white Christian image and so set the terms in which 'others' – defined as 'less than human' because living closer to nature – had to prove themselves. Again it was the West alone that could take its human-ity for granted.

If 'others' were to prove themselves members of the magic circle of human-ity they had to prove their rationality in terms provided by the West. If people were to be 'modern' they had to be ready to imitate the West, even if this meant they had to be *false* to their own traditions and cultures, which came to be diminished in their own eyes as they were conceived as 'backward' and 'uncivilized'. Franz Fanon in *Black Skin, White Mask* (1970) shares how he came to think and feel about himself through the workings of colonialism. He learnt to feel ashamed of his own customs and traditions in Martinique as he learnt to identify culture and modernity with Paris. He felt diminished in his own eyes and shared with others an unacknowledged feeling of inade-quacy. It was as if they were not 'good enough' as they were, so that they had to aspire to become 'other' than what they were. It was only when Fanon eventually got to Paris as a student and was forced to confront the everyday realities of racism that he recognized that he was not 'white', for he had unknowingly learnt to see himself *through* the colonial eyes of France and to judge himself accordingly. He had believed a central myth of a humanist modernity: that differences of race could easily be transcended as people learn to relate to each other as equal human beings. He felt betrayed.

Myth and Nature

Modernity is strangely blind to the myths that enforce it, for it presents itself as having transcended myths to be able to face reality in terms of reason and science. Fanon can help us recognize the power of modernity as a myth and the ways it works to devalue colonial peoples in their own eyes. The myths and traditions of Martinique had to be forsaken for they were the products of unreason and nature. Only through a separation from nature could we recognize that progress within modernity involves the control and domination of nature. Within modernity we learn to despise and devalue connections with nature for they serve to prove our own 'backwardness'. We are assured that it is only through following a movement from 'nature' to 'culture' that we are on a path towards modernity.

Feminism and ecology have helped us identify and acknowledge some of the myths which have organized modernity. In important respects these movements cut across the traditional political distinctions between left and right since both capitalist and state socialist societies were blighted by eco-logical devastation. In their different ways they each manifested a concep-tion of progress tied to the domination of nature. This was also linked to the subordination of women who were deemed to be closer to nature, for the societies shared a rationalist conception of modernity which treated reason alone as a source of knowledge. The authority given to a detached concep-tion of scientific knowledge has its source in the scientific revolution and its disenchanting of the world. This followed from the death of nature which came to be conceived as matter governed by scientific laws. These conver-gences illuminated the importance of shifting the terms of political and cul-tural discussion so that it was not exclusively concerned with arguments between capitalism and socialism but recognized how both were shaped in different ways by a Eurocentric tradition of Enlightenment rationalism.

The devaluation of nature has gone hand in hand with the devaluation of women, who were conceived of as being 'closer to nature'.[7] When feminism is not theorized in structuralist terms that impose a categorical split between 'nature' and 'culture', there are significant resonances between feminism and ecology. As women were silenced within a modernity which identified dominant white Christian masculinity with reason, so nature was also silenced for it has no voice of its own. As reason is separated from nature and comes to be seen as the exclusive source of meanings and values, so nature is also denied as a source of values and meanings. There are no longer *intrinsic* values which we have to respect and honour in our relation-ships with nature, for we are no longer to conceive of ourselves as part of nature; rather, our 'humanity' comes to be defined in radical opposition to it. Reason sets us apart from nature.

The modernist identification of masculinity with reason reveals the inner relation between feminism and ecology. As men we learn to silence our 'inner natures' for they are experienced as a threat to the rule of reason. We learn to live without emotional needs which become deemed as a sign of weakness. To be soft and tender is to be 'feminine' and this often connects to a fear of gayness – homophobia – in many heterosexual men. We do not have much relationship with these aspects of ourselves, for within modernity we have learnt to *discount* them as a way of affirming dominant heterosexual male identities. In the ways we learn to tell ourselves as dominant men that we don't have needs and that we can survive on our own if we have to, we also learn to do without myths. In identifying with reason we learn to prove that we can live without the consolations of myth. It is only children who need myths, for myths essentially reflect a 'childish' level of development. It is a sign of regression to speak of the power of myths or the ways they might speak more directly to our experience through their emotional language. Rather we learn that if we have reason then we don't need myth.

We learn to think of myth not as working within its own terms and through its own channels, but as an inferior and defective form of reason.

There is little that it can teach us that we do not already know through reason but there are many ways that it can lead us astray. To recognize that myths can operate on an emotional or feeling level of experience makes it all the easier to reject them within the terms of an Enlightenment rationalism, because we assume that they are attempting to influence and determine our behaviour externally. This is why it is so crucial for Kant (1959) to argue that we can *only* sustain an inner relationship with our reason, which is why it is only when we act according to reason that we are supposedly exercising our freedom and autonomy. So Kant manages to sustain a remarkable reversal that becomes a powerful myth within modernity, namely that we are left with an external and estranged relationship with our experience. In a significant respect it is not 'ours' for it is 'subjective' and seeks to influence our behaviour externally as a form of unfreedom.

With Kant we come to have an externalized relationship with our 'natures', which are radically separated from reason and deemed 'animal natures'. Whatever experience has its source in our natures can form no part of our identities as rational selves. When Kant talks of 'human nature' it is reason which constitutes the 'human' and it is expressed through 'rising above' our 'animal natures'.[8] What is crucial here is that though reason is a quality which men can take for granted in their interactions with women, for it is men who are supposedly the 'rational sex', masculinity is *not* something that we can ever take for granted as men. Masculinity is something that we have to be constantly ready to prove. It isn't anything we can feel easy or relaxed with because we have to be constantly vigilant and on guard to prove that, for instance, we are not 'soft' or 'sissies'. Since masculinity is very much defined as a relation of exclusion it is constantly shadowed by homophobic feelings, for it is threatened by any behaviour that might be regarded as 'soft' or 'effeminate'. This is probably why still relatively few men have engaged in processes of change.

Robert Bly's *Iron John* has been able to touch the experience of many men partly through its recognition of the power of myth. It has explored different ways of speaking to the experience of men which sidestep a rationalism that so often acts as a form of defensiveness. Bly has been able to speak to the heart and souls of men that have long been starved of recognition and nourishment. But part of the appeal of Bly's work lies also in his promise that if men engage in an exploration of their inherited forms of masculinity, they won't be 'feminized'. Men are guaranteed that they will not become 'soft', with all the threatening homophobic associations this presents to contemporary masculinities. This is a guarantee that you seem to be offered before you even begin any process of exploration.

But even here Bly touches an important chord, for he understands that many men have found it difficult to relate to feminism. Some have been tempted into feeling that masculinity itself is a relationship of power which oppresses women so that there are no ways for it to be redeemed or changed. This has led men to sometimes reject masculinity in their identification with feminism, feeling that the women's movement would set the agenda for them. This has fostered a politics of *self-denial* which left many

heterosexual men feeling uncertain in their masculinity. Bly seems to be
offering a third way that allows men to escape from the macho image of
masculinity that was dominant in the 1950s and which we still live to an
extent Bly readily acknowledges, even though it does not fit the historical
framework that he has prepared for himself. Bly talks about how the unfeeling and distant macho man who was totally focused on a job and individual
achievement within the public realm of work was replaced by the 'feminized' and 'naive man' of the 1970s and 1980s. The history is much more
complex but it allows Bly to present in *Iron John* a new way that can supposedly escape the pitfalls of both conceptions of masculinity. But this can
easily mislead us about the processes through which men can change. It also
fails to engage enough with men's relationships with women and the impacts
of feminisms on these relationships.

Notes

1 Feminism was decisive in getting heterosexual men from different backgrounds to think
about the power they had so long taken for granted within relationships. This was a central
concern in the relationship between men and feminism. This is explored in *Between Men and
Feminism*, edited by David Porter (1993). It is also a central theme in Victor J. Seidler, *Rediscovering Masculinity: Reason, Language and Sexuality* (1989).

2 Some of the predicaments we face within a postmodern world which too often refuses to
acknowledge the continuing impact of modernity are explored in Zygmunt Bauman's *Modernity and Ambivalence* (1993) and in his essays *Intimations of Postmodernity* (1994). See also
Marshall Berman, *All That Is Solid Melts into Air* (1982). For a brief introduction see Barry
Smart, *Postmodernism* (1993).

3 For a helpful discussion of postmodern identities see, for instance, *Forget Baudrillard*,
edited by Chris Rojek and Bryan Turner (1994); Sadie Plant, *The Most Radical Gesture* (1992);
Place and the Politics of Identity, edited by Michael Keith and Steve Pile (1993); and *Mapping
the Subject: Geographies of Cultural Transformation*, edited by Steve Pile and Nigel Thrift
(1996).

4 A sense of Baudrillard's trajectory can be gained from the critical early text *Symbolic
Exchange and Death* (1995).

5 The way in which reason is defined in fundamental opposition to nature within modernity
is a central theme in *Nature, Culture, Gender*, edited by M. McCormack and M. Strathern
(1980). It is also central to Max Weber's recognition of the disenchantment of nature within
modernity: see his introduction to *The Sociology of Religion* (1967).

6 The way that fathers traditionally have to exist as external authorities in relation to the
family are explored in Victor J. Seidler, 'Fathering, Authority and Masculinity', in *Male Order:
Unwrapping Masculinity*, edited by R. Chapman and J. Rutherford (1988, pp. 272–302). I make
connections to Kant's ethical writings, particularly his text *Education* (1960) where he explores
the role of fathers in moral education.

7 The way that the devaluation of women had gone hand in hand with the devaluation of
nature is explored in Caroline Merchant, *The Death of Nature: Women, Ecology and the Scientific Revolution* (1980). It is also a central theme in E. Fox Keller, *Reflections on Gender and
Science* (1984); K. Stern, *The Flight from Women* (1986); and R. Radford Ruether, *New
Woman, New Earth: Sexist Ideologies and Human Liberation* (1995).

8 I have explored how for Kant it is reason that defines what is 'human' in human nature,
so established a rationalist form of humanism, in *Kant, Respect and Injustice: The Limits of
Liberal Moral Theory* (1986). It is because ethics is defined in terms of 'rising above' animal
nature that it is so difficult to rethink the relation between ethics and ecology.

3
Aspects of Self

Masculine and Feminine

Men have responded to feminism in different ways and we have to think carefully about how men can change in relationships with women. The way that Bly presents the history assumes that men have already 'got in touch with the feminine', have somehow already learnt to accept their emotional aspects so that they might be ready to take the path that he sets out within *Iron John*. This partly explains Bly's silence about feminism and the ease with which he can say that his concern is elsewhere, namely with men's relationships with their masculinities. This allows Bly to focus upon awakening the 'inner warrior' that has been allowed to fall asleep within contemporary cultures of masculinity. It is this language that can so easily be misconstrued, especially by men who are looking to challenge the modest gains that feminism has made over the last 20 years. Bly's language carries historical resonances that can cut across the mythological contexts that he carefully provides for them. It has been used by men 'to stand up to feminism' as part of a backlash that Bly very much regrets.[1] In part he cannot be held responsible for the uses made of his work, but he does carry responsibility for the language he uses.

Where Bly is onto something important is in questioning those men who have felt that the issues they face in changing are adequately dealt with in terms of 'recovering' feminine aspects within themselves. The problem with this Jungian language is that it leaves the masculine as unreconstructed, as if men will automatically assume a new shape through this process of exploring feminine aspects.[2] Seeing the process of personal growth and integration in these terms can encourage men to accept emotions and feelings that they have traditionally learnt to reject. But it tends to reinforce a *split* which would treat reason as 'masculine' while emotions and feelings are regarded as 'feminine', thus underwriting some of the critical dualities of modernity.[3]

Nevertheless this can be a useful way of thinking and encourages men into a sensitivity to processes of personal change and development. At least it leads men to think about aspects of their experience which they have rejected and devalued. It also fosters a vision of growth that is at odds with the mechanistic notions of change that have characterized men's experience within modernity. These are organized around the idea of self-control as involving the domination of emotional and sensitive life so that it cannot 'interfere' with the direction we set ourselves through reason. We learn to regret our 'inclination', in Kant's (1959) term, thinking that we would fulfil ourselves as rational beings if we did not have the temptations of nature to deal with. Jung (1956) helps us to challenge prevailing rationalist traditions and helps us connect to other areas of experience. We are left with a very different conception of fulfilment as human beings, even if we find it hard to come to terms with issues of class, race, gender and ethnicity which are still treated within modernity as aspects we have to learn to 'rise above' to be able to recognize others in their humanity. Jung's vision opens up some crucial concerns which challenge the terms of modernity, while at the same time closing others.[4]

Men can often experience a division within themselves as a struggle between different parts. This is something Howard Cooper has expressed well:

> I could say that I am suffering from a split consciousness. There are two forces inside of me, each seeking to dominate the other. One I experience as a masculine, assertive force. I am manipulative and egocentric, and I have an urge to be dominating and authoritarian. My intellect enjoys having answers, possessing truths. Mind, will and logic dominate . . . The other force is not concerned with having and using. It is concerned with feeling and sensitivity, dreams, creativity, fantasy . . . It is intuitive, gentle and strong. It allows me to be receptive, allowing and accepting. When I live from this still centre I do not need to manipulate people and events to suit my own needs. I experience this force as a powerful feminine one, in which my ego submits to a power greater than myself. Its concern is my growth, development and change as a human being. (1990: 352)

This is a powerful voice that can speak to us movingly, but it talks in terms of two independent forces, which is often the way that we think about 'masculine' and 'feminine' principles under Jung's influence. This way of thinking has proved insightful to both men and women when it reminds us of aspects of our experience which the dominant rationalist culture teaches us to separate from and reject. It can help men reconsider the vulnerability and tender feelings that they have learned to discount and can raise questions about a culture that makes it so hard to acknowledge and accept these aspects of their experience. Within a Protestant moral culture, men and women in different ways inherit a sense of the *evilness* of their natures as human beings, even if this has been given a secular expression and moderated within a liberal moral culture. It still leaves men in particular feeling uneasy about their bodies and emotions which they can experience as 'distractions' and 'temptations' from the real 'business of life' that lies in individual achievement and success. In this sense as heterosexual men we are divided *against* ourselves, for we are set in a constant struggle against an evil nature – represented by our sexualities and desires – which needs to be curbed if we are to maintain 'control' over ourselves.

Within modernity the masculine is defined in opposition to the feminine, for we have to constantly prove as boys that we are not 'soft' or 'weak'. This inner fear of 'being weak' stays with us long into our adult lives as men. It is part of living out the dominant myths of masculinity and it connects to a pervasive sense that we will only be 'real men' if we have fought in battle. Even if we have rejected these notions intellectually, we might be surprised

at feeling regret that, say, we are too old to have participated in the Falk-
lands War. It is as if the possibilities of 'manhood' could have passed by a
whole generation who had not been tested at war. Again it is a matter of
listening to unconscious emotions and learning from them, even if they do
not fit with our rational conceptions of ourselves. But the ways we learn to
listen to our unconscious are also structured in particular ways within different psychoanalytic traditions. Freud (1922) was more keen to recognize the
workings of repressed sexual desires which can somehow get lost in Jung.

It is difficult not to feel that sometimes the 'feminine' remains idealized
within the Jungian framework. Somehow it seems to lead us to deeper connections with the self while the masculine seems to be trapped in 'having
and using'. While we might recognize the place of these different qualities
within our experience we might wonder how far it takes us to identify them
as 'feminine' and 'masculine', though no doubt these terms carry their particular cultural resonances. This language still seems to have a way of
deceiving us about the ways the feminine remains 'other' to us as men and
the *difficulties* that we often have in relating to women as people in their
own right with their own sexualities, desires and ideas. There is a danger of
appropriating the 'feminine' at the same time as we idealize women. It
remains an open question whether 'coming to terms with our feminine
aspects' will shift the ways that we relate more equally to women. It could
work in different ways. Both Freud and Jung seemed trapped in different
ways in seeing female sexuality as an 'enigma' because they accepted masculinity as a norm that 'others' were to be judged from. To this extent they
remain within the terms of a Eurocentric modernity, showing different
aspects of the identification of masculinity with reason.[5]

Jung's language can be helpful to men in raising questions about the connections we have with aspects of our experience, that we so easily devalue
as we live out dominant myths of masculinity within a Protestant moral
culture. Bly also has doubts about the ways the notion of 'anima' has been
used to refer to the 'female principle' as it operates within men. The point
is that this principle is operating within our experience, even if we are
unaware of it. But this makes it difficult to *identify* the limitations and
restrictions that have been structured into men's experience through the
particular identification of masculinity with reason as power. This also helps
illuminate the difficulties that heterosexual men have in coming to terms
with their 'feminine aspect'. Rather it is because dominant men have learnt
to place their identities through an identification with reason that emotions
and feelings have become threatening within a dominant Protestant tradition of modernity.

Men from different class and ethnic backgrounds can express particular
emotions like anger and frustration without bringing their masculinity into
question. These emotions can affirm traditional masculinities so that men
often learn to act out of anger, for instance, as a way of protecting themselves from softer and more threatening emotions like fear, sadness and
vulnerability. It is the 'weaker' emotions that we deny because they

compromise dominant Western myths of masculinity as independent and self-sufficient. As men growing up in Protestant cultures it is often difficult to acknowledge our needs for others, for it is easy to feel that we will be overwhelmed if we 'give in' to emotions we have so long denied. Often it is easier to move into irritation and anger, especially with those we are closest to, as a way of holding less acceptable emotions in check. We can act out of anger often as a cover for emotions which we find it harder to acknowledge.

It might be that part of the appeal of Bly's *Iron John* is that he allows men to contact their emotions of loss, hurt and vulnerability while at the same time being able to offer a guarantee to their masculinity. This allows men, often for the first time, to share their feelings and emotions with other men secure in their own 'warrior' status. Bly's language can work as a form of reassurance for men who would fear that exposing sadness or loss might be a sign of homosexual feelings. This means that men do not have to *work through* their homophobic feelings as part of being close and intimate with other men. This helps explain the broad appeal of *Iron John*, which is in many ways a difficult book to read because of its many cultural references. By providing men with a sense of security in advance it allows many men who have not been touched by feminism to engage in a process of self-exploration. This is to be welcomed as long as it does not sustain a backlash to feminism. But is less able to appreciate the need to rework relations with women and question the forms of power that men can so often take for granted within the larger patriarchal society.

Needs and Dependency

Within the rationalist culture which has dominated modernity and worked to marginalize romantic voices to an autonomous realm of culture, heterosexual men have often learnt to despise their emotions. We tacitly learn to treat our emotions as an 'inconvenience' that gets in the way of being able to govern our lives through reason alone. It is a powerful myth that men's lives would be so much simpler if we did not have to deal with emotions at all. A central myth within modernity is that men do *not* have needs of their own but can live independent and self-sufficient lives guided by reason. To admit that we have emotional needs, even to ourselves, is to acknowledge 'weakness' and 'failure'.

As white heterosexual men we learn that emotional needs have to do with a childish dependency that we should have left behind on the path towards manhood. To acknowledge needs is a sign that we have failed to make a proper transition to manhood. This is the way we weaken a connection to our 'inner child' who we abandon in order to prove our masculinity. At some level we carry a sense of betrayal as if we have betrayed a source of inner knowledge and wisdom. We often learn to separate from our childhood experiences and relationships, thinking that they can only compromise our masculine identity. Rather we prove that we have made it to manhood through forsaking our 'childish' experiences. This is a price that we have to pay, though at some level we can feel guilty about it. It is as if we have given up some precious part of ourselves in order to find favour within the broader culture. Often we do this to secure the approval and love of our parents, giving up what we know so that we can be acceptable to them. But we also do this to live out particular myths within the broader patriarchal culture. For a liberal moral culture is still strongly informed by an abiding Protestant sense of inadequacy, a sense that we are not 'good enough' as we are. This is part of how we *prove* our masculinity to be 'independent' and 'self-sufficient'.[6]

With masculinity identified with reason we learn to be suspicious of our spontaneity. This is part of a more pervasive uncertainty about natural emotions and feelings which are deemed to be a sign of lack of 'self-control'. Spontaneity has its place but it it severely restricted. It has to do with fun and entertainment, not with the serious business of life. Reason alone is a source of meanings and values. When Bly talks about 'wildness', a term so often misinterpreted, he means the opposite of 'tameness', and he ties this to men's loss of spontaneity. This is an aspect of the administration of life that has become so endemic within the corporate culture in which people are taught to identify with their firms. Bly tracks this back to the industrial revolution and he surmises that with each passing generation we have experienced a weakening in our capacity for spontaneous living.

As men it is easy to experience spontaneity as a threat to an ordered and rational life. In *Recreating Sexual Politics* (1991a) I talked about this in terms of the 'externalization' of men's experience, the ways men come to evaluate their experience according to external standards alone. It is so often a matter of whether we are 'good enough' according to unquestioned cultural standards, and we are left haunted by a sense of inadequacy. This is an effect of the degradation of inner emotional life and sensitivity, which have been given a secular form within modernity. In traditions of social theory set in rationalist terms, we disdain spontaneous feelings, for we learn to treat them as 'lacking' reason and direction. We treat them as signs of 'inadequacy' rather than as an embodiment of a movement beyond the conscious control of the mind. Within a rationalist tradition we have lost a sense of sources of wisdom that might lie beyond the control of the rational mind. Rather our spontaneous feelings are yet another symptom of a childishness we have failed to control. They reflect an inability to curb our 'animal natures'. So it is that we can only prove ourselves to be 'in control' as rational selves by silencing and denying the promptings of our inner selves.

Thus men often learn to fear their own spontaneous emotions for they indicate an 'animal nature' that has still to be controlled. But it can be misleading to call these neglected and hidden aspects of ourselves 'wild', as when Bly talks about connecting to the 'wildman' within, the Iron John who lives at the bottom of the lake waiting to be bucketed out, as the Grimm's fairy story tells. Bly's book *Iron John* consists of an extended meditation on this story, an attempt to recover the truths that we have lost and redeem the power of the mythology it expresses. In many ways it is a rewarding story but Bly threatens to universalize a story that is not every boy's story of his path towards manhood. It resonates with a particular experience of boyhood and a set of struggles, but we have to be careful not to generalize too quickly. The fact that it has struck a chord for so many different men, particularly in the United States, reflects a need that some men feel to discover different ways of being men in the 1990s.

A Jungian tradition often presents archetypes as operating in a realm of their own, waiting to be discovered. It suggests a universalism that, underlying differences of culture, history and tradition, there exists a universal language that illuminates human experience. This is a claim also hovering over Bly's text that we have to treat very carefully, for there is always a danger that we will unwittingly universalize a particular cultural experience. This is the thrust of Lucy Goodison's work *Moving Heaven and Earth* (1992) which works to recover a culture in ancient Crete which is organized around the symbolic experience of women. She shows the centrality of women's bodies to the rituals that mark the passages of the seasons and people's lives. There is a celebration of the body and nature as sources of wisdom, a refusal to make a categorical distinction between the heavens as the source of truth and goodness and the earth as the place of nature and evil. Here we find a challenge to Jung's (1971) vision of the Greek gods who occupy a heavenly space of their own, for we can recognize this as part of a move towards a patriarchal society in which women lost their power. The suggestion is that Jung has generalized from this classical Greek situation and so universalized on the basis of a particular male experience and power.[7]

Within modernity men learn to be 'independent' and 'self-sufficient' through *denying* emotional needs and desires. It is 'others', namely women and children, who show their weakness by having needs. Men are there to support others through moments of emotional difficulty, but we supposedly do not need to support ourselves. When the chips are down we are well able to look after ourselves. This is a myth that many men find it hard to break with, for we fear the weakness and inadequacy that it will show. We fear losing face in front of others and our place on the hierarchy of power positions. But as we grow up through our twenties and we witness certain patterns taking shape in our relationships we can sometimes recognize a fear of contact and intimacy. We can wonder, especially as white middle class heterosexual men, whether ways we have learnt to silence and deny our inner emotional lives are not creating difficulties for ourselves in close and intimate relationships. But this forces us as men to confront some central myths about 'strength' and 'weakness' that govern so many contemporary masculinities.

Often our dependency upon the emotional work that women do for us in heterosexual relationships is hidden because we persist on seeing ourselves as 'independent'. It means that we reject the love and support being offered to us, while at some level feeding off it. We devalue the emotional work that our partners often do, taking it for granted. It is as if we have little sense as men of the emotional work that goes into sustaining a relationship. Once in place we can take relationships for granted as part of the background against which we live out our individual lives as men.[8] With male identities largely established within the public realm of work, that is the arena that counts in men's sense of achievement and self-esteem. This means that we often take relationships for granted, whatever lip-service we might give them. This is structured into the ways that male identities are affirmed within the public realm of work. It means we devalue much of the work that partners do, for it threatens the masculine sense of ourselves as self-sufficient. This is emotional work that we somehow have to learn to do for ourselves if we are to take greater responsibility for our emotional lives.

Bly helpfully draws attention to the slow and patient 'bucketing' work that men have to learn to do for themselves. We slowly have to move the water of our emotional lives so that we can help create a different relationship with ourselves. This involves giving up the notion that emotions are a sign of 'weakness' so that we can value and honour the strength that it takes to face our emotions rather than hide from them. There is also courage involved in acknowledging that we *need* others, that we do not have to make it on our own. This is a more honest situation, for so often we are dependent upon women to interpret our emotional lives for us, without even acknowledging the hidden work they do. To learn to take greater responsibility for our emotions and feelings as men doesn't have to make us any the less 'masculine'. It is a way in which we can learn to express and share masculinities with others rather than withdraw into a sullen silence. Nor does it mean that we are any the less 'rational' or 'reasonable', even if it broadens the terms in which we automatically learnt to set reason against nature within modernity.

But the imagery of the wildman can so easily lead us astray, for it can suggest that we have to reverse the dualities of modernity to return from 'civilization' to 'wildness', rather than to challenge the very terms of this modernist framework. It might partly be, as Rousseau (1964) recognized, that we have lost touch with our natures within a modernity that has encouraged us to leave them behind to cultivate a rationalist vision of self. Too often this has meant living up to false images and myths of ourselves as we learn to judge ourselves by terms not of our own making. As boys we are constantly living up to standards, say at school, where we can assume that there must be something wrong with us if we disapprove of the regime of the school. We are told that if we are not 'wimps' or 'wet' then we would get on well, so that if we don't like it, we only have ourselves to blame. We internalize the blame, thinking we are not 'good enough', rather than question the naturalized ideas of masculinity that we feel forced to live up to.

Notes

1 For a helpful discussion of the backlash against feminism in the 1980s see Susan Faludi, *Backlash: The Undeclared War Against American Women* (1992). For an idea of the backlash

against feminism on the part of heterosexual men, see, for instance, David Thomas, *Not Guilty: In Defence of the Modern Man* (1993); and Neil Lyndon, *No More Sex Wars* (1992).

2 Introductions to Jung's work which help to place it in intellectual and historical context are given in Andrew Samuels, *Jung and the Post-Jungians* (1986); and Roger Stevens, *Jung* (1956).

3 Jung's discussion of 'masculine' and 'feminine' is explored in terms of notions of 'anima' and 'animus' in *Aspects of the Feminine* (1986). There is also some discussion in *Man and his Symbols* (1964).

4 To rethink Jung's work in relation to politics see, for instance, Andrew Samuels, *The Political Psyche* (1995).

5 For a sense of how Jung thought about female sexuality see, for instance, Sukie Cosgrove, *The Spirit and the Valley* (1976).

6 The links between a dominant white heterosexual masculinity and a Protestant moral culture are explored in Victor J. Seidler, *Recreating Sexual Politics: Men, Feminism and Politics* (1991a), particularly as they relate to the pressures on men to be independent and self-sufficient.

7 Lucy Goodison, in *Moving Heaven and Earth* (1992), tries to show that Jung's universal archetypes are in fact based upon a particular historical moment in the development of patriarchy. She uncovers a different experience of women's spirituality in Crete, which at the very least makes us aware of alternative possibilities.

8 A sense of the emotional labour that women are often expected to do within intimate relationships is explored by Jean Baker Miller in *Towards a New Psychology of Women* (1976). She shows the way that men's power in relationships so often works to render invisible and devalue the emotional work that women do.

4
Myths of Manhood

Myths and Masculinities

How can we learn to identify the myths of masculinity that are unwittingly
lived out in our everyday lives? Within an Enlightenment vision of modernity we have learnt to think that myths are not 'real' and so cannot affect
the ways we live. We might be told that even if we think they can, 'in reality'
they cannot. This has made it so much harder to appreciate the power of
myths within contemporary lives and the ways they influence both *who* we
want to be and the ways we think and feel about our lives. Robert Bly's *Iron
John* struck a chord in its recognition that within contemporary society the
myths we inherit about who we are to be as men no longer illuminate the
lives and relationships we now live. They create a whole range of expectations about who we 'should' be that can be in tension with a different
reality we want to live. This is part of a crisis of contemporary masculinities.

A central myth of masculinity we inherit within modernity is the idea that
men do not have needs of their own because if they are 'strong' they can
get on by themselves. The traditional conception of the macho man who is
in control of his life and relationships helps to create false expectations and
blinds men to the injuries they do to themselves in aspiring to live up to
these ideals. This has been particularly sharp for middle class boys who in
England have been sent away to boarding schools at around eight years old.
They are often encouraged to feel grateful because their parents are sacri-
ficing to provide them with a good education. They are told that it might be
difficult in the beginning, but they will soon get used to it. In any case it will
be 'good for them' because they will learn to be independent and look after
themselves. If boys continue to feel miserable, this only proves that there
must be something 'wrong' with them. They learn to keep these insecurities
secret because they fear that others will only be given grounds to reject them
if they find out.

This feeling that 'there is something wrong with me' continues to haunt
different masculinities. It encourages boys to hide what they are feeling
because we live in fear that others might 'find out'. For young middle class
boys sent away to boarding school this resonates with a sense of having been
abandoned by your parents. Even though little is said, it can be difficult not
to feel at some level that it is because there is 'something wrong with you'
that they are sending you away. At some level boys carry an unspoken anger
at being rejected by their parents, though this has to be suppressed because

you learn to think of these emotions as 'irrational' – and so as further proof that there is something 'wrong' – since you are so often told that what is being done for you 'is for the best'.

Sometimes it is only many years later in adult life that some of these emotions begin to surface. Men begin to recognize that 'others didn't like it too', so you can begin to give yourself permission to have your own anger rather than to discount it. As Piers Partridge and John Witt have found in workshops that they have run for survivors of public school, men have kept these emotions secret for so long and embodied a way of coping with the world that it is often painful to recall these experiences.[1] The point is that these boys learn to be 'independent' before their time, so that they learn to cope externally with situations that their inner emotional life is hardly ready for. Moreover, they learn to *despise* emotions and feelings and only to value success and achievement in the external world. They learn to rely upon patterns of behaviour that are not appropriate within intimate and personal relationships. Often, men who have these histories carry too much unresolved pain from their childhood experiences to be able to open up emotionally to others. But it can be difficult to identify the 'emptiness' of their emotional lives, for this is what they've learnt to live with from school. They learn to be 'on guard', for it is hard to trust others when there is so much unmet and unresolved needs. It is hard to recognize what you are missing, if you have never experienced it before.

As men grow up to deny their emotional needs, as they learn to live out myths that we have absorbed about 'how men are supposed to be', we hardly appreciate the 'injuries' we do to ourselves through being cut off from our emotional lives. We learn to *present* ourselves as we are 'supposed to be' and we learn to conceal any emotions that might bring this ideal into question. We do not want to know about any emotions or feelings that might compromise the image that we are doing our best to live up to. As men we learn to think that we are 'strong' because we do not have needs and that we are simply there to provide support for others who are 'weaker' than ourselves. Men are also encouraged to feel that we know what is best for others, for reason is essentially a masculine quality, so that we carry a responsibility for legislating for others.

Though it is crucially important to recognize the particular experience of different masculinities of class, race, ethnicity, generation and sexual orientation, it can also help to keep open resonances that can sound across these differences. This does not at all mean that underlying these differences there exist universal structures of masculinity that are modulated in different ways, through different cultures, histories, traditions and experiences. This tendency towards exposing underlying patterns that supposedly characterize universal forms of 'human nature' is a strong feature of modernity. This particular humanist vision works to undermine the reality of differences, and suggests that we can 'rise above' these supposedly arbitrary and contingent differences.[2] We have to be wary of a tradition of rational humanism because, despite its claims, it so often worked as a relationship

of exclusion. It so often normalized a particular pattern of human relationship and treated 'others' – women, blacks, Jews, gays and lesbians – as
'lacking' some essential element that would have allowed them to participate equally in the magic circle of humanity. We have to be ready to listen
and honour the differences that exist and the different voices in which they
are expressed without losing touch with visions of equality, freedom and
justice that were part of an inheritance of modernity. But we might have to
conceive these values differently.[3]

Power and Emotion

Men's power in relation to women was given a particular form within modernity. Often this is difficult for men to appreciate because individual men
can feel so unsure and powerless themselves. They find it hard to recognize
themselves in the powerful images that feminist theory often presents of
men, for they seem to bear such little relation to their own insecurities and
fears of rejection. This helped create a resentment towards feminism and
fuelled a backlash in the 1980s, especially when men saw women increasingly in powerful positions in industry, the media and public life. At the
same time it was easy for other anti-sexist men to feel that feminism had the
answers, and only later to resent the ways these were presented. Bly's
silence about feminism in *Iron John* has left him open to being used as part
of a backlash to feminism that he says he would in no way support.

Somehow we need to be able to acknowledge the power that men have
in society without thereby feeding a myth that all men feel powerful in their
individual lives. For if we are to openly and honestly explore the sources of
our different masculinities we have also to recognize our inherited sense of
superiority in relation to women. It is easy for many men to feel that women
are there as subordinates to serve the needs of men. We need to explore
unconscious emotions and desires which could foster a backlash, for
instance the notion that 'because this is their proper place they only have
themselves to blame if they are punished for trying to escape it.' Often this
is a hidden source of male anger and violence. Anger against feminism so
easily slides into rage against women, which we can discern in such backlash writing as Neil Lyndon's *No More Sex Wars* (1992).[4]

We have inherited a sense as men that the public world is a man's world
and that women have no right to enter it unless they are prepared to
conform to the same standards. The rules of membership are taken to be
fair and impartial, so there is resentment when it is pointed out that these
are rules which reflect the experience of men. As women enter the traditional male workspace there is often resentment because it threatens the
ways that men are used to relating to each other.[5] It is men who no longer
know how to be with each other when women are around. Traditionally this
has gone along with the idea that the home is the 'proper place' for women,
so that their presence in the workplace is an aberration. Men are prepared

to 'help out' within the domestic realm and with children, but basically this is still an area that women should have responsibility for. This vision of 'separate but equal' has informed the traditional structures that men have often grown up with and taken for granted in their own families. This links to the ways that masculinity still remains tied to the notion of men as 'breadwinners', since male identities are still very much defined within the public realm of work.[6]

These notions still work as sources of resentment as men feel unsettled and disturbed by the challenges of feminism. There is a more widespread sense of equality as fairness, which means that more men appreciate that it isn't *fair* for women to be left with responsibility for the domestic realm and childcare, but this often stops short of questioning men's careers. Then men fall back on reason, which allows men to legislate 'what is best' not only for themselves but also for others. It is 'rational' for them to sustain their careers because they can earn more. So it is one thing for men to 'help out' but quite another to talk seriously about job sharing. But we shouldn't minimize some of the changes that have taken place, even if it means that men still do relatively little around the house. There is a gap between the different ways men now talk about themselves and what men actually do.[7]

Even if some of these contradictions can sometimes be talked about in reasonable tones, what is at issue is a shift in men's power that men often resent at an unconscious level. If men want to live out different myths about themselves, threat and violence may not be very far from the surface. For if men have learnt to think of reason as their own, they are used to getting their own way. We are used to 'knowing what is best', so it is threatening to be told that women have their own ways of thinking about things and have their own values and priorities. For this is to challenge reason as providing a single scale upon which different preferences can somehow be weighed. This assumes that different preferences and priorities can be made compatible with each other. But often this is not true in a relationship, when women want time and space for themselves to work out how they want to live and relate.

As men learn to create new myths about themselves it is important to recognize that we might accept something rationally, but feel quite different about it emotionally. This is why it has been important for men to discover a space in which we can safely explore the different levels of our experience. Men will feel anger and resentment at the loss of power they are being asked to accept, and they need a space in which these negative emotions can be explored. This questions the idea that men can control their experience through reason and will alone, as if we can discount emotions we would rather not have. We have learnt that 'if they are not acknowledged, then they do not exist.' But this is part of a myth of control *as domination* of our inner emotional lives that leaves us constantly fitting and adjusting our experience to rational ideals we have worked out for ourselves. Often this leaves men in tension with themselves, for there is frustration about having to live up to ideals of masculinity that are not of our own making.

Both feminism and psychotherapy can help challenge the terms of a modernity which assumes that ideals can be worked out by reason alone. This leaves men constantly trying to live up to myths of ourselves and feeling we 'should' feel and behave in particular ways. This can make us strangely intolerant of ourselves, for we refuse to admit into our conscious awareness any thoughts or emotions which do not fit the ideals we have accepted for ourselves. This has created an impersonalization of men's experience governed by reason that makes a more personal voice difficult. As men have been challenged by women to share themselves more emotionally and personally, this has touched deep fears which need to be appreciated.

It isn't that men are being stubborn and withdrawn, for often they would dearly love to have more contact with themselves emotionally. The identification of masculinity with reason has made it difficult for men to be more emotionally responsive, and this isn't anything that can be changed by will and determination.[8] To share what we feel about ourselves emotionally can so easily threaten our sense of ourselves as men. We can go rigid out of fear that our male identities will disintegrate and we will be left with nothing. This is why it has often been easier for men to feel that feminism has to do with the opportunities available to women, but nothing to do with themselves as men.

As we begin to identify some of the diverse myths that we live by as men, so we can start to recognize how much effort has gone into sustaining these images of ourselves. It is so easy to feel that we have 'failed' because we are 'not good enough'. So, for instance, boarding school boys often learn to turn their anger against themselves, for it is difficult to appreciate that the practice of sending boys away so young is barbaric. We are so used to keeping our emotions secret that it is hard to share them without feeling that we will be humiliated and made to feel small. It is only as we recognize that we are not the only boys who have felt this way that we can gain the courage to share more of ourselves. As we learn to honour the courage that it takes to share emotions with others, as part of a process of exploration, we learn to recognize the integrity of emotional life. As we learn that it is important to be as true to our emotions and feelings as to our thoughts, we learn that there is nothing shameful in having needs and asking for help. Rather this is the only way that we can grow in our individuality, for it gives us an experience that others *can* be there for us although they were not there when we were young. It is part of a process of healing the wounds that we carry from the past and learning *how* to relate differently in the present.

Myths and Emotional Life

The myths that we inherit within modernity no longer speak to our condition as men and the diverse challenges that we face. This encourages Bly to look for different sources in ancient myths and fairy tales that can remind us of qualities we have lost and carry a wisdom that we can still learn from.

As we awaken to the significance of myths within our lives we can appreciate literatures that we have too readily forsaken within modernity. We have learnt to treat reason as an exclusive source of knowledge so that we have lost the capacity to discern wisdom and understanding. Myths do not offer us false consolations but they have a power to illuminate predicaments that we still face in making a significant transition from boyhood to manhood. Bly appreciates that Western societies have *lost* a sense of the importance of this transition so that many boys find themselves stuck, unable to move to manhood. As boys we are often uncertain what it means to be a man, what capacities and skills we need to nourish to make a transition.

Myths and fairy tales have to be explored for the meanings they carry. They do not offer up their meanings in a way that can be gleaned without making individual efforts ourselves. For the learning is personal and cannot be abstracted without taking a risk that meanings will be lost. These stories still have the power to move us, not only because they remind us of childhood, but because they can still illuminate issues that we face. They can remind us of a wisdom that we have lost and identify inner takes that we face in our movement towards manhood. So it is through a recognition of the powers of myth that we can realize that we do not grow into manhood as part of an automatic process or simply through being 'socialized' into the norms and values of the dominant culture. Nor is it a matter of accumulating knowledge and abilities that will prepare us for the world of work. It also involves a different kind of education – an inner education we have lost touch with.

In part this is to recover a sense of spiritual values that have been lost within the cultures of modernity. The fact that these tales can still talk to us, even if the meanings they have for us can only be grasped within the context of contemporary lives, shows a possibility of a conversation across generations and cultures. There seems to be a hunger for a wisdom which modernity too easily dismissed. While its visions of the rational self guided through life by the light of reason alone have exhausted itself, people have been looking round for traditions which can speak to different levels of their being. Modernity had been trapped in its struggle against religion so that reason was to take the place of faith. But this was to mistakenly identify religion with spirituality and to assume that science would *replace* the need for both.

Reason was established in a struggle against forms of 'unreason' that worked to suppress emotions and feelings as sources of knowledge. But myths do not operate at a conscious level of claim and counter-claim that can be heard on the tribunal of reason. If they 'make sense' it is partly in speaking to our emotions and feelings and so to a level that we are not used to acknowledging within a rationalistic culture. But it is also true that myths do not operate in an autonomous sphere of their own, for they reflect assumptions at work within the dominant culture, even if they work to subvert crucial meanings at the same time. This is why we have to be careful about the particular myths we choose to focus upon while at the same time not simply judging them by the prevailing cultural standards. The appeal of fairy tales which often seem violent speak to the experience of children who are dealing with unconscious fears and horrors. As Bettelheim (1975) tried to explain it, the meanings fairy tales carry often speak more profoundly to the conflicts young children are working with than a rationalist culture has wanted to admit. This means we have to be careful before we seek to edit aspects of myths which we deem 'unsuitable' for children. But we also have to be aware of the particular gender, class, 'race' and ethnic presuppositions they carry.[9]

The language of myth has resonances that we cannot easily control and so can speak to us more directly and vividly than ordinary prose. It might be that men have resonated with it recently because their experience has been so trapped within the rationalist terms of modernity. It seems to offer an escape and a way of revisioning masculinity. But it also carries its own dangers for it can provide an escape into a separate realm that men think they can control and identify with. So it is easy for men to be seduced by the grand title of 'warrior' or 'king' or 'magician' as representing different possibilities for men that have somehow been closed off within the routines and administered lives of industrial societies. But this can also serve as another form of withholding, for it can so easily provide an escape from having *to deal* with the everyday realities of emotional relationships. In this regard it echoes a pervasive temptation for men to idealize their experience, which in part is a consequence of suppressing so much of our inner emotional lives. Again this is something I explored in *Recreating Sexual Politics* (1991a) where I talked about the ease with which men seem able to fantasize about their experience and relationships. It seems much harder to deal with the emotional work of sustaining everyday relationships.

When Robert Bly shares his insights in reading the story of *Iron John* he is sharing the fruits of an exploration over many years. It is part of a long process of development that led him eventually to explore his relationship with his father. The painful experiences that are shared are part of coming to terms with an alcoholic father and Bly readily talks about how long it took to deal with this aspect of his experience. He mentions how it is like living with an elephant in the room but nobody is mentioning it. We all live with our own denials and in our own time we have to work with them if we are to grow in our individuality. Freud (1922) understood that you cannot deny emotions because they only return to haunt unconscious lives. He questions a modernity which suggests that we can turn away from difficult emotional lives, as temptations that lead us astray from following the aims and goals we have set for ourselves.[10]

Myths and Language

But there is a danger in myths that men think that they can gather the fruits before they have done the emotional work themselves. As the story of *Iron*

John shows, there is no easy path. We have to go through the different steps in our own time and in our own way. It is through such a process that we gain experiences that help connect us to the languages of myth. But this is a journey that we have to take for ourselves, since others cannot take it for us. In part it is a journey into the depths of our own despair and grief, for it is only if we have fully tasted the bitter fruit that we can begin to ascend from the 'ashes work' Bly so movingly talks about. We cannot wish ourselves to be 'wildmen' or 'warriors' because we have learnt to talk this way. The language will only have weight *if* it resonates with an experience that can give it meaning.

Bly is clear that when he talks about 'wildness' he means the opposite of the 'tameness' of the corporate executive who is very careful not to put a foot wrong, and when he talks about the 'warrior' he is talking about the person who is able to stand their inner ground, someone who is clearly defined in their individuality. But within Western cultures a language of 'warrior' and 'wildness' carries its own histories and meanings. For to be a warrior is not to be a 'wimp', so that it can so easily slip into meaning not allowing yourself to be pushed around by feminists or anyone else. It can so easily reinforce the sense of a man who is prepared to go it alone and who does not need others. In many ways it is an unfortunate term for it tempts Bly into talking about conflict, battle and war as he slips from psychological and spiritual languages into talk of politics and social life. These transitions can easily be made but, unless we are very scrupulous in distinguishing the levels we are talking about, they can help foster the very values which Bly wants to challenge. He was strongly against the Vietnam War and has a long and honourable record in the peace movement, for instance recognizing the importance for the men's movement to grieve the loss of the thousands who were brutally slaughtered in the Gulf War.

While acknowledging the different ways that mythical language can speak to the experience of men through providing different visions of maleness, we have to be aware of the histories that myths bring with them. If we are to appreciate cultures which have maintained traditions of initiation that help mark a passage from boyhood to manhood and which continue to value what men can learn from each other, we also need to be aware of the cultural settings. We can certainly learn, for instance, from the traditions of native Americans about the reverence for nature which we have lost with the disenchanting of the natural world that characterized modernity. This is important learning that is often blocked by notions of cultural relativism which would treat values and traditions as relative to particular cultures. Far from seeing peoples who live 'closer to nature' as 'backward' and 'primitive' within the terms of an Enlightenment modernity, we are beginning to be able to listen to what they say and to learn about values and ways of being that we have lost within a tradition of secular rationalism.[11]

If we can honour the noble traditions of being a 'warrior' which existed for many tribes and appreciate the distinction that Bly draws between the 'savage' and the 'warrior', where the warrior is the one who faces his wounds, we also have to be careful about the easy appropriation of anthropological work. For it is so easy for myths to connect with the traditions of a patriarchal culture which diminishes the experience of women and children who are there to serve the needs of men. Bly might well say that it is time to reevaluate the experiences of patriarchal cultures, for there are values and traditions that we have lost which illuminate what men can teach each other. He might be right about the importance of recovering certain traditions, say of storytelling through which wisdom and guidance were passed from one generation of men to the next. In the last 20 years men have absorbed so many negative images of masculinity that it is time to rethink and recover traditions which show *different* ways that men can be with each other.

But it is important to recognize what particular qualities men can learn from each other without failing to appreciate the need to rework the relations of power and subordination that have characterized men's relationships with women. It might well be that it is important for men to learn how to listen to each other for a while, for we have lost a capacity to trust other men. Within the competitive cultures of masculinity which have characterized industrial societies we have grown wary and suspicious of other men, feeling that they will put us down the moment that our defences are lowered. This is why so many men talk about feeling closer to women than to men. But they draw from this the idea that they don't need to talk to men because feminism provides no challenge to them since they have 'no problems' with women.

This is reflected in difficulties that heterosexual men often share in being able to reach out towards each other for help or support. Somehow it is so much easier to reach out when we are up and so difficult to ask for help when we feel down. It is as if there is something shameful in needing the support and comfort of other men, especially if we are down. It might be that we are just too vulnerable then to take the risk. It feels easier to withdraw and to lick our own wounds. Often it is at times like this that we will reject the love and support that our partners might be able to give. At the very moment that we need it most it seems impossible to take it in. Even as we are hugging someone close to us, we cannot absorb the nourishment that they have to offer. This pattern is deeply set in contemporary masculinities, for as men we learn to affirm our male identities by *not* needing others. Since we don't have emotional needs we cannot admit that we need nourishment, nor can we provide such nourishment for ourselves. It is as if when we are down we have to hold more tightly to male identities so that we have to push away what others might give, for to admit that we need threatens our male identities. We give out the message that we don't need others, when the truth is often that we are desperate for contact but cannot take the risk of reaching out.

Language carries the scars of its own cultural and historical inheritance. We need to critically engage with the meanings it carries, for otherwise it can so easily be abused. Even if it is no part of Bly's intention we have to be aware that he cannot define terms as he would want without at the same time questioning some of the historical resonances they have carried. It becomes difficult to talk about 'warriors' without appreciating the ways the term has traditionally marginalized and devalued the experience of women. This language might still be able to teach us important lessons about manliness which are the lessons that Bly wants to draw. But if 'manliness' also involves an appreciation of how men are to conceive their relationships with women and children then these considerations cannot be left till later.

It might well be that heterosexual men need to create time and space with each other to explore aspects of their experience as men that they can only explore with each other. Often men have unspoken fears about being together as men, especially if this brings back echoes of painful experiences at school. But it might be that men can help each other to face these fears and insecurities and that through this emotional process men can learn to trust each other a little more. There are wounds that we carry as men that other men can recognize from their own experience so they can help us heal. Through consciousness-raising and men's therapy groups many men have learnt to share more of their experience with each other. Sometimes this is a frustrating process because, as men brought up to identify with our minds, we find it so much easier to 'talk about' an experience than to share it in its emotional intensity. Often this has provided space and time in which men can reconsider and *rework* diverse forms of what it means to be a man. It also involves questioning the ways we have been brought up to relate to women and to take responsibility for children. It involves sharing some of the wounds we have covered over from childhood, as we gradually come into contact with them. Often, as with all first steps on a new path, it is tentative and takes its own time.

Notes

1 Work with men who have survived the experience of public schools can be difficult, for they have often learnt that they have had such privileges that they have no right to their emotions. In different ways this experience can serve as an acute reminder of the separations that men from quite diverse masculinities are often expected to endure in silence. The particular workshops I refer to here can be contacted through Spectrum in North London.

2 For some helpful reflections upon the ways we learn to conceive of the relationship between identity and difference within modernity see, for instance, *Modernity and Identity*, edited by J. Freedman and S. Lasch (1990); and *Beyond Equality and Difference*, edited by Gisela Bock and Susan James (1992). The ways that we learn to treat differences as contingent forms of an unfreedom that we have to 'rise above' within a dominant Kantian tradition is a central theme in Victor J. Seidler, *Kant, Respect and Injustice: The Limits of Liberal Moral Theory* (1986).

3 Some interesting discussion about coming to terms with difference without forsaking aspirations towards equality and justice is given in Martha Minow, *Making All the Difference* (1990); Elizabeth Spellman, *Inessential Women* (1990); and Iris Marion Young, *Justice and the Politics of Difference* (1990).

4 This masculinist writing is still more influential in the United States where it helps to sustain a men's rights movement. Some of its latest manifestations connect to aspects of the

Christian right in the Promise Keepers. It remains crucial to engage with these movements to understand what is drawing men to them, rather than to simplistically dismiss them as expressions of an anti-feminist backlash.

5 Reflections on changing patterns of work relations as women increasingly enter what were traditionally male occupations are provided by Cynthia Cockburn, *Brothers: Male Dominance and Technical Change* (1983) and *Machinery of Dominance: Women, Men and Technical Knowledge* (1985).

6 To think about the ways that masculinities have been shaped within the pubic sphere see Arthur Brittan, *Masculinity and Power* (1989); Jeff Hearn, *Men in the Public Eye: The Construction and Deconstruction of Public Men and Public Patriarchies* (1992); and David Morgan, *Discovering Men: Sociology and Masculinities* (1991).

7 Some of the changes taking place within the organization of the domestic economy and the changing relations between men and women are reflected upon in Arlie Hochschild, *The Second Shift: Working Parents and the Revolution at Home* (1989); and Jane Wheelock, *Husbands at Home: The Domestic Economy in a Post-Industrial Society* (1990).

8 The identification of a dominant masculinity with reason and the issues this raises for men in their emotional lives is explored in Victor J. Seidler, *Rediscovering Masculinity: Reason, Language and Sexuality* (1989). It is also a central theme in Shere Hite, *Men and Intimacy: Personal Accounts Exploring the Dilemmas of Modern Male Sexuality* (1990). See also Deborah Tannen, *You Just Don't Understand: Women and Men in Conversation* (1991).

9 Bruno Bettelheim discusses the appeal of myths and fairy stories in *The Uses of Enchantment* (1975).

10 Freud reflects upon the repression of sexuality and emotional life within the conditions of modernity in *Civilization and its Discontents* (1961). This theme is explored in Philip Rieff, *Freud: The Mind of the Moralist* (1965) and Octavio Mannoni, *Freud* (1991).

11 An exploration of some of the difficulties of thinking about values within much postmodern writings which so often sustain notions of cultural relativism is provided in *Principled Positions: Postmodernism and the Rediscovery of Value*, edited by Judith Squires (1993). It is also a theme in Jeffrey Weeks, *Inventing Moralities* (1996) and Michael Walzer, *The Company of Critics* (1989).

5
Wounds

Hidden Injuries

As men we often learn to hide and conceal our emotional wounds as part of proving our masculinity. In so many different ways we learn to affirm our masculinities by showing that we can carry our wounds and that we have been able to harden ourselves against them. We learn to *minimize* the pain we have suffered both in ourselves and in what we are ready to show to others. We learn to tell ourselves 'it didn't hurt' and 'it was nothing really' as we harden our hearts and prove that we could 'take it'. In this sense many men are survivors from difficult childhoods because as boys they found little recognition of their emotional needs. Since 'boys don't cry' they learnt to carry their hurts within themselves, hardly recognizing them for the wounds they are. We learn to believe that 'sticks and stones may break our bones but words will never hurt us.' But this is not true, for we often do hurt inside. But then we take this as a sign that there is something 'wrong' with us, that we are not 'acceptable' and so we are 'different' from other boys. We live in fear that others might find out and reject us, so that often we are wary in our relationships.

Within an Enlightenment culture of modernity it is hard for men to acknowledge the wounds that they carry. In this chapter I want to provide an explanation for this and explore some of its theoretical and personal implications. Often we learn as boys that it is only girls who have feelings. If we have suffered in childhood, say in being left alone in hospital for a few weeks, we can carry such a deep sense of abandonment that we cut ourselves off from our feelings, because it would be too painful to feel. As a young boy we might feel abandoned and feel that this only confirms that there must be something 'wrong' with us, because otherwise we would not have been left. After such an experience it might be hard to trust that others can be there for us. We might feel that there is no way that we could be a part of a family that has treated us in such a way, and so be left with a sense of being an 'outsider' unable to connect emotionally with those around.

For boys it is often easy to disconnect from our feelings because we are not supposed to have them anyway. We learn to trust only ourselves because it is too risky to reach out towards others. We become self-sufficient, often learning to do what is expected of us in relation to others, but having little feeling for what we do. Since we have learnt to survive on our own we do not experience needing others, even those we are closer to, so it might strike us as strange, both theoretically and personally, when we hear other men talk about 'needing contact' because we have little in our inner experience which resonates with this. In part this is to live out the dominant white, Protestant, heterosexual masculine ideals of modernity, for it is to exist as a rational self working our lives out through our thoughts. We learn to do what is expected of us and in Kantian terms we do our duties so that others have no grounds to complain. We might even enjoy contact with others, but we *could* also survive well without it. At some level we are always on our own, for we don't really have feelings for others.

Often men from diverse backgrounds feel envious of the contact women seem able to establish with each other. It seems as if women often find it easier to sustain relationships with each other, while for middle class heterosexual men it feels more precarious to reach out. I know how hard I can often find it to sustain relationships, as if they dissolve into a series of discrete experiences. It is partly that I am so used to getting on without them that I still have to learn *how* to take care of my friendships. Somehow women often seem more in touch with their need for contact with each other. This is a need that we have learnt to deny as men and it goes some way to explaining how isolated and alone men often feel. If we are to relearn a talent for friendship it will involve learning how to appreciate the contact we can have with other men and allowing it to nourish our selves.[1]

In some ways feminism has also made it harder for men from diverse class, 'race' and ethnic backgrounds to acknowledge their wounds. It is easy to feel that because we have power in relation to women and within the larger society, whatever we suffer pales into insignificance when compared with the systematic oppression of women. This can encourage men to grin and bear it, affirming their masculinities through showing that whatever the obstacles they have been able to 'win through'. But it can also leave men feeling bad about themselves as men, as if we cannot escape feeling guilty for all the suffering that has been done to women through patriarchy. In the last 20 years men have felt confused and uneasy in their responses to feminism, feeling that they are carrying the blame for misery and suffering which they have not created themselves. There is often a disparity between the ways men feel individually in relation to women and the ways they feel collectively represented. This has created its own forms of resentment that can break the surface in acts of frustration and violence against women and children. At some level men have very little understanding of themselves and they can feel cheated, unable any longer to rely upon women to interpret their experience for them.

In *Iron John*, Bly makes clear that the sufferings of men can in no way be compared with what women have had to suffer through long years of patriarchy. But at the same time it is important not to diminish what men go through themselves and to identify the sources of their oppression, even if these are not institutionalized in the same way. Bly focuses upon the 200 years that have passed since the early development of capitalist industrialization which took men out of the home, so separating them from everyday contact with their families. He argues that each generation of men has been gradually weakened through a loss of contact with fathers who no longer share their skills and concerns with their sons. Concerned with the experience of boys and the difficulties they encounter in the West in making their transition to 'manhood', he argues that boys have lost the nourishment they often need from everyday contact with their fathers.

Bly relies less on historical evidence than on his own childhood experience growing up on a farm in the Midwest. He sees himself as part of a generation whose experience has not been passed on and he recognizes that significantly he found it easier to bring up his daughters than he did his sons. We need to be careful in not romanticizing relationships between fathers and sons and the kind of contact and communication they shared with each other. Of course what matters is not only what people say to each other but also the activities they share with each other. The stories that men used to tell each other need to be recovered in an age when the TV has become a central means of communication. Bly talks in physical terms about a 'substance' that passes from fathers to children and which they need as a vital need of the soul. For boys it seems to be important in a particular way for it is part of growing into manhood.

The chord that *Iron John* touches is the loss that many men feel for contact with their fathers and the hole that this has left in men's lives. There is often an unrecognized sense of shame in the ways men have been demeaned within contemporary culture, as if the father is a figure who can easily be ridiculed and put aside. This might well be part of an act of revenge against the father who has failed his sons and daughters, but there is also guilt and anger that needs to be recognized. Bly talks about how men have been starved of *contact* with their fathers and so have failed to be properly initiated into manhood. This is part of what allows him to say provocatively that 'there are so many boys in the culture and so few men.' But this can easily sound like John Wayne resonating with a traditional chord in the culture, for as men it is easy to grow up feeling that we are not 'man enough'. Bly touches this traditional anxiety too and seems to offer men a path to manhood with a guarantee that they will not be 'feminized' in the process. Bly talks with these different voices for in some ways he does seem to want to reinstate the values of traditional masculinity that have been falsely challenged by feminism. This remains an unresolved and central tension in his writings.

The silence around feminism and relationships with women goes to the heart of *Iron John*, for Bly is ambivalent about the place of women and relationships. If he helps us recognize the wounds that men carry, the notion of 'manhood' that he espouses does not include references to women and children. In part this is because we have to explore our masculinities with other men and create and honour a space and time in which men can share these explorations with each other. I think that men need such 'sacred space' as women have discerned for themselves in consciousness-raising groups. The idea might be that only later when we have been affirmed in our manhood can we begin to think helpfully about more equal relationships with women and children. But there is something important missing in this vision of manhood.

Bly often says that he does not want to repeat the Freudian story that blames mothers for the ills of their sons, as if it is only because women are so possessive in relationships that boys cannot find their own path. It is true that he thinks that fathers have failed in their responsibilities towards their children and that men have to take a much more active part in the lives of young children. But even if he calls fathers to account there is still an abiding feeling that it is when women enter the lives of men that all kinds of trouble and complications begin. This is part of the silence in relation to feminism and women in *Iron John*. It is as if women get in the way of men being able to achieve their manhood, rather than helping to *redefine* the terms this manhood has traditionally taken. For in the end we are still left with a traditional picture of masculinity and of the path that boys have to take. There is little sense in which our manhood might be enriched and transformed through sharing in a different contact with women and children. It also affects our understanding and grasp of the inner wounds that diverse men often carry in their relation to masculinities.

Fathers and Sons

In the West in the 1990s men are increasingly recognizing a feeling of loss when they consider the contact they have had with their fathers. Often we experience a sense of sadness that has been difficult to express. Men from different backgrounds are talking more openly about wanting to have been acknowledged, recognized and blessed by their fathers in ways they never were. This has remained a deep and largely unacknowledged wound that *Iron John* and the mythopoetic men's movement has helped to bring to the surface. Bly has helped men to experience a wounding that they rarely allowed themselves to feel before, for as boys we often learnt that we could not cry for our fathers. It was 'unreasonable' to expect that our fathers might have been able to spend more time with us; 'they had to go out to work' for it was their role to provide support for the rest of the family.

As boys we often learnt that it was 'irrational' to have emotions and feelings that cannot be realized. It was easy to be made to feel 'silly' and 'stupid' for wanting to have more contact than a father is prepared to give. If we learn within a rationalist culture that 'fathers are doing their best working for the family' it can seem 'unreasonable' to want any different, for fathers are doing what they are supposed to do. So as boys growing up in the 1950s and 1960s we learnt to silence and discount our needs and turned the blame against ourselves for wanting something that we were not supposed to want. It only proved that there must be something wrong with us for wanting to have more contact, so that we soon learnt to keep our feelings to ourselves. With time we learnt to alter our expectations and came to expect very little from our fathers. We learnt to swallow our anger and disappointment that our fathers seemed to do so little with us. But often these feelings went unacknowledged and we just felt uneasy and awkward, unable to express much of what we were feeling. Other boys did not seem to see their fathers much more either, so it was 'normal'.[2]

Some men share in men's groups the ingenuity they showed in finding ways of spending more time with their fathers. They might remember hanging around the garden shed so that they were there when their father needed some tools held, or offering to fill shelves when their dad was working in the shop. Having to accept that their fathers 'had important things to do' and little time to play, boys found other ways of seeking them out. They learnt that they were really not entitled to hope that their fathers could play with them. Often boys are expected to grow up quickly so that they can learn to amuse themselves, for needing others soon becomes a sign of weakness. This is especially true of older brothers who sometimes have to watch their fathers play with their little sisters. They can feel rejected and unwanted, only to take their anger out on their sisters when the opportunity arises.

I can also remember listening to the pain and disappointment that a middle class man chose to relive in a men's therapy group as he expressed the rejection he felt when his father stopped holding his hand when he was eight. It was as if the father had been embarrassed when the boy held out his hand. He as left feeling that he was 'too old' to have his father hold his hand, and that if he persisted it only proved that there was something 'wrong with him'. But as the hand is rejected often little is said, because it is somehow communicated that 'you should know better.' There had to be a hidden inadequacy that also separated him from other boys for simply wanting to continue to hold his father's hand. If this is true of this desire, it is easy to fear that it must be true for many others too. So often as boys we learn to deny and extinguish these similar desires in ourselves. We reject these feelings when they begin to surface so that we soon fail to acknowledge their existence at all. We tell ourselves that 'now we are eight' we would not dream of reaching out to hold our father's hand. But so it is that dreams turn sour and, as boys growing into young men, we fail to recognize what we want from others. Since it is 'unreasonable' to want more contact with our father, we learn to *deny* these feelings within ourselves.

Such experiences influence the ways we learn to talk to ourselves as boys. As we discount these impulses for contact, recognizing them as signs of weakness that need to be carefully hidden, we damage our spontaneity or 'wildness' as Bly has it. As we learn to discount our needs so we begin to talk to ourselves in *false* ways, helping to sustain a reality we choose to live since it seems 'irrational' and 'pointless' to hope for any other. At some level we reverse the truth of our feelings so that we can strengthen ourselves to live with a pain we cannot acknowledge out of a fear that others will put us down. We tell ourselves 'I don't need any contact with my father', 'I'm big enough to look after myself', 'I'm old enough to do without the love and support of my dad.' These become ways of proving our male identities and help to sustain men's particular relationship to language, for often language becomes used as a form of self-protection.[3] In the competitive worlds of masculinities we learn to protect ourselves when we are still very young.

But Bly helps us recognize that this is often an exercise in denial, for at another level we are hungry for a different kind of contact. It might be a contact that we are never going to receive, so that we have to learn to look to others and to ourselves to provide the nourishment and recognition we need. Bly recognizes that we also carry hurt, anger and disappointment for the *absence* of our fathers which lies buried within our inner emotional lives. Often these are emotions we do not want to touch, for it can feel like an act of betrayal towards a father who was 'doing his best'. It is also easier to think that we can't have many feelings about our fathers, because we had such little contact with them. We tell ourselves that since we were such strangers to them, it is hard to have any feelings about them. Sometimes men from diverse backgrounds can only remember the atmosphere that would dominate the family when their fathers came back from work. They learnt to 'be seen and not heard', for their dads were unapproachable and they were scared that they would be reproved if they made any sound.

Until quite recently fathering in white middle class and working class settings existed as a clearly defined role and set of responsibilities and men knew what was expected of them. It was their task to serve as breadwinners and to act as a source of authority in the disciplining of their children. Boys were often told to 'wait for your father to come home and he will sort you out', and this goes across quite diverse class, race and ethnic differences. Men would draw some pride from their identities as authorities within the family, especially when this was so often denied to them at work. But it meant also that fathers were not supposed to get too close to their children for this would interfere with their being able to sustain the distance that was considered necessary to exerting clear and impartial authority.[4]

It is only with the challenges of feminism that men have had their authority and power within the family questioned. Within the patriarchal form of family it was assumed that the 'father rules the house' following a line of authority that flowed directly from God.[5] It was as if the father represented the source of law and authority within the family, so that his word could not be questioned without bringing into question the nature of authority itself. So it was that fathers could expect to get their way. It was only two generations back in working class Glasgow that fathers would expect to eat whatever meat was available while the scraps would be shared out between the others. The children would often live in fear as their father was someone to be avoided. In the generations that followed this might have moderated itself, but the father still expected 'to get his way' and the family was still largely organized around his work. He still expected to be obeyed immediately when he told the children what to do.

The idea that 'I'm your father and you have to obey my word' was given a different form within the middle class, but often children were forced to live in a space of their own having relatively little daily contact with their fathers. To question your father's authority was to show a lack of respect and so to prove that you deserved punishment, for it was the father's duty to discipline his children. If children were not behaving correctly this reflected badly on the parents. Only recently have we had the idea that respect is something that parents also have to earn in their relationships with their children, for this notion would have made little sense in Victorian times.[6] Generally it was not clear what contact children in different social classes and ethnic communities could really expect with their fathers, for it was often thought to be the mother's work to 'bring up the children'. Fathering was more of a relationship of authority that was exercised as part of a final court of appeal.

Again we have to be careful not to generalize. We have to be careful before assuming, as Bly tends to do, that fathers who worked in closer proximity to their children sustained closer relationships with them. There might be more contact where fathers are concerned to teach their sons a trade and initiate them into particular traditions of skill, for this meant that different generations were at least doing things with each other. It is often through doing things that men learn to communicate with each other and find ways of connecting. This creates a space in which attitudes and values are shared, even if they are not directly talked about. We should be careful not to underestimate the context of shared practical activities, but at the same time we have to investigate what is shared and what is withheld within these contexts. Often boys want a more direct contact that is not forthcoming, while they still can treasure the time that they share with their fathers doing things together. Again we need to explore these different cultures of masculinity, learning how to appreciate the different forms in which communication works. But if fathers had learnt to withhold their own emotional expression, this would often remain a silence with their children who might learn that emotions and feelings are *not* shared for they have no place in a 'man's world'.

Loss and Denial

Often it can be hard to acknowledge, within the context of diverse masculinities, that we feel the loss of a 'closer' relationship with our fathers. When we have learnt to expect so little it can be hard to touch our wounds about the disappointments we have carried into adult life. Of course men have enjoyed many different kinds of relationships with their fathers but it can be difficult to explore these differences within a dominant culture of modernity which teaches men to deny and eradicate their emotional needs. As long as men learn to treat emotions as a sign of weakness that compromises their male identities, it will be hard to share our emotions with each other. We learn in so many different ways to say that 'it doesn't matter' and so to *minimize* the wounds that we have received, somehow turning them into their opposites as badges of our masculinity, ways of proving ourselves as men.

Robert Bly's *Iron John* helped men to experience at a *feeling* level a sense of longing for their fathers that had long gone unrecognized. In helping to illuminate the cultural processes through which men learn to conceal and hide their emotions, we implicitly challenge notions of cultural and historical relativism that are so prominent in the human sciences. As Freud (1922) grasped it, the fact that we learn to conceal and hide our wounds does not mean that they go away, for they still exist as wounds in our inner emotional lives, waiting to be recognized. It is a false sign of manhood to think that we affirm our masculinity by eradicating our 'softer' emotions and feelings. Yet this is a crucial aspect of the identification of masculinity with reason that has structured dominant Western visions of modernity. With Kant (1959) we learn to discount our emotions and feelings as sources of 'unfreedom' so that we can act out of a sense of reason alone. As we learn to challenge our identities as rational selves, we question the distinction between reason and nature that sustains them.

Freud understood that if we are to grow and develop in our individuality we have to learn to face and acknowledge our emotional wounds.[7] For Bly the warrior is the man who is ready to face his wounds, rather than to slide away from them. This is a sign of courage and 'manhood' rather than a sign of weakness as it is so often portrayed. Part of this involves recognizing the hurt we often carry as well as the anger and rage at the absence of our fathers, either physically or emotionally. This does not mean that these emotions have waited in a pristine form to be acknowledged, for this is not a process that can be governed by will and determination alone. We have to be ripe for this kind of work on ourselves and this is work that is always done in the present, even if it involves regression to earlier moments in our relationships with our fathers.

Within modernity men have learnt to deny their emotional lives, so it is hardly surprising if we lack an adequate language to explore the workings of emotional development. It might well be that the notion of 'repression' suggests a hydraulic conception of emotional life, as Foucault (1980) describes it, as if our emotions are lying in the unconscious waiting to be retrieved.[8] But different images inform different traditions of psychotherapy and it can be misleading to present a homogenized notion only to subvert it. It is too easy to suggest that we might be able to abandon a notion of 'repression' because it suggests to some that we can reach a state in which there is no repression. When Foucault (1980) in his later writings explored traditions of caring for the self, he seemed to discover a new sympathy for what might be involved in individuals 'working on themselves'. He maintained a healthy suspicion of any notion that a 'professional' could somehow tell you what you were feeling, when this has no reality for yourself. He rightly challenged the pretensions of a psychoanalytic tradition that too often regards itself as the exclusive possessor of 'knowledge' that clients are struggling to achieve for themselves. He was too aware of the links between knowledge and power to let this pass.[9]

At the same time it is important to recognize that a man might learn to cope with feeling abandoned by his father by saying that 'it didn't matter to me . . . I didn't like him anyway.' It might well be that many men will feel completely relieved at not having more contact with fathers who were abusive, violent or negligent, while at the same time carrying emotions that remain unresolved. This is a complex process but it is important to be aware of the therapeutic balance of power and authority so that we know when it is slipping away from the person himself. This remains a crucial demarcation for alternative forms of psychotherapy, though analysts who are working with sensitivity will often be careful not to impose their own interpretations but to leave space for people to make their own discoveries. It is a tricky balance, and it remains helpful to recognize ways we defend ourselves against feeling hurt or pain that we are not ready to deal with. This is part of a process which has its own rhythm and timing. People have to find their *own way*, though they can be guided through the insight and experiences of others who have taken the same path themselves.

I know what some of this father loss has meant from my own personal experience. I spent many years feeling ashamed that I didn't have a father when other children at school did. I spent many years searching, trying to fill a dark hole that had been created by the death of my father when I was just five. I cried for many nights when he died, saying that 'if I was good, perhaps he would come back', and I felt, like many children, that there must have been something wrong or defective in me that explained why he had to die. It was somehow easier at that age to blame myself than to discover and explore the sources of my anger at having been abandoned so young. I felt that there must be something wrong with me because 'I didn't have a Daddy'. This feeling did not leave me when a stepfather came into my life, for it was hard to accept him properly if I was to stay loyal to my 'real' father.

Somehow I got locked into a pattern of having to prove myself to my father and for many years, till quite recently in my late forties, I seemed to live in his shadow. It was as if proving myself to him was a way of giving my life meaning. At some level the shame that I felt at not having a father connected to a sense that I was somehow 'inadequate' as a human being, as if without a father in 1950s England I was hardly entitled to exist. I didn't want other boys at school to ask me about what had happened, so I learnt to live as if I still had a father at home. This was living a lie and meant that in some ways I rendered myself 'invisible' because I did not want to be noticed, for this was threatening because it meant that others might ask. I don't think this way of dealing with a father's death is so unfamiliar. I saw how my nieces had to cope in a later generation when my brother died.

In the 1950s people did not talk easily about death. It was as if it was catching if you talked about it. Children were to be protected and I don't think that I was ever properly told about my father's death. The truth was too painful so it had to be hidden and it was deemed preferable not to tell the children the truth if it was painful. My parents' generation had to deal with all the sufferings of the war and the destruction of their families in Hitler's gas chambers. In their different ways they were all survivors. They had somehow to get on with life so they had to learn to put the past behind them. As refugees from Hitler's Europe they soon learnt that people didn't want to know their stories. They soon realized that they were expected to pretend that they were 'like everyone else'.[10] This is what we learnt as children. We were to melt into the background, feeling grateful that the country had been generous enough to 'let us in'. Only later did I learn how few were allowed in from Nazi Europe. Even though they had nowhere to go, the doors were often shut in the faces of the Jewish refugees. A story of generosity became the myth that my generation absorbed, because again the truth was too hard to bear. In any case we were the lucky ones.

As I grew up in a Jewish refugee family, children were to be protected from the truth. If we did not know what had happened, it could not mark and disturb our 'normal' childhoods. As children of refugees we did not want to draw attention to ourselves so we learnt to live in the shadows, doing as well as we could to prove ourselves. We carried the hopes and expectations of our parents, for their careers had often been cut short when Hitler came to power. But our parents shared very little of what they had experienced, so it was as if we were going into the world with very little history of our own. We carried painful gaps that were rarely to be filled. Looking back I can realize that it was hard for adults to share emotions with children if they had had to close off emotions themselves. It was done in the name of 'protecting the children' but the adults were also protecting themselves because they did not want to be reminded of their own pain. But so it was that the children were made to carry their parents' own unresolved guilts and anxieties. Unknowingly as boys and girls we carried emotions and feelings that were passed on from our parents. They were passed on in silence for often there was no space within which to talk about them.

We learnt that our parents had all suffered enough, even though they were not prepared to go into details. As children we learnt that we did not want to add to their suffering so we had to be 'good'. A strange familiar reversal took place when the children were supposed to look after their parents and to protect them from any difficult emotions. I learnt *not* to ask too many questions about my father or really to share my hurt and anger at his death. I learnt that it was 'unreasonable' to feel anger because he hadn't chosen to die, or so the story went, so I learnt to swallow my anger and to go along with the notion that I had a 'happy childhood' and that I did not miss anything. It was only as a young adult that I learnt otherwise and that I found the space in which I could begin to come to terms emotionally with my father's death. It was only then that I appreciated how many unresolved emotions and feelings I had carried inside over the years.

Mothers and Sons

As I was growing up in a middle class Jewish family I was protected from pain, even from the pain of my father's death. It was felt that I had no right to my own feelings of pain, for my mother saw it as her task to protect us from pain. To say that I was upset or depressed somehow worked as an attack on her mothering, even when it was truthful. Over the years I have learnt to respect the truth and be suspicious of traditions which would undervalue its search, for it was treated as a dispensable quality while I was growing up. So it was that the 'truth' was in short supply and I was constantly told by adults that I was 'very happy' and that I had 'all the things that a child could possibly ask for'. Being told this so many times made it clear that, if I was still unhappy, it meant that there had to be something wrong with me.

The fact that my father had died and my mother was forced to go out to work to support four children was somehow beside the point, since it was crucial for my mother to feel that she was not failing us. It was a difficult situation and we were all very proud of the work she was doing as the first woman in the fur trade. In the early 1950s the prevailing myth was that mothers should be at home with their children, so she must have felt guilty at having to work. As children we wanted to make things easier for her. It was hard enough for her to leave us, though she felt fulfilled at work and probably guilty also for feeling so. But she could not stand to hear that we might be sad or unhappy for this was only to add to the burdens of her life, or so we were told. She had 'enough to deal with' without having to hear that we were not happy, so we learnt to be 'happy' and to accommodate to whatever was offered us as children. We became adults before our time, for in many ways we became adults the moment that our father died.

So it was that I felt that if I was sad or unhappy I was somehow hurting my mother who was already making so many sacrifices for us. Having these emotions made me feel ungrateful, so it was hardly surprising that I learnt to *suppress* them. If anyone asks me how I am, the question still throws me off balance. I often say that I am feeling fine before I have really stopped to consider what I am saying. As I was growing up there was no space within which I could safely express my feelings of loss at my father's death or the anger that he'd left me with. I learnt to keep these feelings to myself, especially when I felt 'unfair' at feeling the way I did, which only made me feel worse about myself. I learnt to internalize my own grief and loss so that with time I was barely aware of how they shadowed my waking life. I learnt to accept the myth that I lived a 'happy childhood' so that I did not really have anything to complain about. I learnt to be grateful for the blessings that I had, for after all my mother was still alive. Still as an adult I can feel a sense of betrayal when I talk about the loneliness and unhappiness that I experienced in childhood.

I don't know how much of this has to do with being boys and the notion that boys are *not* supposed to have feelings at all. Probably it was tied up with proving that we could cope as boys with the carefully regulated life we lived being looked after by our grandmother. Somehow it was hard to have our own feelings of sadness or loss without thinking that they reflected in some way on my mother. It was as if she was the source of all the emotions and feelings in the family and as if she had all the feelings for the rest of us. We were to be seen and not heard in the new regime with my stepfather. We were not to remind my mother of the past, for she did not want us to disturb the order that she had created for us. We were to feel grateful that she had 'provided us with a father', for in the 1950s it was difficult to acknowledge that boys could grow up perfectly well without fathers. Somehow to be unhappy was to be ungrateful. We learnt to keep our reservations to ourselves.

Boys often carry a feeling that their childhood was cut short and that they had to become 'adults' before their time. This is partly because boys are taught that being 'independent' means having to deny your emotional needs and live without the support of others. Often this creates a false sense of independence for it works to suppress the emotional needs boys have. We learn how to live *without* being held or cared for emotionally, for these are all signs of weakness. We learn to separate from our mothers and from the love they can give us for we have to prove that we can do without. We find ourselves despising emotions as signs of weakness and as symbolic of a failure to grow into boyhood. We tell ourselves that we can get on perfectly well without the loving support and care of others, for we fear that this threatens and somehow drains away our masculinity. We learn that it is only girls who have emotions.

Often this cuts short our emotional growth as boys, but this becomes difficult to identify within a culture that lacks an adequate language of emotional development. Too often we think of maturity in terms of an 'ability to cope' but as boys we learn to cope on our own while cutting off from our inner emotional lives. If we think about emotional development it is in the Kantian terms of control *as* suppression of an 'animal nature'. Too often we can only conceive of emotions as getting in the way of reason, as a disturbance on the path of achieving 'ends' and 'goals' that have been set by reason alone. Often, as boys living out different masculinities, we learn to swallow our softer emotions for we do not want others to know what we are feeling. It can become a form of revenge since we do not want others to have the pleasure of seeing our tears. So, for instance, we can think of the boys who refused to come down to see their parents off when they left them at boarding school. They learn to *reject* as a way of coping with their feelings of rejection. As boys we learn in different ways to harden our hearts to the pain we often feel inside.

As boys we often have a feeling of being abandoned, left on our own to grow up as best we can. This is part of learning to be 'independent' before it is appropriate. Boys who are sent away to school can experience it as a silent death, for they are given little space to mourn the separation from their families. This act of cruelty is presented as a gift of kindness, for they are supposedly being offered a 'privilege' that other boys are denied. If you are supposed to feel grateful, it is hard to show your suffering: it only proves that you are 'inadequate', for other boys 'soon get over it'. But in other ways the boarding school, or the reform school for working class boys, remains

symbolic of the ways that boys were expected to be. It gives a physical form
to a separation from care and concern that all boys are expected to make,
for within modernity boys are often expected after a certain age to live
without emotional needs. As boys we are expected to separate from parts
of our selves, as we learn to disdain our inner emotional lives. It is hardly
surprising that as men we have such difficulties in sustaining relationships.
Often it can be too painful to 'open up' after the long years of neglecting
our inner emotional needs.

I experienced a sharp separation when my father died and my mother had
to go out to work full time when I was just five. The playfulness and spontaneity of childhood was cut short and we four brothers were expected to
be older than our age. We were to be responsible and as boys we were constantly told that we had to 'look after our mother'. I didn't really know what
this meant, other than that we should be careful not to add to her burdens.
I was identified with my father and I was supposed to be 'clever' in the way
that he was. This left me with a special sense of responsibility to look after
my younger brothers, even though I was not the eldest. This created its own
double bind, for I felt guilty in relation to my older brother and also resentful. It also meant that I felt a special responsibility to keep the memory of
my father alive, to stay *loyal* to his existence. But in some ways this put me
outside the stepfamily that was being created. I was an 'outsider' even in my
own family.

At another level I felt too connected to my mother, as if I was somehow
to provide her with emotional support and to 'take the place of my father'.
When I read Freud's story of the Oedipal myth it struck deep chords, as if
it had been written for me personally. I was about 11 or 12 and had got a
book on Freud out of the library. I was searching for a way of understanding. At some level I can recognize that I wanted to have my mother all to
myself and that I wanted to be the 'favoured son' who had somehow
replaced my father in my mother's affections. I don't know how much my
feelings of loyalty for my father helped me cope with the guilt at feeling that
I had somehow 'killed him off'. Somehow I had allowed myself to feel
'special' because I had been breast-fed by my mother for a longer period
than the other boys. I felt that I had a special connection and love.

Freud (1953) helps to illuminate the sexual feelings that boys often have
for their mothers and the complexity of the relationship. This operates at
the level of unconscious desire, as psychoanalysis has it, but it also reflects
the unresolved sexual feelings that go on between the adults. As boys we
are often drawn into seductive relationships with our mothers, who are
feeling frustrated and unfulfilled in the lives they are forced to live within a
patriarchal society. Since women within patriarchal societies were traditionally denied forms of social and personal expression and expected to
live in the shadows of their husbands, this set up all kinds of unmet needs
and emotions that were often played out in the sexual dynamics between
mothers and sons. As men with diverse masculinities have traditionally
expressed little of themselves within relationships, women often look

towards their infants and children to fulfil emotional needs. Sometimes they take out the anger and frustration of their sexual relationships by drawing their sons into intimacies that set them against their fathers. So it is that we cannot separate the dynamics of emotional life from the gender relations of power, as psychoanalysis often tends to do. Rather than treating relationships as manifestations of universal patterns, we have to be aware of a relation between power, emotion and sexuality.

Freud doesn't appreciate how important fathers can be in the emotional lives of their children. In this regard he reflected the Viennese culture of his time. As Freud has it, it is the father's task to separate sons and daughters from the intimate embraces with their mothers. The danger is that mothers will hold on emotionally and will not allow their children to move towards emotional autonomy and independence. In this Freud shares with Kant the notion that development comes as a movement from dependence *to* independence. In this way the need for dependence becomes a sign of immaturity. It is the identification of masculinity with independence and self-sufficiency that gives men the authority and distance to separate mothers from their sons and daughters at this crucial stage. This break takes a particular form as it involves, as Freud has it, a fear of castration for boys. In learning to identify with their fathers they supposedly no longer experience them as competitors for their mothers' love.

The identification between sons and fathers is 'abstract' in Freud's story because it doesn't grow from an ongoing relationship, since fathers are so taken up with the demands of work. Boys cannot know their fathers in the way they know their mothers who care for them every day. This can leave boys with an idealized vision of their fathers and a disdainful notion of their mothers. So the lack of balance that exists in the relationships between men and women is reflected in the uneasy relationships boys often have with their fathers and mothers. As boys we might love our mothers but we also know that we have to be different. It can be difficult to *accept* their love and concern if we feel that as boys we eventually have to learn to live without it. Often we defined ourselves as boys in opposition to our mothers, because we felt we had to prove we were 'not' female. But the story is always complex and the way we learn to feel about our mothers can so often be tied up with how they are treated by and experience their partners. It also depends upon how much love and warmth we received in our early years from either parent, for this can crucially affect how we learn to give and receive affection and love in our later lives.

Love and Separation

Some boys are 'mothers' boys' and others are 'fathers' boys'. I was a mothers' boy who was probably saved by the fact that my mother went out to work most of the time and also insisted on living her own life. Though she often talks about the ways she has sacrificed her life for her children, this was very much the expectation of her generation. Fortunately she also had the wisdom to do otherwise. But it has still been difficult to make an inner separation and it is still easy to be drawn back into the hope that I will receive the affirmation and recognition I can still long for. It takes time to learn that our parents will not change and that we remain trapped as long as we live in the expectation that they are about to. Rather we can change in the ways we relate to them and so bring a different dynamic into the relationship.

Freud understood that separation is a more complex process than we culturally recognize. We think that when we have left home, that is the end of the story. Only gradually in our relationships do we sometimes recognize *how* we live out certain patterns of giving and receiving that resonate with ways we related to our parents. In our twenties it can be easier to lay the blame on our partners, thinking that things will be very different with someone else. Only when we recognize that, in new relationships, similar issues emerge that don't seem to go away, do we appreciate that we are trapped in certain patterns. But it can still be hard to accept that we need help to sort out the emotional ties that bind us, for as men we experience this as a sign of failure. We often imagine that we should be able to work things out on our own. Often we are suspicious of any form of psychotherapy, which strikes us as a sign of self-indulgence. It remains tempting to blame others through projecting responsibility on to them, since within a Protestant culture we are constantly trapped into proving that 'it wasn't our fault.'

The story of *Iron John* tells the tale of a boy who is forced to steal the key from under his mother's pillow so that he can release the hairy man who is caught in a cage and who will eventually take him on his shoulders into the forest. It is by the side of a lake in the forest that he is to be tested. Bly is right to emphasize that the boy cannot negotiate for the key with his mother but has to be ready to make a break. He cannot expect her to understand, but he has to do it *for himself*. He has to be prepared to steal the key while she is asleep. The point is that if you wait for your mother's approval or want to take it with her blessing, you will probably never establish the separation. Some boys never make the break and this is a choice that they have somehow made for themselves. But there is a price that has to be paid.

David Astor, for many years the influential editor of *The Observer*, had to cut his links with his dominating mother Nancy Astor before he could come into his own identity. Such is not a single event, as the story of *Iron John* can suggest, but can be part of a much longer process that involves much inner work. Will and determination might be significant ingredients in the situation but they are not by themselves enough. As Richard Cockett describes it in 'Escaping from Nancy' (*The Observer*, 22 September 1991), it was hard for David because he was the closest to Nancy of all her children. She was very possessive of her children and, as David has remarked, 'She loved me . . . she just did not know how to go about it in the right way.' As Cockett describes it, 'Nancy could not bear to let any of her children succeed or shine on any but her own terms and was constantly directing them to this end. They were not allowed an independent life, or to search for their own particular spiritual or political path.'

David was forced to break totally with his mother in order to survive. She was most possessive of him, pinning her hopes on him as the son who would become a Christian Science 'practitioner'. At Clevedon, Nancy used to say to David, as a joke, 'I wish you'd been born an ugly girl, then you couldn't leave me.' David's difficulties with Nancy accentuated a natural shyness and diffidence and damaged his self-confidence. Eventually he went to see his father to say that he could no longer endure his mother's attitude towards him. He probably understood the problem and only asked David to keep in touch before letting him go. It is fair to say, as Cockett does, that 'David's break with his mother, painful though it was, was the making of him, allowing him to develop a greater degree of independence than any other member of the family.'

Freud understood the necessity of making the break. It is something that we all have to struggle with ourselves for it is something that others cannot do for us. It is *inner work* we have to do for ourselves, as we face our fear of the anger and rage we might have to endure during this process of separation. The fact that we separate does not mean that we do not love our parents, for often we have confused love with attachment and codependency. At some level we fear that we cannot survive without the attention of a parent. But families have quite different dynamics, and as boys and girls we have to find our own ways of separating from both our mothers and our fathers if we are to learn to live in our own light. This process can take many years to complete, for once we have broken the physical ties we also have to work our way loose from the inner emotional ties.[11] It was only with great difficulty that I recognized how far into adult life I was still writing to please my father, to win some kind of approval from the heavens. Somehow I was still struggling to prove myself to him, even though he had been dead for over forty years, so that I was still living in his shadow.

As boys we inherit different qualities from our parents, partly dependent upon the particular dynamics that worked themselves out in the family. Often it is far from clear what qualities we have learnt from which parent. It took me time to recognize how much of the anger and power that I had expected to inherit from my father was in fact drawn from my mother and had to do with accepting the 'feminine' aspect of myself. It was only as I was acting out in a psychodrama the ways I learnt to relate to my mother at the dinner table that I recognized the enormous power and energy that had been tied up and was now released as I took up her role. It was an enormous liberation to recognize how much of my power and energy had been withheld as I learnt to separate from the 'feminine'. Having accepted the cultural myth which identified the 'active' with the 'masculine', I had forsaken the power tied up with my mother. It was energy that was available to me as soon as I began to accept the qualities that my mother had represented and expressed in my life. Again, it was something I discovered through this process of exploration that I could in no way have predicted in advance. This is part of the joy and self-discovery of psychodrama. It was only as I took on the part of my mother that I became aware of the enormous energy and excitement that I had long suppressed.[12]

So in working on our relationships emotionally, it is a matter of acknowledging and *facing* not only our wounds and hurts as part of the process of daring to be more honest with ourselves, but also the sources of our energy, power and identity. If we are to begin a revision of our different masculinities we have to explore the different messages we have unconsciously absorbed from our parents and the larger culture about what it means to be a man. Often what they have bequeathed to us was never talked about consciously within the family but was communicated through bodily movements, tensions and silences. Often we learn more through what is *not* said, which is part of the weakness of a discourse theory that relies too heavily upon what is expressed through language as the source of meaning. In many families what matters most is rarely put into words, and as children we so want to have the approval and recognition of our parents that we are often ready to forsake our inner truth, to become what they want us to be. This is a complex process that is mediated through class, gender and ethnic relations. Our parents have such power over us as small children that it is hardly surprising that what we so often forsake is ourselves.

Freud's most important challenge to the common sense of modernity is possibly his recognition that we have to face our pain and wounds if we want to grow in our individuality. We often learn that we can put our experience and history aside to grow in our freedom and autonomy as rational selves. But this is the way that modernity leaves us divided against ourselves and offers us a false vision of our individuality. It is part of the reason we often feel so 'unreal' within a postmodern society, though the theorists of postmodernity have usually attempted to teach us to celebrate our malaise. Freud knew otherwise. He recognized that in denying our emotions and feelings we are *denying* ourselves, for our feelings are as much a source of our truth and integrity as are our ideas and thoughts. What is more, it is mistaken to think that our beliefs have their source in reason alone, for, as I hope to show later, it is often what we feel most deeply that is the source of our beliefs.

We learn that we cannot put our wounds aside in the hope that they will go away if we do not give them any attention. We often learn that to dwell upon our emotions is only to feed them. Sometimes this might be true, but it doesn't work as a general rule, for the wounds and hurts that we learn to avoid or 'rise above' often have the habit of returning to haunt our dreams and fantasies. If we are to face ourselves we have to be prepared to *rework* our histories and experiences, for this is a path through which we can regain some of the grounds of our being. As we define what we feel and what we have lived through, however painful it was, so we define ourselves more clearly. This is an important first step in a process of initiation, for it promises us greater truth and reality as less of our energies are taken up with denying what we experience and presenting ourselves as we would want to be. In part this is to unlock emotions and feelings that for many of us men have been buried for so long. It is not shameful to carry hurts from the past; rather, if we are to revision our different masculinities, an important first step is to find the courage to share more of what we have silently carried inside us for so long.

Notes

1 Reflections upon the nature of friendships that men growing up into diverse masculinities have with each other are offered in Stuart Miller, *Men and Friendship* (1983) and *Men's Friendships*, edited by Peter Nardi (1992).

2 For some thoughts upon the changing relationships of fatherhood and the ways that boys from diverse backgrounds learn not to expect much contact from their fathers see, for instance, *Fathers and Sons*, edited by John Hoyland (1992) and the collection *Fatherhood*, edited by Sean French (1992).

3 The way that men brought up within a dominant masculinity can learn to use language as a form of self-protection is explored in my *Rediscovering Masculinity: Reason, Language and Sexuality* (1989, Chapter 7).

4 The way that traditional fathering is sustained through maintaining an emotional distance that allows for impartial authority is explored in Victor J. Seidler, 'Fathering, Authority and Masculinity', in *Male Order*, edited by R. Chapman and J. Rutherford (1988). See also the discussions in R. Sennett's *Authority* (1981) and in his *The Fall of Public Man* (1980).

5 The ways that particular religious traditions have sustained patriarchal male superiority need to be carefully explored. I question the assumed identification of Judaism with patriarchy and hence the blaming of the Jewish sources of Christianity for the continuing patriarchy within Christianity. These are false readings of the relationship between the two traditions. See, for instance, Daniel Boyarin's *Carnal Israel* (1993) and his *A Radical Jew: Paul and the Politics of Identity* (1994). For some important feminist contributions see, for instance, M. Daly's *Beyond God the Father* (1973) and her *The Church and the Second Sex* (1968); R. Radford Ruether's *Sexism and God-Talk: Towards a Feminist Theology* (1983) and her edited *Religion and Sexism: Images of Women in the Jewish and Christian Traditions* (1974); and Judith Plaskow, *Standing again at Sinai* (1990).

6 For reflections on changing notions of respect in relationships between parents and children see, for instance, Robin Skynner, *One Flesh: Separate Persons* (1976) and the helpful introduction he wrote with John Cleese, *Families and How To Survive Them* (1983).

7 For a sense of the development of Freud's work see his *Introductory Lectures* (1922). For a grasp of the social and historical context out of which psychoanalysis was developing see Peter Gay, *Freud: A Life in Our Time* (1988).

8 Foucault's challenge to Freud's hydraulic conception of repression, as he grasps it, is in *A History of Sexuality* (1980). I have explored these issues in 'Reason, Desire and Male Sexuality', in *The Cultural Construction of Sexuality*, edited by Pat Caplan (1987).

9 For a sense of how Foucault's understanding of the self developed in his later writings see his essay in *Technologies of the Self*, edited by L. Martin et al. (1988), where he shares the break with the work on sexuality which *The Care of the Self* (1990) represented. It does seem as if a very significant shift was taking place, possibly later encouraged by his own experience of AIDS.

10 Kitty Hart, in *Return to Auschwitz* (1981), gives a striking account of how difficult it was to share her experience in these early post-war years. People just did not want to hear and she learnt to keep her history to herself. Growing up in this atmosphere left you with a tendency to silence. We had survived so we were the lucky ones, but we were also shamed.

11 For a helpful critical engagement with Freud on the different ways that boys and girls

might separate from their mothers through the processes of development, see Nancy Chodorow, *The Reproduction of Mothering* (1978).

12 For a way of grasping some of the ideas that informed the development of alternative forms of psychotherapy see, for instance. F. Capra, *Uncommon Wisdom* (1988). For a particular introduction to psychodrama in the context of other therapies see S. Ernst and L. Goodison, *In Our Own Hands* (1981).

6
Initiations

Initiation and Memory

Western conceptions of modernity tend to treat identity as an issue of reason and rationality alone. We need to shift the terms of identity. We are 'initiated' into our families but much of what we have absorbed and learnt remains unconscious, for we have learnt it through our emotions and feelings. We all carry histories that go back beyond an existence as rational selves to the point of conception. Psychotherapies increasingly recognize that how we are acknowledged within the womb and how we are responded to and welcomed when we first emerge *can* profoundly affect the ways we learn to be both with ourselves and with others. Often this is a learning that takes place before we have come into the experience of language and so it does not have a cognitive or conceptual form, though it might well affect the ways we learn to express ourselves through language. Forms of social theory which assume that experience is provided for us through language give little space to such learning. Sadly they have made it almost impossible to illuminate the diverse sources of misery and suffering in many lives. In this crucial regard at least, cultural theory has yet to come to terms with the insights of Freud and psychoanalysis.

New psychologies, in a renewed connection with social theory and philosophy, will recognize that these hurts are not a matter of will and intention alone. Our mothers might well have dearly wanted to welcome us but they have communicated a different, sharper message with their eyes. A piercing look and a coldness of touch can leave us with a very different message. As babies we come into the world with an expectation, as Simone Will (1962) puts it, that good and not evil will be done to us and that we will not be harmed. But until very recently what we experience as babies was hardly recognized for it was assumed that with no memory babies could *not* feel pain and so they could not be harmed. A striking insensitivity marked the medical relationship with babies, which tells us a great deal about the mechanistic vision of medical science that fosters such notions. Most of us who are in our twenties, thirties and forties were born before the influence of Leboyer (1977), and so were born under the glare of sharp lights and were separated very quickly from the breast to be kept away in nurseries so that we would not disturb. Our early protests at this treatment were not heeded or responded to, for it was widely believed that babies did not feel pain.[1]

Birth was our initiation into life. For many of us it was not an easy beginning. In the rationalist terms of modernity it was rarely appreciated. Within the first few hours mothers were often told that they 'had to show who was boss' and so should not respond to the cries of their babies. I remember hearing this just 15 years ago when our child Daniel was born. The folk wisdom had it that 'you would make a rod for your back' unless you showed the baby 'who was in control'. If things have changed the initiatives have often not come from within the medical profession itself. It was pregnant women themselves, in the West in the 1980s, who demanded the right to have natural birth and who questioned the wisdom that women should give birth with their legs in the air. For birth had been appropriated as an event within medical science rather than a natural event in a woman's life in which she might want to be actively involved. How we have thought about birth until very recently says a great deal about how children are treated within the broader culture.[2]

As babies we are initiated into a world of feeling and this subtly guides our understanding. There is nothing 'natural' in the sense of being auto-matic in the response between mothers and babies, for women have been brought up, as have men in Western culture, feeling uneasy about emotional expression. We all learn to wear our own *masks*, wary of showing ourselves more openly and honestly towards others, often out of a fear of rejection. Sometimes it can be painful to hold a new-born baby, because we are reminded of how little we were touched and held ourselves as babies. If we are unable to touch our own feelings so that we are unable to respond with warmth and love, the baby can sometimes feel a silent rage. A baby can be sensitive to a false smile, so wanting at some level to rip the mask off her mother's or father's face.

At some level we all learn to wear our masks, for we learn to adapt to what is expected of us within the dominant culture. Often we fear rejection if we show more of ourselves. As men we learn not to show our feelings but to keep them to ourselves. Adapting to what is expected of us, say by our parents, becomes a way of protecting ourselves against hurt. At some crucial level we are initiated into the society, but *not* initiated into ourselves. Rationalist forms of social theory serve to silence the lived contradictions this helps to create. Even though people talk about individuality, we grow feeling that we want to be 'like everyone else'. As I grew up within a refugee community this was a very strong feeling. We learnt to minimize any quali-ties that might draw attention to ourselves, for we wanted to be accepted. We had little sense of what it might mean to be 'accepted for who you are', for we assumed that we could *only* expect to be accepted if we became 'like everyone else'.

Within contemporary culture the self is often conceived of as an illusion or as an effect of available discourses, for we learn that it is 'socially and his-torically produced' to reflect the values of particular communities. So it is that we learn that our identities are somehow provided for us through the dominant discourses and practices within society. We learn to be suspicious of a liberal vision that treats society as a collection of discrete individuals each with his or her own desires and needs. This tradition fails to appreciate how our subjectivities are moulded within particular cultures. But these poles, which reflect the framework that has dominated an Enlightenment vision of modernity, seem to leave us incapable of illuminating the lived tensions and contradictions between 'who we are' – which is obviously influenced at different levels by the society we live in – and 'what we are expected to be' in order to 'succeed' or 'achieve' within the dominant culture. Feminism has helped women to appreciate this more than men because it recognized that subordination was not a natural condition women could accept, nor could they live simply in relation to men and children. They had to explore their own values and meanings, even if this brought them to question prevailing social relations.[3]

Families and Emotional Life

Living our lives in the West in the 1990s it is doubtful whether the 'normal' family still exists. Growing up in the 1950s it was still possible to believe in such a thing or to feel intensely that the families we happened to grow up in were not 'normal enough'. The family that I grew up in could not be 'normal' for we did not have a father and it wasn't even normal when we had a stepfather, because 'normal families aren't Jewish' or they 'do not have a handicapped child' or they 'do not have a mother who earns more money'. It was easy to feel that however we lived it wasn't 'right', and that we had to do our best 'to be normal'. This was a matter of living up to an ideal that was still very much alive, often just for the sake of what the neighbours might think.

When you looked a little closer at the families that seemed to be able to represent themselves as 'normal' you often discovered that things were not what they seemed and that underneath the all-important appearances there was a different reality. The father might have been severely depressed or the mother might have been coping with her life dependent on alcohol, but often what was going on was being hidden. For what seemed to matter – and in many communities still does – is that the ideal is lived out in front of others, and that the Sunday roast was eaten on time with everyone sitting together round the table regardless.[4] It was partly that the ideal was, as a cultural myth, such a powerful 'reality', especially in the white middle class, that it legislated how people should be and how they should be with each other. So often it involved *living a lie* but this didn't matter if the truth was not out in the neighbourhood. It worked as a form of social regulation to make most people feel bad about themselves, for they were left feeling they 'weren't right' somehow. If you have lived a lie it can make you impatient with the celebration of appearances that is an aspect of postmodern discussions. So often this feels like another form of denial.

Often within the English middle class family there was little space for emotions and feelings. People learnt to show only those emotions that were expected or required of them and they learnt to *deny* any emotions that did not fit with what was expected. It was 'right and proper' that all the family sat down for the same meal together and ate the same things, and it was 'right' that children did not feel angry or sad for they were told by adults that they had nothing that could justify such emotions. Within a rationalist culture it was only if you could defend your emotions with reasons that you could allow yourself to have them. This was particularly true of boys who often felt that emotions were 'silly' or 'girlish', or that they just 'got in the way' of doing what you had to do. Often as boys we learnt to withhold and suppress our emotional lives, as if there was no public space in which we could share inner lives without compromising ourselves. Emotions became too threatening, so that it was easier to learn to live as if we did not have them at all.

We have all been initiated into different family forms, different ways of relating to ourselves and ways of being with others. Within many white middle class families you often learn to pretend, as you learn that love is only available to you if you are 'acceptable' to your parents. You learn to hide and deny any emotions and actions that do not fit with the ideals being lived out in the family. Often you did your best to prove your family was 'normal' even if it meant overlooking your father's depression or your mother's alcoholism. These were treated as 'aberrations' and 'temporary', so that they did not have to be addressed and we could overlook the hurt that we carried about them as children. We learnt that it was 'none of our business' as children, so that we should turn our gaze away or pretend that 'nothing out of the ordinary' was going on at all. You learnt what *not* to talk about. It worked to establish a regime of denial in which you often learnt to keep your ideas and emotions to yourself.

Within the middle class family what often matters most is learning how to behave in front of others. As you are initiated into the rituals of family life as a child you soon learn that what matters is what you do and what you say, while what you feel is a 'subjective' and 'personal' issue that has to be kept firmly in control. So it is that there is often a split between our 'outer' behaviour and our 'inner' experience. They come to exist in separate realms, often with little connection with each other. For at some level, especially as boys growing up in relation to diverse masculinities, we gradually lose connection with what it is we are feeling. At some level, we do not want to know because it is potentially threatening to the images and ideals we have learnt to live out within the context of the family. We are so used to this fragmentation of our experience that it becomes 'second nature', so that we are often unaware of the different ways that we are living out a lie.

In patriarchal families where the father still has a lot of traditional authority, you learn as a child to do what you are told and you learn to do it without question. Questioning what you are told to do can be a sign of disobedience which deserves punishment. The authority of the father has taken different forms and these need to be carefully studied in their context of class, 'race' and ethnic relations. A withering look can be as hurtful as a clout with the back of the hand. We have to be careful how we assess forms of authority and punishment. Sometimes as children we do not consciously register the pain of humiliation, for we are so used to it or have learnt to harden our hearts against it. As boys we often take our revenge by refusing to show others how hurt we feel inside. We take pride in showing that we can 'take it' while often silently feeling hatred at the ways we were treated. Often it is only as adults that we can allow ourselves to feel some of these wounds. We have denied them for so long that it isn't easy to accept them ourselves, let alone share them with others. For it is easy to carry a sense of shame, both for ourselves and for our fathers, that makes it hard to talk about painful experiences. Often it is easier to feel that if we do not talk about them, perhaps they did not happen at all. We learn to deny in this way.

As young boys we learn that what we feel has no relevance, for 'you are only a child', and a child's place is in doing what he is told and not being 'naughty' or 'disobedient'. If you have ideas or emotions of your own you soon learn to keep them to yourself. This upbringing can make it hard for boys to share themselves emotionally without feeling they are being weak. If we have known a wall of silence in our relationships with our fathers, it can be hard to share ourselves emotionally with our sons. If we have experienced a cold and distant fathering, there might well be a tension between the kind of responsive fathers we might want to be and this more authoritarian voice that we have absorbed from our own childhoods. Often this shows itself in anger and frustration with our children. This can be frightening if we have learnt to think of ourselves as calm and well controlled in our emotions, possibly in reaction to our fathers. But if we have never really *worked emotionally* on our relationships with our fathers, it can be difficult to change the ways we relate. If we are not in touch with the sources of our own anger, we will often be taken by surprise and respond unpredictably.

Sometimes we can take courage from hearing the emotional work that other men have done, and share more of our own experience. This is something that gay men have often gone through in their experience of 'coming out'. For it has meant sharing, rather than denying, what they have suffered in having to conceal so much of what they were feeling.[5] There is much that heterosexual men can learn for the revisioning of their own masculinities, for we have often colluded in quite subtle ways in the oppression of others. So, for instance, if we grew up in families in which our mothers were being constantly put down by our fathers, we might feel shame at the ways that we sided with our father to win approval for ourselves. We might have sensed our mother's anger for the love and attention that she was not getting and the anger that she felt that the little her husband had to offer emotionally was not going in her direction. She might well have resented her children because of this, finding it difficult to confront her husband more directly.

It can work in different ways too. I remember in my childhood how terrified I felt as my mother was getting furious at my stepfather for some incident at the dinner table. Somehow it seemed to trigger an overwhelming anger as she used her power to humiliate him telling him to get out of the house. As young boys we felt it impossible to effectively intervene to stop what was going on, though we would often try. We would be shouted at ourselves, being told that it was none of our business and that we should not interfere. But it could feel terrible as a child, for it seemed as if your whole world was being ripped apart. I just wanted it to stop because I felt so scared of what was going on. It taught me that emotions could so easily overwhelm and destroy so that it was hardly surprising that I felt wary of them. At some level the emotions seemed to be completely out of proportion with the incident that triggered them, which often had to do with food. Somehow food in our Jewish family had become symbolic of love, so that if you didn't feel like eating, it was experienced as a rejection of the love my mother had to offer. Mealtimes were often tense and charged, especially around special occasions. My stepfather simply had to remark that he wasn't hungry to challenge my mother's power. Often this was a form of passive aggression since it was a sure way of getting his own back, though sometimes it got completely out of control.

What goes on between the parents can be so crucial in establishing a balance of energies within the family. What is *not* expressed can carry as much weight as what is talked about, in terms of its impact upon the emotional holding of the children. This is a valuable insight that has been embodied within traditions of family therapy which refuse to treat individual emotional lives in isolation from what is going on in the rest of the family. Sometimes systems theory has been useful in pointing out the particular 'roles' that individuals play out within the family. Often it is the youngest child who has to carry much of the unresolved emotions.[6] In *Iron John*, Bly talks helpfully about how children are often used as 'psychic copper' to conduct their parents' anger and grief. As children we often want to make 'things better' so we carry our parents' unexpressed feelings for them. This is particularly clear in families of survivors of concentration camps. It is often that the children are carrying the grief which their parents could not express themselves. The children end up looking after their parents whose lives were cut short in childhood. They learn unconsciously that they need to succeed in the world to prove that their parents were not defeated. But carrying the hopes of your parents, who have in part lived their lives through you, can make it hard to establish your own feelings and life. It can be as if you are *not entitled* to your own life.[7]

Often children grow up caught in the emotional crossfires between their parents, wanting to keep the peace between them and carrying emotions and feelings that remain unresolved. It can be hard to disentangle our own emotions as children, for it can be difficult to feel entitled to them in the first place. Within such families it can be hard to find ourselves, for we are so concerned with the well-being of others that we cease to exist for ourselves. This is part of a process of identification and dependency and it can take time and space to sort out what we feel for ourselves. Learning to live for ourselves can be a long and challenging process and involves recognizing the integrity of *our* own emotions and feelings, recognizing that we have our *own* lives to live, our own mistakes to make. We cannot live our parents' lives or prevent them from making their own mistakes. It isn't easy to free ourselves from taking responsibility for others, but it might be important to take more responsibility for our emotional lives ourselves.

As families have changed in the last 30 years, so they no longer conform to a single pattern, if they ever did, and children are often left with even more complex emotional relationships, especially if they are part of different family networks. We can celebrate the existence of different family forms in a postmodern world, while still recognizing how often children blame themselves when a family breaks up. It seems easy for them to feel that if they had only somehow behaved differently, things could have worked out. If children have the chance to mourn what they have lost, then they can respond more easily to a new situation. It is much more difficult if parents pretend that nothing has really changed, for this serves to *invalidate* the experience of children themselves. It leaves them feeling as if there has to be something wrong with them personally for not being able to take things more easily. As more children share a similar predicament it becomes easier for children to talk to each other and to learn from each other's experience. There is no longer the same kind of stigma attached to separation and divorce, so that it is not something that children always feel they have to hide. It is not an easy situation, but it doesn't have to make children feel inadequate in themselves, when so many people in their class at school seem to have gone through something similar. There are still the same insensitivities to deal with as the dominant social institutions of state, education and welfare persist in refusing to acknowledge the new realities of family life.[8]

Bly does not help us here, for he often seems to miss the stability of traditional family forms. It is possible to regret the absence of older men playing significant parts in boys' lives, without nostalgically hoping for the return of a traditional family. Focusing as he does on the role of the father in initiating boys into manhood, he doesn't explore sufficiently the workings of power and subordination within the traditional family and the tensions this left in children's lives. The subordination of women into domestic life and childcare, with the restrictions in their participation in the public sphere, built all kinds of unresolved tensions and unspoken needs into the everyday realities of family life. This affects the initiation of both girls and boys into themselves in diverse ways, for it affects the ways they learn to relate emotionally. It might well be that families are not so prepared to stay together 'for the sake of the children' and the consequences have to be considered carefully for everyone involved, but this can bring greater truth and honesty into relationships as both genders are finding different visions for themselves.[9] It is in this new context that we often have to *rethink* the relationships between parents and children and the ways both girls and boys grow into a strong and clearly defined sense of themselves.

Private and Public

Bly sees the initiation of boys very much in the traditional terms of a movement from the 'mother's house' to the 'father's house'. He sees boys in particular as having to make a move from the private realm of love, emotion
and domestic life to the public world of hunting and adventure. This is a
transition that fathers have to help boys to make if they are to recover a
'true' sense of manhood. As far as Bly is concerned these reflect natural
differences which contemporary culture has wanted to avoid, in its attempt
to treat gender differences as a result of culture and socialization alone. Bly
wants a world in which men are 'not afraid to be men'. He touches a chord
in many men, especially in the United States, who feel that in their ambivalent responses to feminism they have denied some deep sense of masculinity
within themselves and who have worked hard to become 'other' than they
are as men. While there is something refreshing in this recognition of difference, there is also something misleading. We have to be far more careful
about the ways we think about gender differences, if we are not to reinvent
the terms of women's subordination and oppression.

While Bly expresses a deep respect for feminism he feels that women
should be willing to listen and validate men's pain. This is not something
that women have to deal with themselves, for he is clear that it is up to men
to take greater responsibility for their emotional lives. He recognizes that
traditionally women have been made to do the emotional work for men, so
that they have felt responsible for the well-being and happiness of their
partners. Because of the power that men continued to exercise over
women's lives it was in women's interests to 'keep their men happy', for it
was hard to exist without them. So it is that in *Iron John* at least Bly blames
men for not learning *how* to care for themselves emotionally. He is adamant
that he is not repeating the Freudian story which blames the mother for
being too possessive and demanding in her relationship with her son, so that
he has to be rescued by the external intervention of the father. Bly insists
that the people who are failing their children are not their mothers, who are
doing their job well and with feminism have found new sources of strength
and creativity, but the older generation of men who have failed to initiate
and take responsibility for their children, especially their sons for whom
they have a particular responsibility.

But while it is helpful to focus more clearly upon the role of fathers, there
is a continuing theme in *Iron John* which can easily be read as laying the
blame on feminism and the media for demeaning the image of the father,
as someone who is 'good for nothing'. This is a complex issue and we need
to assess the ways that recently, under the impact of feminism, men have
been marginalized within relationships and made to feel incapable because
they cannot relate emotionally. Sometimes Bly seems to hint that this is to
expect men to behave like women and he touches a raw nerve of anger
about the ways men have been represented recently within contemporary
culture. As Bly has it, often a younger generation of men have colluded in

this, angry as they are because of the lack of relationship they enjoyed with their fathers. But at another level these same men can feel guilty and ashamed at the ways their fathers' generation has been portrayed, knowing that there is another side of the story that is not being told. While seeming to blame fathers, Bly is also providing a space in which men can honour their fathers and appreciate what they passed on to them, even if they might have wanted more or wanted something different.

Bly has helped restore a link and conversation between different generations of men. He has done this in a traditional way by excluding women from the picture completely, but at least he has done it. He was created a time and space in which men can experience the loss and love they hold for their fathers. He has helped men feel the guilt and the longing, the anger and the yearning that was held but *not spoken*. This has helped many men reconsider the ways they were brought up to be men and the kind of myths and silent messages they received about what it was to grow into manhood. This has brought to the surface a hidden connection between fathers and sons as men learn to appreciate what was not said as much as what was said.

But in important respects Bly still blames the mother for holding too tightly and possessively to her children, even if he also wants to call older men to account. He still seems to see the mother in roughly Freudian terms and tends to feel that fathers have failed to carry through the responsibilities for separating mother from son, which Freud assigned to them. He adds to this the charge of demeaning the father in the eyes of the children, without analysing how the unequal relationship of power between the parents is often the source of women taking out their frustrations on their children. Again it is a failure to engage sensitively enough with the feminist critiques of relations of power and subordination within the family that has tempted him to treat the father in this way. It is as if Bly thought he would be able to put issues of relationships with women aside because not enough attention has been paid to the relationships between fathers and sons.

There is little doubt that feminist discussions until quite recently have often avoided thinking about relations between fathers and daughters. They have found it easier to recover the complexities of the mother's relationships with her daughters. It has been too easy to identify fathers exclusively with patriarchal power or to identify masculinity with male power. This makes it difficult to explore men's often ambiguous relationship to dominant forms of masculinity, as I tried to explore in *Rediscovering Masculinity* (1989). Where feminists have been concerned with issues of sexual difference, they have often been concerned to disentangle themselves from the influence of patriarchal meanings and values to open up a psychic space which expressed women's own experience and values. Often the focus, especially within Italian feminism, has been on birth as an experience that potentially gives women access to values and intuitions that men have little connection with.[10] In this context of sexual difference, it can seem as if any concern with relationships with fathers only serves as a distraction from the central task of constructing a women centred symbolic realm, in ways often hinted at by Luce Irigaray (1985).[11] But this can mean denying the pain and silence that remains unresolved in relations between fathers and daughters. Sometimes the relationship carries so much guilt and anger that it seems easier not to deal with it at all.[12]

There will be a temptation in feminist discussions to think that since the father was often absent and played a marginal role within the family, he played a small part in the emotional development of girls. Thankfully this silence has been broken and women have begun to explore their often un-resolved relationships with their fathers. It becomes clear that 'absence' does not mean less influence, for fathers can often play a very crucial part in the ways women have grown up to think and feel about themselves and the ways they relate. Ridicule of fathers can serve as a defence against having to experience the pain that is still carried in relation to them. Within a Catholic tradition women often grow up with uneasy feelings about the body and sexuality. Life too easily becomes a struggle against the sins of the flesh. Identified with purity and with images of the Virgin Mary, it is easy to feel haunted by guilt and inadequacy for you are inevitably going to fall short of the ideal.[13] Within this context boys are often identified with the threat of sexuality. It can seem easier to live without them at all, while at the same time there is often a strong attraction because of the very temp-tations they offer.

We are initiated into different traditions which can have a very strong influence upon our emotional and sexual lives. If boys learn that the body is sinful and that masturbation is an evil, it will be easy to feel that there is something *wrong* with them. It creates an intense sense of interior guilt. Within Christianity you often learn that life is a 'veil of tears' and that the only meaning to life is to reach heaven and to make sure that one's soul has not been darkened. There is an abiding split between the earthly and the spiritual. Within a Catholic tradition it is easy for men and women in differ-ent ways to feel that sexuality is sinful and that it represents a falling away from an ideal of celibacy. It is only in its procreative role that sexuality can be celebrated, which makes it very hard traditionally not to condemn homo-sexual and lesbian relationships. There is a continual attempt to separate the commitment, love and sharing from the 'dirtiness' of sexuality itself. Somehow we need to recognize that the repressions of our private lives cannot be neatly separated from who we are in our public lives.

Bly tends to think that boys learn about emotions and develop an emotional language in relationship to their mothers, only to find it hard later to communicate with their fathers who have different – but equally valid – ways of being and relating. For Bly men live in a different emotional world from women and it is through a relationship with fathers or mentors that boys can be initiated into the emotional world of men. Again I think we can learn to appreciate what men can share with each other, while at the same time recognizing how historically this has often been at the expense of women. I think it is important for men from different class, 'race' and ethnic backgrounds to learn how to share ourselves emotionally with each other and to do things that can bring joy and fulfilment as men. It is crucial if we are to revision masculinity to break the hold of its dominant notions that teach men that we can do without the love and support of others. As men we have needs that we should not be ashamed of or learn to treat as a sign of weakness. Often we sustain our male identities by starving ourselves of emotional nourishment that could otherwise satisfy and fulfil. As we have learnt to deny our needs, so we have learnt to deny ourselves as men.

But if we need contact with our fathers we also need contact with our mothers. It might well be that we have to learn how to give nourishment to ourselves before we can accept it from others. Often we have to accept as we grow up that we are not going to receive what we want from our parents, so that we have to learn how to accept what we need from those who are willing and able to give. This is not to underestimate the importance of contact between fathers and sons. It remains helpful to investigate how men *can* learn from each other in the context of relations between older and younger men. Sometimes the apprenticeship system provided a helpful context in which skills were passed on and wisdom shared across generations of men. With changes in the division of labour fathers are more often not in a position to pass on their jobs to their sons and this can weaken their sense of what they have to give. It can be striking for older men to consider in particular historical contexts what it is they have been able to give of themselves to their children. Traditionally men have often felt locked into their positions of authority in relation to their children which has fostered distance and reserve.

Authority and Fathering

Horkheimer (1972) and the Frankfurt School noted the decline of patriarchal authority and the difficulties this created for sons in particular in establishing a clearly defined sense of identity. For within the Freudian story it seems as if the child has to have a father to define himself against, and it is through such a process that he comes to define his ego.[14] Of course, as Kafka (1954) describes his relationship to his father, he could also be too powerful and dominating a presence in a boy's life so that he crushes his son's sense of autonomy and independence.[15] So it was that for Kafka 'initiation' into manhood meant finding ways of *separating* from his father's influence. The father was such an overwhelming influence within the 'mother's house', where his atmosphere and pressure were everywhere, that he could not easily be escaped. This did not only involve a physical separation, for Kafka knew that he carried his father inside of him so that he was present in his dreams and fantasies.

Kafka's *Letter to My Father* helps us appreciate that initiation has also to do with self-identity and independence. It has to do with becoming a person in one's own right, though this is not a single event in a person's life, as Freud and Jung appreciated in their different terms, but often involves a lifetime of working on oneself to integrate and come to terms with the different aspects of being that we learnt within modernity to deny and discount. Kafka understood this himself, for he had his own ways of working on himself. He had learnt that the path to autonomy and independence went beyond the rationalistic terms provided by Kant for modernity. Autonomy does not just mean exercising the control of reason over the temptations of nature so that we exist as rational selves alone. It is not only through a struggle with our 'animal natures' that we can be initiated into ourselves. Somehow we also have to challenge the dominant terms of modernity to appreciate the integrity of our emotional and somatic lives.

Within the masculinist terms of modernity, as I have explored them in *Unreasonable Men* (1994), being 'rational' means *not* being 'emotional'. You prove yourself to be a 'rational agent' by showing that you can control your emotions and feelings and guide your life by reason alone. So it is that we learn 'self-control' as men, as involving the domination of our emotional lives. If we have emotions we learn not to show them but to keep them to ourselves, for it is hard not to feel that they shame us in front of others. This has established a particular relationship to our emotional lives, especially as middle class men. It has helped form dominant traditional notions of white heterosexual masculinity and has had an important bearing upon what fathers felt they could pass on to their sons. Often men learnt to control their emotions by being distant and cold, thereby thinking that they would encourage their sons to be 'strong' and 'independent'.

To focus, as Bly does, on the weakening connections between fathers and sons which have flowed from the industrial revolution and men leaving home to work away in factories, can be to miss the cultural and historical forces also at work within the relationship. This is what the Frankfurt School can help us understand, especially in Mitscherlich's influential work *Society without Fathers* (1970).[16] They also recognized how the father's position and status within the family was influenced by the skills that fathers could pass on with their jobs and that promised a means of livelihood and continuity. Many skilled working class occupations allowed fathers to feel pride and self-worth as they appreciated that they had something to pass on to their sons. This gave working class men power and self-confidence within the family, though this could also be abused as fathers insisted that families had to be organized around their needs and that 'what they said went'. But the self-esteem and pride men felt at work could also moderate their presence at home, for they could feel that they had less to prove to others. With changes in assembly-line production and the deskilling of work in the post-war period, men often carried home a sense of frustration and bitterness at the repetitiveness of work that was released at the expense of partners and children.

Possibly it is when fathers feel less secure in their skills and when work has been deskilled and degraded so that it only exists as a way of 'earning some bread' that there is greater tension and frustration. Work becomes something that is left behind at the factory gates. It becomes something that working class fathers do not want to be asked about or reminded of till they have to go back to it. Certainly it isn't an experience that men want to share with the rest of their families. Work becomes something that they have to do, but it is no longer something that they take much pride in. So it is that working class children often learn not to talk about work with their dads. It is passed over in silence as men are anxious to prove themselves in other spheres of their lives. Again we have to be careful not to generalize about the changing place of work in men's lives. It might encourage some men to be more involved in the home, taking pride in the work they do to maintain the home, if not being more involved with the children. But it could also be related to incidences of domestic violence and difficulties that men have in defining a new role for themselves, especially if their partners are bringing as much money into the house.

Since the Second World War there have been significant shifts in the organization of work that have had their bearing upon father's authority and power within the family. As work becomes a matter of earning money and money alone becomes the source of status within the family, fathers establish themselves more often through what they can buy for their children. Men seem to have shifted their relation to themselves as consumers, since traditionally this was completely left to mothers. But men can also feel they aren't earning enough so this creates a new pressure, especially as men feel shamed that they cannot afford to buy what they want to. So toys often become a marker and reminder of a father's status and part of the connection between fathers and sons. Buying what the children have seen on TV becomes a way that fathers sustain their status and authority within the family. In the 1980s consumption assumed a new importance. It also became a way that some men could deal with their frustrations at work.

Consumerism has worked to shift the terms of class relations but class remains a crucial factor in the construction of different masculinities. The middle class clerical worker or corporation man can feel equally ashamed of their work. They can feel that they have little to pass on and that they want to forget the office when they are not there, but they might feel more control when it comes to advising their children on education which has become a dominant factor in job allocation and career prospects. Working class fathers can feel less confident in discounting education than they once did while still feeling uneasy in their contact with the school. It can be difficult for fathers to help their children for they fear being shown up if they cannot do the homework. This can leave working class men feeling unsure and brittle about what they can give to their sons. Often sport assumes a central importance in the communication, such as when fathers and sons go off to football together.

But men can also feel uneasy with the challenges of feminism and with women working in different jobs. Men still largely define themselves as breadwinners and as providers but at the same time they can feel that they should participate much more in the home and with children. Significant shifts have taken place: men can feel they should be doing more, but often

just help out. In many working class and middle class families it is still left
to women to take responsibility for thinking out what should happen,
though men might help more with looking after children or doing the shop-
ping. There is a sense of 'fairness' amongst people growing up after the
1960s, a sense that men and women should be more equal and that women
should no longer be treated as 'second class citizens'. But there is enormous
tension in the ways this is being worked out which cut across differences of
class, race and ethnicity. Heterosexual men are coming to terms with a loss
of power and authority within the family as they search for a different identity as men from what was passed on to them from their fathers. Little seems
to have prepared men to negotiate with their partners, especially when
there are no clear models of how men are to be. What is clear is that many
women are just not prepared to put up with what they had before.

Men have had to respond to the challenges of feminism from within the
different masculinities they live. Often men have learnt very different ways
of getting their own way and being in control, though these structures may
remain invisible as men live out a more equal vision of themselves. Often it
has been difficult for men to adjust to the new powers that women claim
within relationships. As women learn to give priority to their relationships
with friends, refusing to put arrangements aside to be available for their
partners, it is easy for men to feel resentful and rejected. It is as if men find
it hard *not* to interpret this as a sign that their partners do not care for them
enough, for otherwise they would make themselves available. If this is a traditional pattern of relationships that boys grew up to take for granted, it is
often carried unconsciously as an expectation. This is part of a crisis of
masculinity that takes different forms in working class and middle class settings. Often this reflects a pervading cultural uncertainty about how men
are supposed to be in relation to women and children.

It is partly because heterosexual men are brought up to think they should
always be *in control* of their lives, and so always know what to do and how
to behave, that it can be so unsettling when women challenge the ways men
are. Men will often react violently when they feel that their authority is
being threatened, especially if they think they have been 'reasonable' in the
changes they have made. Sometimes men withdraw into a sullen silence,
feeling like strangers in their own homes, and often home life will continue
as if they are not there. This can be painful, but men often learn to swallow
the situation as women refuse to defer to their husbands in traditional ways,
or possibly only in public to keep up appearances. This shift of power and
authority has affected men from different class, ethnic and racial backgrounds. As men learn to cope with a new situation there is often enormous
tension that breaks through the surface of relationships at unexpected
times. At some level there can be a stubborn resistance as men find it hard
not to feel bad because they feel they are no longer respected in their own
homes. If this is not the situation, it can be hard for men not to feel it this
way emotionally.

Sometimes men have felt resigned to the loss of power and authority in the family. They might have tried to assert their authority and got angry at the ease with which others 'talk back', thinking that respect should be automatic 'because I'm your father'. It can be difficult to accept that respect is something that has to be earned, yet in the West this has become a common notion since the early 1970s. In part this reflects a shift towards a postmodern conception of relationships where individuals deem themselves to be free from the demands of tradition, able to make their identities and relationships for themselves. It is this shift away from traditional forms of authority that marks a postmodern vision. Somehow it is connected to a sense that people have to act as their *own* authorities, for there are no longer certainties that can be relied upon and no way that reason alone can legislate what is 'right' and 'wrong' for people.

With the challenge to modernity has come a distrust in reason as an independent and autonomous faculty able to guide and control life. It opens up questions about the extent to which life is something that we can expect to control and possibly a vision that there might be larger forces of nature that we have to learn to live with. For instance, people die suddenly or find themselves with critical illnesses, but little prepares us to accept these as events in people's lives rather than as 'interferences' that we want to put aside as soon as possible. Both men and women in different ways have learnt to live 'in their heads' within a rationalist vision of modernity. There is little space for feeling, for it is too easy to believe that we are 'bothering others' when we show our grief to them, say when someone close has died. It is as if we have all somehow learnt to deny death and to believe that those closest to us will go on for ever. If we have feelings we learn to keep them to ourselves since otherwise we are 'burdening' others or somehow 'taking advantage of them'. It is not only men who feel this way; women too are brought up within a rationalistic culture to treat their emotions as a sign of weakness. Often this reinforces women in their subordination since it seems to 'confirm' that women are the 'weaker' sex.

In crucial respects masculinity is tied up with our visions of modernity since they have been so shaped around the authority of reason. Feminism has helped to question the abiding modernist distinction between reason and emotion and so has helped to reinstate emotions, feelings and imagination as sources of knowledge. Men have traditionally learnt to legitimate their authority as flowing from the universal voice of reason. It is the 'impersonality' and 'universality' of reason that have allowed men to legislate for others and so to feel that they 'know best' what is good for others. Often it has meant that men do not have to listen to the experience of women, for reason operates independently of experience and carries its own authority. In challenging the sovereignty of a reason separated from nature, feminism has brought into question the fundamental terms of modernity. Since men are initiated into a central position within modernity through the identification of a dominant white, Christian, heterosexual masculinity with reason, it can be hard for men *to listen* to the questionings of feminism. It is too easy to discount what women are saying, for their voice is already devalued as 'subjective', 'personal' and 'emotional'. So it is hard for their voices to carry weight with men.

As men are challenged by women around them they will often withdraw, feeling upset, for little has prepared them to listen to what is being said. They might disappear into themselves, hoping that the 'madness' will pass and that others will 'return to reason'. Men might escape into work or into alcohol, not wanting to admit that others might be right. It can be hard for men to acknowledge that there might be different truths, for modernity has taught men that reason is theirs to be relied upon on all occasions. The authority of men has been tied up with the authority of reason which has allowed men to assume that any challenge to a conception of reason separated from nature has to be 'irrational' – a challenge to reason itself. But it is important to recognize that there are *different* conceptions of reason without thinking this leaves us with the relativism of so much postmodern theory. For as authority becomes redefined, as we learn to appreciate that it has an inner aspect and doesn't just exist as external rules, so we are also left with a recognition that both men and women can grow in their own authority.

Difference and Integrity

Within modernity it has been difficult to recognize that there might be different paths to the truth. We learnt that reason alone could be relied upon and that science was the exclusive source of truth. As white, heterosexual, middle class men we were initiated into particular privileges within modernity, for reason was to be identified with masculinity. So it was that modernity was largely cast within men's terms, though it was presented as a universal aspiration that was open to all. It was a vision that was to be increasingly tied to the power of capital and, as Marx appreciated, its capacity to subvert different forms of value so that monetary exchange provided the exclusive source of meaning and value. There was an intimate relationship between a universal conception of reason and the sovereignty of exchange values within a capitalist society. This is something that Max Weber helpfully illuminated in *The Protestant Ethic and the Spirit of Capitalism* (1930), though the connections to masculinity are left largely implicit.[17]

Women learnt that if they were to know truth and reason, as Kant defined it for modernity, they could *only* discover it in relation to men. It was men alone who could know reason and morality. There was a single path and there was a universal set of principles that could be discerned through reason alone. Women could not have their own meanings and values if they wanted to find emancipation. So it was that Jews and blacks also learnt about the conditions of modernity. They had to be ready to dispense with their particularistic traditions, customs and values if they wanted to aspire to the universal dreams of the 'rights of men'. So it was that modernity was identified with the dream of emancipation and it was felt that any 'differences' that divided peoples were artificial and needed to be put aside.[18] But this vision of a 'common humanity' was very much set in dominant masculinist terms. This is not to deny the values of freedom and equality it offered, but to appreciate the terms.

But there is a powerful tension between recognizing the particularity of women's experience and values and accepting the universality of the 'age of reason'. Women were made to feel that they had everything to gain and nothing to lose in following the guidance of reason. But this involved its own 'dis-memberment', as Mary Daly has presented it, for it involves *denying* the pain and terror of the witch burnings which accompanied this new ordering of gender relations.[19] It was the 'unreasonable' voice of a reason that had learnt through the sixteenth and seventeenth centuries to disdain nature, and was ready to condemn so many women who had been involved in healing and herbalism as 'witches'. This was a 'victory' that is reenacted every year in the symbolism of Hallowe'en as children learn to fear the wisdom that witches might bring. Women learn to separate themselves from their own histories, somehow identifying themselves with a universal history of freedom and progress. Often this is presented as the defeat of unreason and superstition, as we learn to accept science alone as the source of knowledge and belief.

The West has also sought to treat slavery as part of a story of developing freedom and progress, so avoiding painful questions about the collusions of the Enlightenment with the legitimation of slavery.[20] As nature became disenchanted, in Weber's terms it could only be treated as a 'threat' to civilization. This was to diminish Africans in their own eyes, as they were deemed to be part of nature and so excluded from 'civilization'. The West had used reason and science to set modernity in its own Eurocentric image, which was largely white and masculinist. The West was able to legitimate the slave trade right into the middle of the nineteenth century. Christianity had its part to play in this legitimation, for science and Christianity often went hand in hand as 'benefits' that the West could bring to otherwise 'uncivilized' peoples who should be 'grateful' for the 'good news' that the West was bringing. They were being given a chance to escape from the barbarism of nature. If they refused to recognize what 'was good for them' then they would have to be destroyed because they had put themselves 'beyond the pale of reason'. The threat they presented could not be tolerated, for it showed ingratitude. Genocide has still to be recognized as also a terrifying fruit of modernity.

Many religious Jews also yearned to be part of the universal fellowship of reason and to reconstruct their religion and self-identity in its terms. They learnt to despise the particularity of Jewish experience when set against the universality of Enlightenment modernity. The moral vision which set universality in sharp opposition to particularity could *not* appreciate any universal message that might be conveyed by Jewish existence and persistence. Jonathan Sachs, in his *Crisis and Covenant: Jewish Thought after the Holocaust* (1990), has conceived of the Enlightenment as a cultural language 'into which Judaism could not be translated. Two systems of thought, each opaque to the other, met in headlong confrontation.' For Sachs the covenant between God and the Jewish people is expressed in Torah and is interpreted through midrash which is a form of biblical exegesis. Crucially it treats Torah as a teaching, not as a text, for 'Torah is not information, but instruction.' As Sachs explains it, 'There is no more exact opposition than that between midrashic and historicist approaches to textuality, the one seeking to transport ancient worlds alive into the here-and-now, the other confining their meanings and imperatives to the there-and-then.'

Midrash challenges the universalitism of an Enlightenment modernity that claims that there is a single path to truth that can be legislated through reason alone. For midrash is essentially an open form of exploration that traverses boundaries, as Maimonides gave midrash an Aristotelian emphasis drawing upon Greek sources (for a helpful introduction to Maimonides see, for instance, David Hartman). Midrash echoes the possibilities of postmodernity while aspiring to elucidate different truths, because it is essentially ambiguous and has multiple truth values, and seems to invite further – and often contrary – exegesis.[21] It accepts the validity of *different authorities* and refuses to accept the sovereignty of a single source, for there are different sources of revelation. There might be lessons to learn from this tradition as we struggle to validate the integrity of different cultures and traditions without falling for the fashionable relativism of so much postmodern theory. We have to learn how to listen to the different voices, rather than subsume them under a single authority.

Men have gained enormous power and privileges within modernity, for it has largely universalized on the basis of the white, male, Christian heterosexual voice. It has meant that as men we still expect to get our way and to legislate 'what is best' for others. As different voices have insisted upon being heard, men have sought to listen to them within the *rationalist* framework of much postmodernism. This has sought to sidestep rather than to meet the challenges of feminism and ecology, especially their early questioning of the split between reason and emotion. As modern Western men have learnt to identify with their minds, they have treated their bodies as machines and learnt to despise their emotions as signs of weakness. It makes it hard to listen to others if we have never learnt how to listen to ourselves. At some level we experience feelings as involving a loss of power and a lack of self-control. So it is that we have learnt not to feel. We operate at a different level of ourselves, learning to cope with whatever is expected of us. Like packhorses we are so used to carrying the load that we are barely aware of the strain and pressure and that we often live with as men.

As I have argued, we are initiated into a 'man's world' when we are still very young but we learn not to complain. As babies, boys in the Protestant North are usually held less by their mothers but fed more. It is as if baby boys are supposed not to need so much touching. It is interesting to note the gender differences which mean that, in some families, boys can be expected to put up with the smaller room without the carpet for they are expected to 'do without'. It is this rugged individualism that men are expected to conform to. Often, as boys growing into manhood, we can be expected to sleep in cold rooms because it is 'soft' to expect a duvet, or to be nurtured by our surroundings. As boys from different class, 'race' and ethnic backgrounds we learn to pride ourselves with being able to *do without*. It is hardly surprising that as men we find it hard to communicate our emotional needs within relationships, given the ways we have been treated within the dominant culture of masculinity. It isn't that men are essentially any the less caring and loving, but within the dominant culture we have learnt to forsake inner connections with ourselves.

Because of the privileges that men have had within modernity in relation to women, it can be difficult to recognize that men have also often had to work within oppressive work situations. We have to think about masculinities in relation to class, race and ethnicities if we are to think of the relations of power between men that have served to marginalize different men's experiences. It is often factory and office work that provides some men with control over other men's lives, other men with far less control over the everyday conditions of their own lives. Rather than treating men exclusively as a 'problem' because of the power they have in relation to women, we *also* have to validate men's own hurts and sufferings and the ambiguous relationship they often have to the dominant notions of masculinity and male power. Gay men have long talked about the ways they feel oppressed by heterosexist norms. Somehow we also have to find ways of validating diverse heterosexual men in their different experiences, rather than simply identifying them with a relation of power.

It is too easy to simply leave boys feeling bad about themselves, for instance in school because of the time and space they take in the classroom. This echoes an abiding cultural message that says that boys are 'no good' and that whatever we do we will not 'make anything of ourselves'. We can feel trapped in an endless round of obligations, thinking that 'when this is over' we will begin to live for ourselves. It is as if men are often trapped into leaving themselves aside, because at some level we inherit such a weak sense of personal self. It is as if we are defined by what others expect of us – by work, relationships, children, which all carry their own obligations. Often men are dutifully supporting their partners, doing their best to pick up the pieces and keep things going. Often it has been too easy for feminism to deride what men do, partly because men have such little sense of what they have to give more personally, beyond fulfilling what is expected of them in the different roles they perform. But often men are still much less responsible at home, allowing themselves to do less than they do at work where they may be driven and compulsive. Sometimes it is easier, when men find it hard to make time and space for themselves, that they say so rather than pretend otherwise.

Initiation and Self

As men we are often initiated into different roles and responsibilities but not initiated into a relationship with our personal self. Since our male identities as working class and middle class men with jobs are established within the public realm of work, it is often hard to give ourselves in our personal and sexual relationships. It is easy to leave these aspects of our lives to our partners, and feminism has often intensified this sense in its notions that men do not know how to relate emotionally. Men have often withdrawn into themselves rather than take greater responsibility for their emotional lives and relationships. For there is an abiding tension between the ways that men expect to get their way and to know 'what is best' for others and the ways men learn to deny their emotional needs. Often men are trapped into activities which leave them little time and space for themselves. Somehow it becomes easier to *deny* these personal needs for it is still easy to feel that emotional needs are a sign of weakness.

As middle class boys we have often learnt to do without. This is the way we have learnt to affirm our male identities. We become insensitive to ourselves, for at some level we do not listen to ourselves. Often we do not stop even when we are tired but insist, within a Protestant culture, on pushing through the barrier of our tiredness, as a way of feeling good about ourselves. We resist our own mortality and have little sense of limits. Having learnt within a Cartesian tradition to treat our bodies as machines, we do not expect them to let us down. This is reflected in the ways men often resist going to doctors, unless there are unmistakable signs of illness. Too often we dismiss the signs, thinking that 'it is nothing', for we have constantly learnt to minimize the deprivations we are supposed to endure as men. This is the way we have learnt to test ourselves, which is part of an endless process since our masculinity is rarely anything that we can take for granted and feel comfortable with. We have to be constantly on our guard to prove it and often we are proving it against ourselves.

Men are often scared of having time and space for themselves. For some men it can feel that if they aren't busy with something they don't exist. It is as if they exist in their activities, but do not exist for themselves. This is partly why men find it harder to care for themselves, often neglecting to look after themselves. It may be easier to do things for others than to face our own emotional needs. We can feel easier carrying the burdens of a difficult relationship, while at the same time finding it hard to express our need for others. This can serve as a defence against having to feel ourselves. For many of us who have been brought up in families where we learnt to live without feelings, it can be easier to let our partners carry the emotional weight of the relationships. Rather than feeling our own anger we allow our partners to carry it for us.

But this creates an emotional imbalance in the relationship which allows men to blame their partners for being 'so emotional' when it does not suit them. But often it is more helpful if men ask what they have learnt to do with their own emotions and feelings. This encourages us to rethink our histories in our families so that we can begin to reclaim ourselves emotionally as we learn how it was that we learnt not to feel. Within the Protestant moral cultures of the West it was easy to treat emotions as a childish embarrassment we should learn to live without. Often we do what is expected of us in relation to others, for we have little sense of what we really feel for them. We are anxious to be seen as not interfering in the lives of others, and we learn to be independent and self-sufficient. We exist within the modern West as rational agents, not as emotional beings. Often we want our partners to recognize our emotional needs for us because we feel uneasy with sharing our vulnerability. Yet we can so easily resent them for being intrusive at the same time. Often we feel more comfortable at a distance, which is why we have such difficulties with the everyday realities of intimacy and contact. At an early age boys internalize a message that to need others is a sign of weakness. It seems easier to live without feelings at all.

Though Bly recognizes the importance of men reclaiming their emotional lives and honours what men can learn to share with each other, he fails to appreciate how we are *also* initiated into our manhoods in relationships with women and children. The process of initiation has different aspects, each with its own sacred time and space. It is not simply that the West has lost the capacity to mark an initiation from boyhood to manhood, for we have also gained through a recognition that men have emotional needs too. We have to be wary of drawing too quickly from the examples of different cultures unless we also appreciate what the different forms of initiation have meant for the quality of relationship between men, women and children. Bly cannot do this because he works within a framework which sees initiation as part of a movement from the mother's house to the father's house. It reflects the move from dependency towards independence that is also integral to the masculinist structure of much Freudian psychoanalytic theory.

Bly is aware of the 'psychic hole' that exists in boys' relationships with their fathers. This is filled by all kinds of demons, such as the dishonouring and demeaning of older men within the culture. Sometimes Bly seems to blame women for diminishing men in the eyes of their sons, but at other times he accepts this is part of a natural process that will go on as long as boys learn their emotional language from their mothers. This makes it hard for boys to appreciate the different emotional worlds of their fathers. But we have to be careful about the ways we talk about men having a different gender ground and so a different way of feeling and relating. It might be important to appreciate what it is that men can share with each other, the skills and stories that share a particular experience, while at the same time recognizing how within patriarchal societies these have worked to limit options and possibilities for women. Feminism has been crucially important in making visible the subordination and oppression of women. Sometimes it has also made it harder for men to validate their own pain and hurt but this is crucial if more open and equal relationships are to be sustained.

As long as we identify men with their power alone, we fail to appreciate the contradictory experiences of men's lives. Talk about gender ground might help us recognize a difference which too often is lost within the universalistic language of modernity. Women have traditionally been judged according to masculinist standards and found wanting because we assumed that reason provides us with an impartial and objective standard. So, for example, women have been treated as less moral than men according to the scales prepared by Kohlberg (1981) because they are less likely to conceive of morality in terms of universal principles. But the work of Jean Baker Miller (1976) and Carol Gilligan (1982) has helped us to an awareness that women might conceive of morality in the different terms of care and concern.[22] This brings into focus a different way of conceiving moral issues, which is more attuned to the persons involved. These different voices have been too readily related as an ethic of care and concern as opposed to an ethic of rights and justice, somehow connected to the different experiences of men and women. But it is also important to relate these differences to issues of power and the central place of dominant White heterosexual masculinity within our inherited visions of modernity.

But if we are to recognize the integrity of differences and validate people's different experiences, we have to be careful *not* to subsume and assimilate people's experiences inappropriately. We have to recognize the ways men are brought up with a thin connection to self and emotional lives, while being careful at the same time that we don't simply evaluate men's experience according to the standards and values of women. We might recognize that men have different ways of going about things without thereby excusing the ways men are within patriarchy. For instance, with the early challenges of feminism towards the institution of mothering, there was an emphasis upon parenting as a discrete set of activities that can be shared more equally between partners. It might be important for men learning from this to redefine their responsibilities to their children, bonding with them from the first moments, whilst *also* recognizing that fathering involves its own particular joys and responsibilities. This does not have to be a way of getting men 'off the hook', but is one of appreciating difference.

Men from quite different class, 'race' and ethnic backgrounds are looking in the 1990s to create different experiences of fathering from what they had experienced themselves. While wanting to do more they have also been trapped by the intensification of work that has been a feature of the 1980s and 1990s. Bonding with our children at a very early time is part of an initiation into a different vision of manhood. While Bly recognizes the importance of fathers being involved with small children, there is little space for this within the framework that he has prepared for himself. For he remains largely trapped by a traditional vision of masculinity which sees it as taking place around the 'father's house'. It is hard to feel that it will not reproduce at some level a disdain for women. Bly has to take some responsibility for the ease with which his work can be appropriated by those men who want to regain ground that they see lost to feminism. They want women to feel

that the home is still the fundamental space for women because it is supposedly where they learn their 'femininity', while it is *elsewhere* that men
have to learn their masculinity.

It can be difficult for men to respond creatively to the challenges of feminism, but this remains crucial work. Bly can seem to cut through this necessary work to give men a clearly defined position which resonates with the
confusions that so many men feel about how to be. It can seem as if it is the
father's role to initiate his sons and to prepare the transition to the 'father's
house'. But this spatial metaphor, appealing as it can seem, only serves to
trap men into traditional visions of masculinity. Bly helps us to recognize
something important about the contact between older and younger men and
the need for men to face their emotional wounds. But he leaves us with a
false clarity by creating a 'man's world' that is at once separate and autonomous from the women's realm which remains domestic and largely in
control of the early years of children. But if we are to be initiated into a
more meaningful masculinity I think that men have to be at home, as
women do, within both the domestic and public worlds. It is not simply
developing a relationship with our inner child that is part of the healing, but
the contact and intimacy that we can share appropriately with our partners
and children. There is a time when separation is crucial but there is also time
for connection and contact.

Notes

1 A sense of these profound changes in the ways birth was to be understood is given in
Frederick Leboyer, *Birth Without Violence* (1977). See also the work by Michel Odent, *Entering the World* (1985) and his later book *Birth Reborn* (1984).

2 For important critical work on the ways children and child-rearing have been conceived
in the West see Alice Miller, *The Drama of the Gifted Child* (1981) and *Though Shalt Not Be
Aware: Society's Betrayal of the Child* (1984). For some cultural and comparative reflections
see Erik Erickson, *Childhood and Society* (1950).

3 Feminism has insisted on women taking their own space to create their own meanings
and values. Through this process they have learnt to appreciate the differences that exist
between women of different class, ethnic and sexual orientations. See, for instance, Jean
Grimshaw, *Feminist Philosophers* (1986); Lynne Segal, *Is the Future Female?* (1987); and bell
hooks, *Ain't I a Woman? Black Women and Feminism* (1981) and *Talking Back: Thinking
Feminist, Thinking Black* (1989).

4 For an exploration of the changes taking place in family life and intimate relations see,
for instance, Sue Lees, *Sugar and Spice* (1993); Sue Sharpe, *Just Like a Girl* (1976); and Judith
Stacey, *Brave New Families* (1980). While it is crucial to recognize changes it is also important
to recognize the ways that ideals and myths operate to make people feel bad about their own
experiences.

5 A sense of the diverse developments within gay men's sexual politics can be gleaned
from Ken Plummer, *Telling Sexual Stories* (1994); Tim Edwards, *Erotics and Politics* (1994);
and Steven Seidman, *Embattled Eros* (1992). For a sense of links with lesbian politics see *We
Are Everywhere*, edited by Mark Blasius and Shane Phelan (1995).

6 An understanding of the developments within family therapy can be gained from the
selected papers of Robin Skynner, *Institutes and How To Survive Them*, edited by John R.
Schlapobersky (1991). He recognizes that it is only when professionals 'include themselves in
the process of change' that mutual growth and learning ensue.

7 Important work with the second generation of Holocaust survivors is shared in Ward's *Memorial Candles: Children of the Holocaust* (1992). In their different ways they illuminate the struggles of the second generation to live in their own light.

8 For a sense of the changes in family relations and what these mean for children growing up in different arrangements see, for instance, *What Is To Be Done about the Family*, edited by Lynne Segal (1983); Sue Sharpe, *Fathers and Daughters* (1994); and *Marriage, Domestic Life and Social Change*, edited by David Clarke (1991).

9 A sense of the emotional realities of changing family relations is explored, at least in relation to heterosexual relations, in *Families and How To Survive Them* by Robin Skynner and John Cleese (1983); and D. Winnicott, *Playing and Reality* (1974). In relation to mental disorder, Bruno Bettelheim's *The Empty Fortress* (1964) is a fascinating study of autism. See also Janet Finch, *Family Obligations and Social Change* (1989).

10 For a sense of Italian feminism and the ways it explores notions of sexual difference see, for instance, Rosi Braidotti, *Patterns of Dissonance: A Study of Women and Contemporary Philosophy* (1991). See also *Knowing the Difference: Feminist Perspectives in Epistemology*, edited by M. Whitford and K. Lennon (1994).

11 An illuminating introduction to the writings of Luce Irigaray is given by Margaret Whitford, *Luce Irigaray: Philosophy in the Feminine* (1991). A helpful introduction to her own development is provided by Luce Irigaray, *Je, Tu, Nous: Towards a Culture of Difference* (1994).

12 Reflections on the relationships between fathers and daughters are given in *Fathers and Daughters*, edited by Ursula Owen (1984); and Sue Sharpe, *Fathers and Daughters* (1994).

13 For studies which can illuminate the relationship between women, bodies and sexualities within a Catholic tradition see, for instance, Marina Warner, *Alone of all her Sex* (1985); and Karen Armstrong, *Paul* (1986).

14 To understand the ways that Horkheimer and the Frankfurt School reflected upon the changing relationships of authority within the family and work, see Max Horkheimer's essay 'Authority and the Family' in his *Critical Theory: Selected Essays* (1972). For a critical engagement see Jessica Benjamin, 'Authority and the Family Revisited: Or, A World without Fathers', in *New German Critique*, Winter 1978.

15 See Kafka's *Letter to My Father* (1954) and the useful discussion of some of the issues it raises in Marthe Robert, *As Lonely as Franz Kafka* (1982).

16 To help place Mitscherlich's *Society without Fathers* (1970) in the context of the Frankfurt School see Martin Jay, *The Dialectical Imagination* (1973).

17 For some helpful discussions that explore the theme of masculinity in *The Protestant Ethic and the Spirit of Capitalism* see David Morgan in *Doing Feminist Research*, edited by Helen Roberts (1981); and Victor J. Seidler, *Recreating Sexual Politics* (1991a, Chapters 2, 3).

18 For reflections upon the relationship of modernity to issues of race and ethnicity see, for instance, Paul Gilroy, *Black Atlantic* (1994); and *Racism, Modernity and Identity*, edited by Ali Rattansi and Sallie Westwood (1994).

19 Mary Daly explores the impact of the burnings on women's historical consciousness and sense of identity in *Pure Lust* (1984).

20 To explore the relationship between the Enlightenment and the institution of slavery in the West see, for instance, D.B. Davis, *The Problem of Slavery in Western Culture* (1989). See also Eric Williams, *Capitalism and Slavery* (1964).

21 For the recovery of Jewish traditions of thought, which have often been sidelined through being designated as 'religious' and so isolated from a Western philosophical tradition, see, for instance, Susan Handelman, *Fragments of Redemption* (1991) and Richard Cohen, *Elevations* (1994).

22 For Jean Baker Miller's work see *Towards a New Psychology of Women* (1976), while for Carol Gilligan's work see *In a Different Voice* (1982). For a sense of the discussion generated by an ethics of care see *An Ethic of Care*, edited by Mary Jeanne Larrabee (1993). An argument for the multiplicity of moral voices is made by Susan J. Heckman, *Moral Voices, Moral Selves: Carol Gilligan and Feminist Moral Theory* (1995).

7

Transitions

Visions of Masculinity

A crisis of masculinity in the late twentieth century takes different forms
within different generations of men. There is no fixed vision of masculinity
that each generation is aspiring to realize, nor is there a falling away from
a golden age 'when men were really men'. Within the mythopoetic men's
movement, Bly can sometimes seem as if he wants to reinstate a vision of
manhood and male bonding that we have lost, especially in the way that he
talks about how men have been weakened progressively through the lack
of contact with their fathers since the industrial revolution. But Bly is often
also aware that in different generations men have to face *different* issues and
realities that little in the past can prepare for. He draws a distinction
between the 'macho' man of the 1950s who is in control and learning to be
tough and hard in the face of life, and what he calls the 'naive' men of the
1970s who have been 'effeminized' through their response to feminism. It
is as if they have not wanted to accept themselves as men because 'to be a
man' was to be oppressive to women. If they have been able to get in touch
with the feminine so long denied within themselves, they have also lost
something crucial in the process.

If this is unfair to the complexities of men's responses to feminism, it
touches something crucial about the confusions men often now feel about
who they are. This is connected to a broader crisis of belief that is part of a
postmodern culture. For if all beliefs are 'relative', what does it mean to
have beliefs at all? Often we learn to adapt to what is expected of us, unable
to formulate beliefs for ourselves. It is part also of a contemporary crisis of
authority, for we have lost confidence in the traditional forms of social and
political authority. Politicians can rarely be trusted, for they are seen as
being out for themselves and they seem prepared to compromise whatever
beliefs they have to get elected. Part of the appeal of Thatcherism in
England was the fact that at least she seemed to believe in something. Bly
talks about how men, under the ambivalences about male identities in the
face of feminism, will often let others challenge and insult them without
being able to stand their own ground. It is because men have become so
uncertain about what they think and feel that it is hard to create boundaries
for themselves. It is as if men allow others to enter their 'psychic houses' to
take what is valuable to them without even registering what has happened.
Of course not all men behave in this way, but it touches a raw nerve.

Bly doesn't allow for different masculinities or help men to challenge homophobia. He seems to guarantee to men that they will not become 'soft' or have to deal with gay feelings, if they allow themselves to share more emotionally with other men. The notion of the wildman seems to allow men to be both tough and tender, for it allows men their tears and anger without compromising a sense of their male identities. Supposedly the wildman movement will protect men from the 'naivety' that befell a generation of anti-sexist men. At some level Bly proudly reasserts biological difference and claims that the fact that men have been hunters for 2000 years has left men with a particular psychic and emotional inheritance that needs to be appreciated and honoured. For Bly it is as if we have fallen for a notion of gender equality that denies the significance of difference and assumes that gender differences are exclusively the product of cultural and social factors. But if we reject a simplistic distinction between 'biology' and 'culture' that has characterized a structuralist tradition, we can still keep an open mind about the nature of 'differences' as long as we are aware of how relations of power and subordination have traditionally formed them.[1]

With *Iron John* we can see the task of reclaiming masculinity as a matter of reconnecting to the 'wildman' within, which we have supposedly abandoned because of the false notion that if there are any gender differences, they are created within the terms of a particular culture. Bly wants to *reassert* the validity of difference without denying the subordination and oppression of women. He strikes a powerful chord in men who feel they have been shamed about who they are as men because their masculinity has been identified with a relationship of power alone. Bly joins those who think that masculinity can be redeemed and redefined, but unfortunately he leaves us with a traditional notion of masculinity as concerned with the 'father's house' alone. If he helps men to draw sustenance and nourishment from what he takes to be intrinsically male activities, it doesn't mean that women cannot do these things for themselves in their own way. But it does block for men possibilities of validating their contact and love with women and children as intrinsic to a reworked vision of masculinity. It also makes it difficult to honour the diversity of masculinities and sexualities.

Initiation for Bly becomes a matter of initiating men into a 'man's world', but often this world is defined in a way that excludes contact with women and children. Rather than facing the difficulties that men have in relationships with women, recognizing how hard we can find it as men to love and care for others, we are encouraged to separate from these aspects of our experience. This threatens to *reinforce* traditional ways that women have been devalued and oppressed, even if this is no part of Bly's intention. The anthropological experience he draws upon reinforces this direction. He mentions approvingly the Hopi custom where the older men prepare a second birth out of a long wooden passage, saying that boys have had a first birth out of their mothers and now need to be reborn out of their fathers. When the boys return from this ritual they have to be introduced again to their mothers who pretend not to recognize them. The women are part of the process for they too recognize the importance of the boy's growth into manhood.

But this creates traditional boundaries between a man's world and the women's world of domesticity. The boy has to leave the mother's realm but this becomes more than a necessary process of separation, for it works to reinforce the notion that the *proper* realm for women is the private realm of domesticity. But this is a boundary that feminism has helped to question and which some men have helped to transgress as they have appreciated, for instance, how important it has been for them to attend the birth of their child and to bond with babies from the very beginning.

Bonding and Separation

There has been a developing sense in the 1990s that men with different masculinities want to have a different relationship with their children than they experienced with their fathers. Over the last decade there has been a growing movement which has encouraged men to be present and active in supporting women giving birth. This is something that men have to have some feeling for, since it often doesn't work if men are present as a matter of duty and obligation. If men are going to sit reading at the end of the bed, it might be better for them not to be there at all. But more men have come to feel more actively involved in the process of pregnancy and this helps them prepare to participate meaningfully in supporting their partners. It is crucial that men do not take over or cut off, but learn to be supportive to what their partner needs at different moments in the birth process. For many men it has proved a profound and transforming, if sometimes difficult and arduous, experience.

From my own experience being present at Daniel's birth at the Mothers' Hospital in Hackney in spring 1982 I know how it helped change my sense of Anna as I appreciated and faced the power and wisdom of birth. At some level it is challenging to men who want to control, for birth is a process that has in part to be surrendered to. It has its own timing and rhythm that need to be respected. The birth had gone much faster than either of us expected and it took time for Anna to accept that she was really in labour. It was a week early and it was easy to feel that it was yet another rehearsal. We did not have time to get to the hospital that we had planned and the ambulance men insisted on taking us to the nearest hospital. Anna was well into the process when we arrived and I can still remember the feelings of panic as we made our way through the open corridors with Anna being pushed in a wheelchair and me following carrying all the bags. Anna was clearly committed to an active birth and she refused to lie back passively as some of the nurses expected.

There was a wonderful African nurse who used her authority to support us, recognizing that this was the way women gave birth 'back home'. There was an enormous feeling of support and warmth in the room as Daniel was born into the world. We had challenged the usual hospital procedures, so other nurses came in to watch and encourage. We insisted that Daniel be allowed to make contact with Anna as soon as he was born, so that the usual procedures of weighing could be put off till later. We were clear what we wanted and Anna had challenged a young male doctor who was sceptical about active birth, saying 'what did he know since he had never given birth himself.'[2] The nurses were patient and supportive and we were allowed to stay together as a new family till the morning. So often men in the past have been turned out into the cold, for there is no place for them to stay in hospital. For us it was a wonderful time of bonding and I can recall the wonder as Daniel first lifted his head to look around the world he had newly entered.

This was an important moment in my initiation into manhood. For long I had carried a fear that I would never really have children of my own. It was as if I was still haunted by a sense that I would probably die young as my father had. I never thought I would become a father myself. Somehow it felt strangely connected to becoming a man in my own right. I felt bonded to Daniel and appreciated the feeling of connectedness. This feeling has not been easy for me to sustain in my life, since I had suffered so many bereavements and separations when I was very young. I had learnt to do without the love of others so that I could survive on my own. I was thrilled to be a father and it lifted some of the burdens and myths that I had carried about myself for so long. I appreciated the time that I spent with Daniel and know at some level that I was nourishing myself: through giving to him I was also finding ways of giving to myself, and in fathering him I was *also* learning to father myself. It also helped to lift the spell of a miscarriage that we had had in Paris five years previously and which could so easily have confirmed some of the worst fears I carried about myself. It had taken time for us to work through the pain of that experience, for we both knew that we had to be finished with it if it was not going to be carried as a shadow by the child to come.

I appreciated the ways I was bonding with Daniel and the love that flowed so easily and naturally towards him, while knowing that I was not having the same kind of relationship Anna was having through breastfeeding him. I didn't feel jealous, though I know other men have felt so. Somehow I had worked through the idea that having an equal relationship did *not* mean having the same relationship. This was a weakness in early libertarian notions which held that women should possibly be discouraged from breastfeeding because with bottle feeding they could have a more equal relationship with their partners from the very beginning. It was a way that fathers could supposedly participate on 'equal' terms. But there seemed something artificial and forced in this egalitarian position and by the time Daniel was born it already felt like an idea from the past. I felt more easy with the idea that at least for a while the primary relationship would be between mother and child and that my role as a father was to support this relationship. I was to sustain and protect it, whilst also developing my own relationship with Daniel.

Freud and Jung both focus upon the bonding of the mother and give little recognition to the bonding that takes place between fathers and infants. They are both, according to Bly, 'mother's boys' who see the father's role as providing the separation between mothers and growing children. This is an important process of separation and many boys only succeed, if they ever do, in making the separation in their adult years. Bly gives a more active role to fathering and he sees that older men have a particular responsibility in initiating their sons into manhood. But Bly's position tends to build upon the separation that Freud and Jung are talking about, rather than appreciating the significance of men *also* bonding with babies. As far as Bly is concerned this is 'mothers' work' and it is wrong for fathers to think that they can do this work too. It can seem as if it is yet another case of men pretending that they can be women. While Bly recognizes the importance of men relating to young children, taking an active part in playgroups and childcare so that children learn that men too can have warm and tender feelings, the framework that he provides in *Iron John* cannot adequately prepare the ground for this.

In contemporary Western societies men often have great difficulties bonding with their fathers. Often they carry such feelings of anger and hurt at the ways their father was not there for them when they were children that it is difficult to feel connected. Sometimes it is only through therapy that men find a space in which they can acknowledge and work through some of their unacknowledged feelings. Only then can they sometimes begin to feel some of the love they have also carried. Quite often men feel that they have few emotions about their fathers, because they had so little relationship with them. It is as if they feel completely disconnected from them. Sometimes this serves as a feeling of self-protection against the hurt and disappointment. But again this cannot be legislated, for people have to explore these emotional realities for themselves. Prevailing poststructuralist theories often lead us astray because they find it hard to appreciate the ways we can carry unexpressed feelings for so long. Operating within a male rationalist tradition they assume that we can control our experience as discourse through assigning it particular meanings. But this often blinds us to the ways we can be surprised at our emotions. They have a movement and rhythm of their own that needs to be acknowledged and followed in its integrity. It is part of a process of exploration that we cannot control through our minds alone.

Since men so often find it hard to bond with their fathers, separating from our fathers is often something that is not achieved until well after their deaths.[3] Sometimes we can continue to live in their shadows, proving our worth to them long after they have gone. This can make it difficult to live in our *own* light, taking more emotional responsibility for our lives and relationships. We can so easily feel trapped as men into continually proving our worth within the public world of work that we find it hard to draw nourishment from our intimate relationships. Even though we might have the power to get our own way, often we do not know what we need and want for ourselves. If we could find more fulfilment in our relationships we might feel *less driven* to be constantly proving ourselves and less need to assuage an underlying feeling on inadequacy we often silently carry. Often we need to maintain control because at some level we fear being exposed and ridiculed. Insecure in our personal selves, it is easy to feel at some level that we are playing some kind of role.

Initiation and Intimacy

As boys grow up within the contemporary cultures of masculinity it is easy to feel that their manhood is something that constantly eludes us. It feels as if there are no rituals which we can believe in which mark a transition from boyhood to manhood. The Jewish ritual of the bar mitzvah when a boy becomes 13 marks a recognition by a broader religious community of the moment when it can be said 'now I am a man.' But I can still remember feeling that I was not really old enough for what was happening. It was an important moment for it is a time that you stand before God and the community, reading from the Torah for others to hear. I felt proud but also unsure of my voice as I had to sing the portion of the law that had been assigned to me. But it was also an initiation into a male privilege, for in the late 1950s there was no equivalent that girls had to go through. It underlined that the responsibilities of men were particular.

My stepfather was there to help me through the process but it was also a moment when I felt a connection with my father. I carried early memories of going to the synagogue with him before he died, when I was just five, and hiding in his prayer shawl – the tallis – as the priestly blessing was made. I peeped out though I wasn't supposed to look. I could feel his physical warmth and protection as I was standing next to him. It is one of the few body memories that I carry. Even though I could sometimes look to his guidance years after his death, as if he was acting like some benevolent force for good, I often looked around for older men who might be able to offer me wisdom and direction. Bly recognizes that we can often not expect our fathers to help us find our ways into manhood and that we may seek out a mentor who can help us on our way. This is an older man who might have followed a similar direction in life and who is willing to hold us in their hearts and offer us guidance. This is a man who we have some *feeling* for. They might serve such a role in our lives, even if we haven't really talked it out with them – though I think it can help to do so.

Robert Bly talks about how Joseph Campbell served as his 'male mother' for many years. What seemed crucial was that there was someone who was ready to believe in what he was doing and who could recognize him for who he is. This can allow us to accept more of ourselves, if we have just one person who is ready to trust and affirm who we are. It is this recognition that we so often miss in our families. Often we feel that we were never really seen or understood for who we are. In the middle class family it is easy to feel that you can only deserve love if you have proved yourself through what you have achieved, say at school or later at work. Often there is little sense of the unconditional love that we need in the early years of our lives. Rather love is treated as a scarce commodity that has to be earned through our actions. For most of the time we are left feeling undeserving. We can also learn to hoard our own love as if it will be devalued if we share it too easily with others. We learn within a white middle class family to be *wary* of giving ourselves too freely. We learn to give things more easily than ourselves. Often we have little experience to draw upon from our own families to recognize what it means to share more of ourselves.

It is hard to generalize about class, but it remains crucial to think carefully about class, race and ethnic relations. In some working class families boys are expected to be tough with themselves if they are not going to become 'soft'. If love is more freely available, it is often tied to correct behaviour rather than to proving ourselves individually. You have to do what your parents tell you for otherwise you are 'disobedient' and 'naughty'. Children have to learn to do what they are told, often without question. The relations of authority are constructed less, as Bernstein (1971) explored it, around the elaboration of linguistic codes.[4] Parents are less likely to offer long explanations justifying the rules that they make. There are more clearly defined expectations of how boys and girls will behave. It would be interesting to explore whether boys and girls are talked to in different ways and whether they develop different relationships to language. Boys seem to use language as a form of *self-protection*, learning very early not to commit themselves. They learn not to put themselves at risk by saying too much. At some level there is an awareness that language is so often used against them by those, like teachers, who have power over their lives.[5]

Boys from different backgrounds might have had relationships with older men who they remember as 'mentors'. But many men have not had the good fortune to discover such mentors who could help them through the transitions to manhood. Many of us might experience ourselves at different times as being stranded between different stages. But probably this is the way it is for most men, and it is as well to acknowledge it rather than to think of 'manhood' as a state that we achieve once and for all. This is part of the problem of talking about initiation as if it was something that was waiting for us to achieve. It can prove a false goal unless men are prepared to engage more openly and honestly with their emotional histories. We have to be prepared to recognize our shadows, rather than to discount them in the way we are often encouraged to do within a rationalist culture that teaches us to 'leave our pasts behind us'. Often if we are not to be trapped by our histories, we have to be ready to acknowledge them.

As boys with diverse masculinities we often grow up wondering what it would be like to be a 'real' man. We watch our fathers or older men for signs that we might be able to imitate or follow. But if it is a status that constantly seems to elude us, it is partly because of the ways that masculinity has been

defined within modernity. Identified as we are with reason, we learn as men
to speak for others before we have learnt to speak for ourselves more personally. It is as if we have learnt to put our emotional and intimate selves
aside so that we can speak in the impartial and universal voice of reason.
But at some level we can also experience this as a false position that we are
taking up to assuage an underlying sense of inadequacy, a sense that we are
not 'good enough' and so have to constantly prove ourselves as men. We
are partly to do this by learning to do without and showing that we can
endure all kinds of unnecessary hardships. We are 'man enough' to do
without the love and support of others. But at some level we often carry our
own resentments as it is hard not to despise others for still having the needs
which we have forsaken. As Freud recognized, we project our unacknowledged needs and desires onto others, for we learn to put ourselves aside.
Often we are locked into unspoken resentments which we do not want to
admit, since they reflect badly on ourselves.

Within modernity men are often brought up with a weak connection to
their inner emotional selves. At some level we learn to treat ourselves as
rational agents so we separate ourselves off from our inner natures which
we learn to despise as signs of weakness. This creates an *imbalance* between
our inner selves and our outer activities which is intensified as men learn to
deny wants and desires. Often we come to have a possessive relationship to
intimate relationships and objects which provide us with substitute forms of
gratification. We can feel ourselves to be eternally dissatisfied, as we seem
to be trapped into constantly comparing ourselves with others. As we can
feel haunted by a sense that whatever we do it is 'not good enough', so we
can feel that we never get enough. Again this is given a different form and
expression in different backgrounds, but it can link back to a sense that we
were never loved and accepted as young children for who we were. Since
boys have to constantly prove themselves it can be difficult to experience
unconditional love. Often we learn to give out to others, but find it hard to
accept the love and support that is offered. At some level we often fear that
it will leave us weak and dependent and so compromise our identities as
men.

This connects to the difficulties men have in establishing boundaries for
themselves in contemporary sexual relationships. Often as men we are still
reacting to the unresolved relationships we had with our fathers, saying that
we want to have a quite different relationship with our children. Many
younger men in the 1990s feel much more bonded and connected with their
children through having been present at the birth and learning to take care
of them at the same time as the mother. This can create a connection that
feels quite new and special in men's lives, for babies bring an unconditional
love and acceptance. Relating to babies can teach us a way of communicating that exists *prior to* language and so help us touch our own physical-
ity and nonverbal expression. Often they implicitly question a poststructuralist tradition that assumes that meanings have their exclusive
source in language, for they can teach us that so much of importance takes

place before language. Or to put it differently, they can help us appreciate different kinds of language and the subtle forms of emotional expression. It can be a nourishing experience for young fathers, unused to accepting love so freely.

Spending time with young babies can also be frustrating and difficult for it involves learning to live a different timing. Babies have their own time, and if we are to respect them we have to learn to *attune* to their timing. Traditionally this is difficult for men who are used to getting things done and who have inherited a fear of 'wasting time'. But it also touches unacknowledged holes in our own experience, for as babies in the 1940s and 1950s we were expected to fit in with adult routines from the very beginning. We were supposed to feed and shit at particular times. Often we carry the tensions in our bodies, as our parents left us on the potty waiting for us to 'perform'. It was as if we owed it to them and were challenging their authority and so risked their anger. At some level we can carry some of the rage and sadness at not having been recognized and affirmed in the muscle tensions of our bodies. We learn to hold ourselves somatically in particular ways in response to some of these primal scenes. But again we *cannot* unlock these unexpressed emotions as a matter of will and determination. They come forward in their own time, often only in spaces in which we can feel safe enough for them to surface.

As we learn to appreciate the time we spend with young babies and infants it can be a way of accepting love and nourishment that we too easily reject from adults. In its own way it is part of an initiation into manhood, for it potentially awakens us to qualities of care and love that we might not have thought ourselves capable of. Bly might well appreciate this but the framework for initiation that he prepares for us in *Iron John* rigidly insists that initiation for men takes place within the public realm. This is unfortunate for it fails to appreciate so much that has been positive for men in their responses to feminism. Feminism has helped many men to open up a more honest and direct means of communication, even if it often brings up anger and rage at the ways women feel constantly taken for granted and have their experience devalued within relationships. Often it has forced men to examine their own unexamined emotional lives as women have asked us to share ourselves more directly with them.[6] This has been difficult for men to learn, especially as we have been so used to living at one remove from our experience. We have often learnt cynicism and disdain as a way of protecting ourselves from being hurt. It can be hard to give these patterns up.

Time and Boundaries

Through spending time with our children we can learn to bond with them. Somehow it seems easier to do this if we are learning with our partners how to take care of them. This is something that women have traditionally had to learn for themselves, for there is nothing 'natural' or automatic about it.

If fathers are learning these skills from the beginning then there is a fluency and naturalness of their touch and contact. It helps if you do not have to defer to your partner, thinking that she already knows what is to be done. This is a powerful form of initiation into our masculinity, for it teaches us that we *can* love and care. This is a crucial learning, for men often carry with them an unspoken fear that they aren't capable of giving or receiving love. We are sometimes wary in our relationships because we fear that others might find this out about us.

There is a learning that men can also do with each other which in part is an unlearning of how we are supposed to be as men. This has been the importance of consciousness-raising and therapy groups for men. We have learnt to listen and share with each other as men. We learnt that we were not the only ones to feel this way, but that others felt similarly.[7] It is also a space where we can explore the reality of our emotions, recognizing that we do *not* feel the way we might want to. Often there is a tension between how we might like to feel and could rationally justify and the ways we do feel in reality. This is a tension that many men feel ashamed about. They have learnt to hide such contradictions in their experience since it serves as further proof that they are 'not right' and so would give other men grounds for rejecting them. At some level we often learn to reject ourselves as men before we give others the chance. It is a strategy that many men can still recall from school as they remember boys who learnt to laugh at themselves before others got a chance to do so. Often it went together with a very low self-esteem. As we learn to explore these painful experiences with other men, we slowly learn to trust them more.

I grew up in a family in which the children were expected to fit into the routines prepared by the adults. We did not expect to be listened to or respected. Our voices were not respected as children and we were often lied to if it suited the adults. If I would eat soup that didn't have meat in, then I would be told that a soup didn't have meat in. Since it was 'good for me' it was done with my best interests in mind. This makes it hard to *trust* adults. I learnt to keep my thoughts and feelings to myself, as did my brothers. At some level it was hard to trust each other because we could so easily be divided, since we all needed whatever adult love was going around. But if you are not respected by the adults, it can also be difficult to learn how to respect yourself. This is especially true within a moral culture that is constantly teaching us to ignore our own emotions and feelings. If we do not listen to ourselves, it becomes difficult to listen to others.

This is one reason why spending time with young children can be so challenging for men. The time can seem endless, for so little seems to happen, It is so easy to be plagued by voices which tell us that we should be getting on with things. But you can get into a terrible fix if you are trying to do your own thing while you are also looking after an infant. It can be terribly frustrating as different timings are involved. It can be easier to give up on the idea of our own projects for a while, though this can be hard for men to do as they fear 'falling behind'. But being with children can teach us a different way of being with ourselves. It can help us to learn what it means to take time in our relationships and to realize how little time we give to ourselves. For as men we are constantly doing things, filling our time with activities. It is very different to give time and attention to ourselves. This can feel like a self-indulgence that we cannot allow ourselves. But this is the way we trap ourselves into established patterns as we continue to talk to ourselves within these Protestant terms. It is because what *matters* to men still takes place within the public realm of work. As soon as an intimate relationship is set in place, that is supposedly the end of the struggle for men, and we then learn to take our partners for granted, expecting support for making our way in the public world.

There is no place within *Iron John* for validating the learning that takes place within relationships and for recognizing how important it is for men to take what we have learnt with other men back into our relationships. It is too easy to see this as a retreat into the 'mother's house', rather than as a space in which we can also express our masculinities. For as we learn to give and receive within our relationships, we are not pretending to be women, but learning how to be men. This is part of learning to have more equal relationships with our partners. As we learn to spend more time with our children, so we are also learning to spend time with ourselves as men. In many ways we have often lost this relationship to ourselves within modernity and we have learnt to relate quite externally. But if we are to restore a sense of the dignity and integrity of men's emotional needs, we will have to find a different balance between our 'inner' and 'outer' lives.

We often learn as men that if we are ready to put value on something then it is important to us. As men we often talk to ourselves, saying that we are doing whatever we do at work 'for our families and children'. But significant as this sentiment is, it is traditionally not reflected in the time we spend with our partners and children. Within modernity we learn to *control* our experience through thinking about it in particular ways. This is what puts men at the centre of their own experience. But if attitude is important, so is the quality of the time that we spend with others. It is part of a post-modern sensibility to recognize that it is not just what we say to our children that matters to them, but who we are with them. They learn from how we relate to them even if we still tell them 'do what I say, not what I do.' This is why it is hard for them to believe that we care so much for them, if we spend such little time with them. If fathers always have 'something important to do' so that they rarely seek out their children to spend time with them, the children get a message. But as we are insensitive to our emotions as men, it is difficult to appreciate how much children *learn* through what is emotionally communicated. Things might never be said, but learning still takes place. Often children have absorbed the lesson that their families do not really care for them individually. It is a painful lesson to live with, but as boys we soon put it aside to get on with life.

I found the early years spending time with Daniel and Lily far easier. I had more experience to fall back on. Despite the frustrations I found it enormously nourishing, as if through giving to them I was also giving something to myself. It was a healing experience as I learnt to take more in for myself. It was through spending quality time with them that I was creating my relationships with them. There were few models around and it felt quite different from my own childhood. In the ways they were related to by their grandparents, I could recognize how I had been treated as a child. As children we were expected to do what we were told. As long as we ate what was on our plates, we were very much left to bring ourselves up. We would be shouted at if we misbehaved and our auditory boundaries were not respected. I catch myself shouting at Daniel and Lily sometimes and it reminds me how much I unconsciously absorbed from how I was treated. Even if I think I am relating differently, every so often I catch myself relating to them very much as I was related to. It is a constant struggle to respect their boundaries, since I experienced so little of this kind of respect myself. It is probably why I have spent so much time writing about respect in a variety of different contexts.

Unless we are clear about our own boundaries, it is difficult for children to learn to respect theirs. Sometimes I have been too available, especially as Daniel was growing up, as if to say 'no' was somehow to deny him. It was easy to feel that authority was related to distance and authoritarian control, for this is the way we often experienced it as children. It seemed hard to live a different *vision of authority* and tempting rather to exist as yet another child within the family. If we had experienced as children our own mothers acting in an arbitrary and authoritarian way, it was often tempting to take the side of our children against their mother. It could feel as if we were somehow standing up against our own mothers whilst we were standing up for our children. But often this is not helpful, and to anyone in the family it is more important for partners to get together and decide upon the rules that will operate within the family. It is only if we are clear in our own authority that we can do this. As I learn to say 'no, I am not available now', I teach my children to respect their own boundaries.

If you have grown up within a middle class family in which you have not been respected and in which your individuality was not fostered and encouraged, it can be hard to pass these qualities on. If you can still hear how you were told to think and feel as a child, for instance that 'nice children do not get angry' or 'you've got nothing to feel upset about', then it can be hard to validate and affirm our children's experience by being prepared to listen to what they have felt. Unless we have done the emotional work to learn how to listen to ourselves, it can be difficult to listen to our children. Even if we want to behave otherwise, we will often find ourselves ignoring or ridiculing what they have to say. Like our parents we might find it hard *to listen* to our children when, for instance, they are in conflict with their teachers. If we experienced betrayal at the hands of our parents who automatically took the teacher's side, assuming that we must have been naughty for otherwise the teacher would not have punished us, it can be difficult to stand up for our children.

It hurts not to be listened to and we learn as children not to share ourselves with our parents for often we cannot stand the humiliation of not being heard. We learn to keep things to ourselves. This can mean that as parents ourselves we often do not share our own fear but hide it so that it does not serve to weaken our children. We falsely assume that they will learn to be 'strong' if we hide our own fears and inadequacies from them. This is a pity, for often we are unwittingly reproducing the silences of our own relationships with our fathers. It can be far more helpful to our sons and daughters to *share* our own feelings of fear when we were at school, say, so they don't end up thinking, as we did, that there must be something wrong with them for feeling this way. In this way we help them to validate their experience, rather than leaving them with the message that 'you've got nothing to be scared about.' We think that we are being reassuring, especially with our sons, but it is quite the reverse. We are often leaving them feeling as lonely and isolated in their experience as we had been as children. Often what our children want is to be listened to without making judgements about what happened.

Respect and Authority

I remember Daniel coming home from primary school feeling upset because he was teased by some of the boys in his class. He'd been having a tough time as the class had become much more divided on gender lines and he was more isolated as the girls he was closer to no longer wanted to play. Between 9 and 10 it seems quite common for the gender culture in classrooms to shift and this can leave some boys stranded, especially if they felt less easy in the dominant boys' culture. One of the boys had thrown a pencil at Daniel and then accused him of hurting his finger. One of the girls stood up for Daniel, saying he wouldn't have done such a thing, but Daniel was confused by the incident and held back his tears as he told the teacher, only to be further teased by another child for not being able to talk properly.

It was a difficult day and I knew that something was wrong as soon as I picked him up from school. Once in the safety of the car he allowed himself to cry. He said that he had recognized his tears forming inside as he had talked in class and said 'it was hard not to let them outside.' Within the class it felt appropriate to hold himself together, but now that he was out of school it was a different matter. Later the same evening he imaginatively put some of the boys who had bullied him on a pillow and, using some Gestalt work, found ways of expressing some of his anger rather than swallowing it. He found some of the words to use that he could not find in class. He followed through a process as different boys came into focus and he discovered that he still had some 'unfinished business' with them.[8] He got very angry and said that he enjoyed it. He felt empowered. He went back into school feeling much more confident that he could tackle the situation, though he knew it would not be easy. As I shared some of my own feelings about being bullied at school he felt much easier knowing that it had happened before and that people survive to tell the tale. As he worked through the situation I could feel easier myself about my own school history.

If we respect ourselves we will more easily say 'no' to our children. This is part of exercising the responsibility of being a parent. It is important not to identify rules with domination, for it can be helpful for children *to know* where they stand with their parents. If there are clear rules and boundaries then children can know what is expected of them, rather than being left to interpret their parents' emotional moods to see what they can get away with. We do not need many rules in the family, but they need to be clearly observed so that children have a clear sense of where they stand. This allows them greater freedom for they understand the boundaries in which they can explore the options available to them. Then, of course, many rules work both ways so that children will feel rightly indignant if an adult has not respected their own space and has, for instance, walked into their room without knocking. If there is an atmosphere of trust children will be able to express their own anger and resentment at their parents without fear of being abandoned or punished for it. To me this is a blessing, for I was always told as a child that 'if you love your parents you won't feel angry at them.' So I learnt to conceal my anger for I did not want to learn that I did not love them. This was a way in which my generation was often tied as children and our experience devalued and discounted.

But as parents we also have to expect anger when we set out boundaries by saying 'no'. Often you have to learn to be unpopular when you limit, for instance, what toys you are prepared to get. It is important to keep your word so that your words have meaning and value, even when it means standing firm against a tantrum. This can be hard for some parents to learn, for they can assume they are being authoritarian when they are only setting firm boundaries. They find it hard to live with the notion of not being liked because they have somehow become dependent on being liked by their own children, often because they have such unresolved feelings about themselves. I know of fathers who find it hard not to buy presents for their children every time they go into a toy shop. This has more to do with their own feelings of deprivation from their own childhood, which have been rarely acknowledged, than with the well-being of their children.

Parents reacting to what they have experienced themselves as children, can find it hard to deny their children. They have often lost confidence in the kind of authority they had experienced in the 1950s and 1960s as children but find it hard to discover a notion of authority they could trust in themselves. This relates not only to the challenges of feminism, as Bly might have it, but to a larger crisis in the nature of *authority* in Western societies. The crisis in parental authority within postmodern families is an aspect of this. It also has to do with fathering in particular, for as Robert Skynner has said about his professional work with families, 'I frequently found that the crucial problem was the father's reluctance to set clearer limits for the children'; and in the work he did with couples with his late wife, 'the problem we met most often was a husband who was passively resisting, and withdrawing emotion-ally from, a wife who had been influenced by the changing roles of women and was becoming increasingly confident, independent and dissatisfied with him' (*The Guardian Weekend*, 19 December 1992: 14).

Men can often move without warning from being permissive to being dog-matic and authoritarian. It often feels difficult to explore the middle ground, so that men can find themselves swinging between these extremes. Somehow this reflects an uncertainty in the 1990s about their own identities and authority as men. It can feel as if men do not feel 'seen' within the terms of feminism and find it hard to respond to their partners' accusations that they are unforthcoming within relationships. It is easy to withdraw into feeling that their partners just do *not* appreciate what they have to cope with. Even when men want to change they often do not know how to. They can feel bitter that the efforts they are making just don't seem to be appreci-ated. It can feel as if nothing they do can make a difference within the relationship, so why bother. At some level for many men there is a well of resentment and anger at the women's movement for having raised these questions in the first place. Even when women do not identify with femin-ism they often demand to be independent and to have their own lives, in ways that are threatening to men. It can be experienced as a challenge to the control men can exert, at the very moment when in an economic reces-sion they feel threatened at work because of the unemployment figures. Often men experience the initiatives of women as a betrayal that they have done nothing to deserve.

This crisis in authority in Western societies in late modernity links to a growing moral uncertainty about how people should behave. It can be hard to set down boundaries if people are *unsure* what they believe in themselves. This is as true in different ways in the middle class family, where children used to be brought up knowing their place, as it is in working class families, where there was a clear sense of what was expected of children. There is an uncertainty that has spread through diverse communities. For example, men and women no longer feel free to discipline children as they did in the 1940s and 1950s. Then it was expected that, in traditional working class com-munities, anyone in the street could tell a child off if they were misbehav-ing. Now people in different classes are more uncertain and they are concerned not to interfere 'in other people's business'. This seems to be par-ticularly affecting working class boys, who are used to more traditional forms of authority. It is an issue when no father or older man is around in a boy's life. It might well be that, in their anti-social behaviour, boys are testing for boundaries that are just not there. If boys do not need fathers they might well need, as Bly insists, relationships with older men who can help them make a transition to manhood.

The 1991 riots in Newcastle raised, in an acute way, questions about the nature of authority in modern societies. If masculinity is what boys are forced to learn on the streets, it is difficult to expect them not to be tough and unfeeling. As a 14-year-old boy expressed it to his neighbour, who was middle aged, 'I want to be harder than my dad. Now I've proved it' (*The Observer*, 15 September 1991: 23). The riot was a way that these boys could prove just how hard they were and they won the attention of the whole nation for it. As a young housewife from Scotswood explained, 'We can't go down to the shops anymore. The yobs control it, shouting and abusing us. We try to send the men down but they are scared too. Would you like to live like this?' (1991: 23). It is not going to be an easy task to rebuild these communities. The bitterness goes very deep at the deprivation that has been suffered for so long. Through the Thatcherite years these communities were largely ignored and left to fend for themselves. The riot was in part against unemployment and deprivation. In this context it is crucial not to reduce the political to the personal. At the same time we have to appreciate how issues of authority, masculinity and power are an integral part of this situation.[9] It also connects with how boys learn to relate to themselves emotionally.

Notes

1 For helpful discussion about the relation of identity and difference see, for instance, Diana Fuss, *Essentially Speaking* (1989); Elspeth Probyn, *Sexing the Self* (1993); and *Identity: Community, Culture and Difference*, edited by J. Rutherford (1990).

2 To think about the relationship of medical power and knowledge, particularly in relation to birth, see, for instance, Sheila Kitzinger, *The Experience of Childbirth* (1967); and Ivan Illich, *Limits to Medicine: Medical Nemesis, The Expropriation of Health* (1976). See also Bryan Turner, *Regulating Bodies: Essays in Medical Sociology* (1994).

3 For some helpful reflections upon men's relationships with their fathers see, for example, Edward Goss, *Father and Son: A Study of Two Temperaments* (1949); F. Kafka, *Letter to My Father* (1954); and Blake Morrison, *When Did You Last See Your Father?* (1994).

4 A helpful introduction to the work of Basil Bernstein on language, class and education is provided by *Class, Codes and Control* (1971).

5 For an exploration of how language is tied into relations of gender power and subordination see, for instance, Dale Spender, *Man-Made Language* (1980); and Deborah Cameron, *Feminism and Linguistic Theory* (1985). See also Debora Tannen, *You Just Don't Understand* (1991).

6 Some of the ways that men have responded to the emotional challenges of feminism are explored in *Men, Sex and Relationships*, edited by Victor J. Seidler (1992).

7 The ways that different men have drawn upon consciousness-raising groups and alternative forms of therapy which put emphasis upon emotional expression are a theme in my *Recreating Sexual Politics* (1991a).

8 A helpful introduction to Gestalt therapy is given by Fritz Perls, *Gestalt Therapy Verbatim* (1971). For a playful autobiography see his *In and Out the Garbage Pail* (1972).

9 For some thoughts on the crisis of contemporary masculinities and the ways issues of masculinity, power and authority are being fought out in different communities see, for instance, Lynne Segal, *Slow Motion: Changing Masculinities, Changing Men* (1990); B. Campbell, *Goliath* (1994); and R.W. Connell, *Masculinities* (1996).

8
Experience

Emotional Lives

As men in late modernity in Western societies we often grow up estranged from our emotional lives and we learn to rely on women to interpret our feelings for us. Robert Bly's *Iron John* fails to appreciate the importance of relationships for he treats them as existing within their own genders. But men often feel isolated and locked into an aloneness that is difficult to carry. Often men want to reach out to share themselves with others, but do not know how to, especially when they are feeling down. I have talked about this as part of a condition of modernity, for it is part of the structure of feelings that has separated our emotions only to disdain them.[1] For it was not only that men were excluded from the home with industrialization, but that emotions were estranged as having no part within the reformulation of masculinity. As men we supposedly exist as rational selves, learning to trust reason alone as a guide to our behaviour.

Within modernity we learn as men to 'rise above' our 'animal natures', for within the framework prepared by Kant (1959) it is only as rational selves that we can be moral beings. This is part of the identification of a dominant white heterosexual masculinity with a vision of reason that is separated from emotions that has characterized modernity. As men we find it hard to recognize that our emotions and feelings *can be* a source of meaning and direction in our lives. We are so accustomed to diminishing and devaluing these aspects of our natures that it becomes difficult to appreciate them as sources of dignity and self-respect. Bly talks about this as 'ascending', in the ways that men so often rise above their emotional lives to find meaning and value elsewhere in their experience. But if we are to appreciate the ease with which men often 'rise above' their everyday emotional lives we have to place it historically and culturally, rather than as a feature of an ahistorical vision of masculinity.

Within the cultural conditions of modernity boys grow into manhood in particular ways. There are enormous differences of class, race and ethnicity which need to be appreciated. But in different ways men are often touched by the aspirations towards modernity, to think of themselves as 'free and equal' within the terms that have been set up by Enlightenment vision of modernity. Masculinity becomes a relationship of superiority because the abiding modernist distinction between reason and nature sets up a disdain for our 'animal natures'. This went hand in hand with a reordering of gender relations, as women were treated as closer to nature.[2] This was the way that boys grew up to disdain girls and the feminine aspects within themselves. For masculinity was very much defined in negative terms as boys had to constantly prove that they were 'not girls'. This was a struggle that boys were involved with as they sought to prove themselves in the eyes of others. This partly explains why the notion that 'boys don't cry' has assumed such a critical position. Within the terms of modernity it acted as a kind of litmus test, as emotions were to be generally disdained as a sign of weakness and 'femininity'.

As boys learnt to 'rise above' their animal natures, so they learnt to disdain girls who were somehow trapped in their natures. At a certain age around eight or nine, boys often seem to separate completely as if they fear some kind of contamination from contact with girls. It is as if emotions might be catching so that the only way that boys can secure themselves is to isolate themselves completely from the company of girls. Some of this has changed with the impact of feminism on the education of young girls, but boys often remain wary, fearful that their precarious masculinity will somehow be compromised. As boys we often learn in different ways to live a lie, for we learn to deny the *reality* of our emotional lives. In important respects this very denial makes it hard for us to grow into our masculinity, for we easily withdraw from the contact with others that can be useful and sometimes necessary for making a transition from boyhood to manhood. At some level this can mean that we remain children in our emotional lives and relationships, for we never learn such crucial lessons as that others can give love to us and we *can* receive love as much as give it.

Experience and Denial

As men we have often learnt to leave our boyhood behind. We prefer not to think about what it was like and what kind of relationships we had with our parents. Often if someone asks us what it was like we say with a false smile, 'it was fine . . . I was quite happy really.' For within a Protestant moral culture we learn not to complain. At some level we feel that to talk about our experience is a form of self-indulgence that compromises our male identity, for it proves that we are not the independent and self-sufficient selves we want to take ourselves to be. We learn to keep quiet and to 'count our blessings', for we always know someone who has had a worse time so that it seems we are 'whinging' if we complain. At some level we do not feel *entitled* to our own emotions and feelings, especially if we know that others have suffered more. There is often the dim echo that seems to constantly repeat itself: 'What do you think you are complaining about? You do not know how lucky you were.' We learn to keep quiet.

As men we often seem to find it harder to share ourselves emotionally within relationships. Sometimes this is because we do not have the connection to our own histories and experiences. We have learnt to put our pasts behind us. At some level we fear that others might reject us if we were to share more of ourselves, for they would no longer see us in such a good light, or so we think. If we shared more of our vulnerability and fears, we would be giving them grounds to reject us, so it can feel much safer to lock our pasts away. We withhold our experiences from ourselves so that it is easy to withhold from others. Within a liberal moral culture we can feel that sharing more of ourselves emotionally can reflect a *lack* of self-control. We think of the truth as relative and this notion can so often serve as a means of self-protection. As men we often learn to control our experiences through controlling the meanings which they carry. This can encourage us to form a vision of truth very much within our own dominant images as men. We learn to defend the meanings we give to ourselves through the reason we possess.

Freud (1961) stands against a rationalist strain within modernity for he understands the ease with which we can rationalize our experience. Though he does not think this through in gender terms, within modernity the particular relationship of a dominant white heterosexual masculinity with reason gives a form to the ways men often rationalize their experience. As men we often learn to believe the stories we tell about ourselves, for it is difficult to appreciate the ways we have learnt to use language as a means of self-defence. Since to be emotional is to be weak, we learn to keep our emotions firmly in check. We do not want to touch them ourselves for we do not want to learn that we might not be the independent and self-sufficient beings we take ourselves to be. We do not want to diminish ourselves in our own eyes, or to give others any reasons to think worse about us. But Freud appreciates the costs of these masculine strategies in the loss of reality they bring. He encourages both men and women to explore the emotional truths about themselves, rather than to conceal and hide. Though Freud often remains trapped in the authority that he gives to the analyst as the source of truth, since it is the analyst who offers 'interpretations' there is a significant strain in Freud's writings that connects 'truth' to 'reality'.[3]

If we refuse to live a lie and seek to face the truth about our relationships, say with our parents, we will eventually find greater reality in our lives. This is to treat 'reality' as something that is *lived*, rather than as having to do with the representations of an 'external reality'. With Freud greater freedom comes from accepting the reality of our emotional lives, rather than rejecting these aspects of our being, as we learn with Kant. In this regard psychoanalysis potentially provides a significant challenge to the terms of modernity and its denigration of nature.[4] Kant (1959) teaches us that we find freedom and self-determination by turning away from our natures and 'rising above' the determinations of our 'inclinations'. We learn to reject these aspects of our being and disdain them as signs of weakness. We fear 'giving in' to our emotions and we learn to look to reason as a firmer guide. But according to Freud this often leaves us with a weakened sense of reality and an insecure sense of self. It is supposedly only through 'working through' the emotions of our childhood, however painful, that we can find greater freedom in our everyday lives.

As men we are constantly living up to images and ideals that we have set for ourselves and we learn to deny anything that might threaten or compromise them. This is partly because masculinity is often an idealized construction that we are attempting to live up to. As boys it is easy to feel that we are not 'man enough' and that we have to prove ourselves as men. This takes diverse forms as different masculinities set their own terms. But somehow the image or ideal often comes to be invested with a greater reality than does our everyday experience which is treated as 'personal' or 'subjective'. There is a gap that opens up between the ways we learn to think of ourselves as men and our inner emotional experience that so easily gets displaced. Rather than challenging this pervasive rationalism there is a way that Bly's symbolic language comes to have a reality of its own. Rather than bringing us *back* to our everyday experience, the truth of this symbolic language supposedly gradually dawns upon us, as we learn to conceive of our experience in its terms. So paradoxically it can serve men as yet another means of escape.

Bly is clear about the definitions he gives to his symbolic terms so that, for instance, the warrior is someone who is able to hold his own ground. As a person who does not let his boundaries be easily invaded he is ready to defend what is of value for him, supposedly in contrast to the 'naive' men who lost a sense of their boundaries through their relationship with feminism. But as I have already argued, this fosters a misleading polarity which can easily serve to reinforce traditional conceptions of masculinity. For it is all very well to say that men have to learn to connect to their tenderness as much as their toughness, but thinking of men as 'warriors' carries its own cultural resonances. It can easily mean standing up for yourself and not allowing others, including women, to push you around. It can foster its own unwitting backlash against feminism, even if this is far from Bly's intention. There is a definite strain in *Iron John* that fosters the idea that women have had their way for too long in damaging the images that men can have of themselves. If this is a misreading, it remains a danger in the symbolic language that is invoked.

Men often need to be brought back in touch with their own experience, for this is so easily discounted within a rationalist culture. The dominant intellectual cultures of modernity have *disdained* experience, for it so readily falls on the side of nature. It was through reason and then through language that we were to order and 'make sense' of our experience. This was an issue of mind over matter. But we cannot control our experience through dominating our natures without, as Freud has it, suffering the consequences ourselves. If we cannot pretend that our lives have been different, we have to be prepared to learn to face ourselves. This means we have to be ready to also return emotionally to our pasts, rather than to assume that we can 'rise above' them. We have to acknowledge that we still carry much of the unresolved pain of our childhoods. This is an insight known to Freud but it is also shared with different spiritual traditions that never accepted the path of modernity. As Bly puts it, if people want to know the truth about themselves, they have to be prepared to descend into the land of ashes. We have to be ready to know our own grief and longing. Since we have chosen to follow this path we can always return without being trapped in it, as so often happens with depression.

Often we carry childhood griefs into our adult lives. We easily think that if we do not give them any attention, then they are not influencing the ways we are. This is then our private concern and does not have to concern others. But Freud (1961) thought otherwise, for he helped return to the West the understandings that had often been lost within the rationalist terms of modernity. He recognized that we could not discount our emotional lives without injuring ourselves. If we are to grow in our own authority then we have to learn *how* to integrate the different experiences that we have been through. In this way Freud helps to restore a historical and emotional dimension to a self that has been too narrowly cast within the rationalist terms of modernity. As we learn to deny our emotions and feelings, so we are denying aspects of ourselves. We make ourselves less sensitive, not only to ourselves, but also to others. We cut off aspects of our experience that leave us with a thinner vision of personal identity. We also deny the integrity of our emotional lives, as we learn to think of ourselves as rational selves alone.

I can still find it hard to acknowledge the difficulties of my childhood, the pain I went through living without a father. It is one thing to accept this intellectually but it takes a longer time to be able to feel this emotionally. It is as if I can know that my father has died intellectually without really being able to accept it emotionally. This is something Freud appreciated in his writings on loss and bereavement. He learnt some of this from the difficulties he went through himself in coming to terms with his own father's death. We begin to appreciate that we are connected to others in ways our intellectual culture finds it hard to name. Possibly Freud drew from a Jewish tradition that recognized that mourning is a *process* that takes time.[5] It is not simply a matter of facing a changed reality in utilitarian terms, as if there is no point in mourning, for we cannot bring back the dead. But this is not a matter of false consolations, as a rationalist culture has it.

Within modernity we have lost a sense of process, for we think too readily in either/or terms. There is little sense that understanding takes time and that it is not simply a matter of the different terms being carefully defined. I know that it took me years to come to terms with my father's death and that in different ways I am still doing it. It was only as an adult that I returned to mourn him properly and then it was only possible once I had allowed myself to feel some of the anger at being abandoned. In some ways I carried these feelings that were never given expression as a child. Of course these emotions go through their own transformations, and whatever grief we might find ourselves carrying as an adult is different from what we might have been able to express in different circumstances as a child. It was partly because I desperately wanted to be 'normal' and 'like everyone else' that it often seemed preferable to pretend that I had a father like others. It didn't feel 'normal' not to have a daddy. I cried for him in my sleep but when I was awake I learnt not to talk about him. Once a year on his *yarzeit* – the anniversary of his death – we would light a candle and remember him in early morning prayers in the synagogue. Otherwise we learnt not to talk about him, as we learnt not to talk about being Jewish. In those days we did not want to be different for we felt scared that we might be picked on. In the 1950s many Jewish people were still hoping to assimilate and were ready then to pay the price in terms of their own cultures and traditions.

Isolation and Connections

Growing up as Jewish within a Christian culture often leaves you feeling isolated and alone. It is hard not to feel shame, especially growing up in the years after the war. So little was talked about. If you learnt to feel proud in the family, you often learnt *not* to talk outside the family. The world was not to be trusted, especially after the destruction of so many Jews during the war. We did not feel safe, for if it could happen in the past, what would stop it happening in the present? As boys we seemed to carry a particular burden for we had to be ready to defend the family, or so we were told. We knew far more than was ever *talked* about, because in the family we were also to be protected. We were never really told that we had so few relations to visit because they had all been killed in the war. It was never really mentioned that my parents were 'refugees' from Nazism and that they had been lucky to escape alive. Rather we were to be 'like everyone else', so these things were not to be talked about. If we tried to raise the subjects we were soon reminded of the pain that was never far from the surface. We learnt that our parents had suffered enough, so we did not want to bring more painful memories up.

We learnt that if you do not talk about something then it does not exist. This was a way that we sought safety. Paradoxically it resonates with much poststructuralist theory that treats meaning as an effect of language. But we also knew at some level that there were other realities that you did not talk about. Even though there was a strong bond between the four of us, as brothers growing up in the same family, there was not much sharing. It was as if we each had to find our own way of dealing with our father's death and our mother's subsequent remarriage. Somehow it was hard to share ourselves emotionally with each other. It seemed easier to cheer each other up and to take warmth from the fact that we were not living through this alone. Somehow we learnt to make our own way, because everything that was painful was hidden away from us, as we were to be protected from the truth. I remember how angry and dejected I felt at 13 when my grandmother died and we were not allowed to go to the funeral. Death was something that as children we were not supposed to know about, though it had been all around us, shadowing us, in childhood. I remember crying bitterly on the step outside the front door, for there was no way I could cry inside the house. It was strange, as if children are not supposed to feel loss or grief because we are 'too young to know'.

But this is an adult's perception, for children often respond to feeling and to atmosphere. As children we often know much more than we are allowed to say. It is as if children are not allowed to have their *own* feelings. It is still common to keep children away from the funerals of even quite close relatives, often out of a fear that they might respond inappropriately. It is said that they might feel uneasy or embarrassed at their parents' tears. I think that this is sad, and that if we shared more of ourselves emotionally with our children it would be much easier for them to have their own emotions and feelings. Again this often has more to do with the difficulties that adults have with their own emotions. It seems easy for men to feel that if they cry in front of their children, they are thereby setting them a bad example of weakness. It seems much better to show them how to be 'strong' in the face of misfortune. But this strikes me as a false and limited vision of strength, for there are times when it seems quite appropriate to feel upset and cry. This does not have to be a compromise of our masculinity.

As long as adults find it hard to accept their own emotions and feelings, they will find it hard to accept these emotions in their children. Often we suppress the emotional expression of our children, for we do not want to be reminded of the grief and hurt that we carry ourselves. If we are to break these circles we have to be prepared to make the moves ourselves as adults. We cannot teach our children what we are not prepared to do ourselves. Often what our children learn is what we are ready to show them, not what we say to them. But parents insist that they do not share their emotions with their children, for they do not want to influence them. Often it is quite right for parents to control themselves from inappropriate emotions that they might otherwise dump on their children because they have not been able to resolve them themselves. Bly is very helpful in the way he talks about 'psychic copper' and the ways children are made to carry their parents' unresolved emotions. It is often the youngest in the family who is made to *carry* emotions that are not being openly acknowledged and dealt with in the family. But more can be safely expressed and shared between adults and children. It is as if we do not know how to be with our children, since the models we have unconsciously inherited from our parents no longer feel right to us.

Bly shares his vision of a spiritual journey towards manhood in *Iron John*, but in many ways this is a journey that everyone needs to take for themselves. The steps that he seems to think boys have to take on their way to manhood represent a particular path that cannot really be generalized. It reinforces the traditional vision of the man alone, seeking his own truth, and leaves little space for men to learn how to share themselves within their relationships. It is hard to be truthful with others before we have learnt to be truthful with ourselves. In the film *Shirley Valentine*, Shirley, a working class woman from Liverpool, talks about how her husband assumes that everything can be made good between them as long as he says 'I love you.'

She knows that these words have no meaning at all and that he doesn't have the first idea what love is about. This touches a chord for many men who, at some level, can recognize that we have never learnt how to love. This has not featured in our education as boys. We might learn to treat love as some kind of precious commodity that we have to be careful not to dispense, since it is a wasting resource. Like money, we learn to be careful with our love.

As boys we often learn how to make it on our own, not how to *care* for others. We distrust the caring that others might offer us, since we are caught in relationships with our mothers that we have never worked through. As far as we are concerned every woman is like our mother, or so we can feel. We can take relationships for granted because the meaning of our lives as men lies elsewhere in the public world of work. This is the arena in which we can know success and achievement and it is here that we can make ourselves as men. So often we take relationships for granted, for we expect our partners to support us in the battles that we have to fight elsewhere. We feel betrayed if they refuse. In Western capitalist democracies the notion of men as breadwinners still has deep roots, despite the aspirations towards greater gender equality. Often men are prepared to share more in domestic work and childcare but they find it hard to take seriously the idea that they might have to give up work completely in the public sphere, since this is so crucial to sustaining their identities as men.[6] Even though it might seem 'reasonable' and 'fair', men still expect that women will take primary responsibility when it comes to the everyday care of children. This exposes the limits of a liberal moral vision that is unable to explore the subtle realities of male power.

Fathers will often find it hard to share emotionally with their children, for they think they have to set them an example of strength that they can live up to. So often we hide our fear and anxiety from our sons and daughters, thinking that if they see these aspects of our experience, they are bound to think less of us. It is partly because we have learnt to treat emotions as a sign of weakness that it becomes so difficult to share them. But if we refuse to acknowledge our fear and vulnerability, finding that we displace these emotions into anger that is less threatening, our sons will learn to do the same. This is a pattern that can be difficult to break within working and middle class masculinities unless we have found the courage to do emotional work on ourselves. As far as our children are concerned, it can leave them feeling alone and isolated in their fear and vulnerability, for it is easy to feel that it shows there is something wrong with them for feeling this way. If we are more prepared to share our fear with our children then we help create a connection with them. We teach them that men have emotions and feelings and that this is part of what it *means* to be a human being. This can help children to acknowledge their own emotions, rather than to feel they have to keep them hidden away.

Often as fathers we can feel uncertain about what to share with our children, for we had such little connection with our fathers. It is as if we do not know how to be, because the traditional models of parent–child relationships no longer fit our experience. It can be hard to claim our authority as parents without being authoritarian. Often this is uncertain ground and we can fall back on an angry voice that is all too familiar from our own childhoods. We have internalized our parental responses so that we often unwittingly fall back on them when we feel unsure how to respond. But it is in this arena of relationships that we are also revisioning our masculinities. In part this means learning to respect our own ways of doing things, rather than thinking that it is a matter of men learning 'how to mother'. Learning to care as a father is part of learning our masculinity, but this is something that Bly cannot acknowledge. If it is important for men to learn to stand their own ground as 'warriors', it is also important to learn *how* to listen and care. This is a matter not simply of owning the pain that we have carried with us from childhood, but of learning *how* to relate differently in our present relationships.

Too often we are trapped by our own language so that thinking of ourselves through the imagery of 'warrior' can leave us feeling we have to make it on our own. It is easy to feel that this is the 'male' way, and Bly does little to challenge this vision. It becomes difficult to acknowledge our fear and vulnerability with our children for, in the traditional societies Bly refers to, men do not share these aspects of themselves. Again we have to be careful about, for instance, drawing from the experiences of native Americans without recognizing that the men often live in a very different world from the women and children. If we are striving for a different quality of contact in our relationships with partners and children, then we have to create an emotional language that illuminates the experience that we live. It is too easy to escape from ourselves, for this is what we have always learnt to do as men. In this situation it takes a particular kind of courage to share ourselves. We often fear being ridiculed and humiliated as men, so that it is easier to conceal and hide aspects of ourselves we have learnt to despise. We do not want to risk shifting the image we live out of ourselves, for it is easy to feel that we will never be the same, and that if we 'lose control' once we will never be able to put ourselves together again. At some level it is hard to acknowledge that we *need* others, when we are used to surviving on our own. It is easy to feel that we will immediately be overwhelmed by a well of unacknowledged needs, if only we would let ourselves begin to feel some of our emotions.

Fear and Anger

It can be important to recognize that men are no less emotional than women, though we have grown up within specific cultures of masculinity to feel estranged from our emotional lives. Within modernity we have got used to the idea that men have to be 'self-sufficient' and able to survive without others. To need others is already a sign of weakness. As a man it is easy to feel that you are very much on your own, so that life in a relationship easily feels scary and threatening. Often we hunger for contact, but we are so used to living without it that we have never learnt *how* to ask for it. We cannot force contact but at the same time we have to learn how to identify what we can take in as nourishment. Within the West we have inherited a fear of bodily contact that makes it hard to reach out and touch others. Often we are left feeling confused about what we need for ourselves. We pretend that we can take the contact but often we have withdrawn into the safety of our inner selves.[7]

The point is that within a rationalist culture we have not learnt how to express our emotions. We have learnt to disown our inner emotional lives so that the very notion that contact with others might nourish our souls seems strange. This is an issue within straight and gay relationships alike, as people learn how to communicate their needs with each other. It is an important first step in which men have been trained to deny and disown their needs. Often we have to formulate very simple requests, for it feels so easy to be overwhelmed. Here the details of everyday life are all-important, for we can recognize that we rarely ask for what we need, possibly out of a fear of rejection. It seems so much simpler not to ask at all. If we have grown up with a mother who has been intrusive, it is often easier to automatically say 'no' as a means of creating some kind of space for ourselves. I know that I do this regularly, as if saying 'no' has become a kind of automatic reaction. I might want the cup of tea that is being offered, but I will find myself saying 'no' all the same. Again each of us has to go through this process of emotional learning for ourselves, for others *cannot* do this for us.[8] But it is a form of learning that we are unfamiliar with, because we grow up within modernity to assume that we can change as a matter of will and determination alone.

Learning to communicate our needs as men within relationships is also part of learning our masculinities. Traditionally men have had power to get their own way but it is important to recognize the ways this power is negotiated. There are areas of vulnerability in men's lives that we have learnt to conceal but this has also served to block communication. At some level there is a tension between the power that men share in the larger society and the ways they often feel about themselves in relationships. Bly fails to illuminate each side of this equation, for the story of *Iron John* remains a traditional story of separation. Supposedly it is only after the boy has separated from his mother and his father that he is ready to find love in the garden. There are moments of great learning on the way, but there is little learning about how to create a more equal and loving relationship within unequal social relations of power and subordination.[9] Possibly it has only been through putting some of these considerations aside that Bly has been able to speak to the hungers that many men live with silently. But there is a loss, for it does not prepare men to live in relation with others without possibly feeling that they are compromising their freedom and autonomy.

As we get to know ourselves more as men, we can recognize how often we might use anger to cover up more threatening emotions of fear and vulnerability. Often there is an imbalance in our emotional expression, when we want to share our sadness but just feel it locked away. Just as a whole range of subtle and diverse emotions are concentrated into anger, so also a whole range of unexpressed needs find themselves *focused* onto sex. We can feel that sexual contact is some kind of salvation that will magically take all our needs and troubles away. Often it carries a burden that is not its own, because as men we have rarely learnt how to identify and differentiate our various needs.[10] It is easy as men brought up within a Protestant culture to be haunted by a feeling that whatever we do is just not 'good enough' and that we should always be striving harder. This partly explains the ways men can learn to use work as a kind of addiction so that we talk of them as 'workaholics'. We can learn to lose ourselves at work and often we find solace there from the troubles of relationships. It can feel as if it is a sphere of life where we know what to do and what is expected of us. In contrast we can feel awkward and unsure when it comes to our emotional lives, so that it can be good to escape them.

If we have learnt within modernity not to let our emotions 'get us down' it is partly because we often experience them as a childish weakness, as we have explored it. It can still be difficult culturally to accept that the way we were treated as children can affect the ways we relate as adults. It seems to reflect a weakness of will on our part if we let our emotions and feelings affect us. We learn that we *should* be able to guide our lives through reason alone, as it is the source of our goals and values. So it is that, with Kant, we learn not to allow our 'inclinations' to distract us from the path we have set for ourselves. We learn to disdain our emotional lives at the same time as we fear too much contact with them, lest they upset and disturb rational plans we have set for ourselves. Similarly we learn that the past is also a form of determination and unfreedom. We learn that since the past has happened it cannot be changed, so that it is pointless to dwell upon it. It can only entrap us, so taking us away from pursuing the goals we have set for ourselves.

In these respects Freud (1961) helps us question the inheritance of modernity. He questions the notion of control as domination of our emotional lives, suggesting that this is a false path since what we have suppressed will return to influence our lives. He exposes the tension between what is explicitly stated and the unexpressed emotions that often hint at a different reality. A discourse theory which treats language in rationalist terms often fails to illuminate these crucial tensions in our lived experience. We learn that there is *no* point in touching the hurts of the past, for this will only loosen our control as they spill over into the present and destroy whatever equilibrium we have been able to establish for ourselves. We learn to order our lives through reason alone, and we come to fear the 'messiness' and 'disorder' of emotional life. We are so used to controlling our emotions through suppression that sometimes as men we no longer feel them at all. Rather it is easy to fear that we will lose whatever precarious control we have managed to create if we were to dwell upon our emotions.

Freud offers us a different vision of control which is based upon creating a relationship *with* our emotional lives. Rather than disconnecting with our emotions so that we can control them, we have to learn to acknowledge and express them in appropriate situations. We have to recognize the integrity of our emotional lives, rather than to block them through suppression. Gradually we might begin to recognize emotions where before we did not know them. We might be all too familiar, for example, with our anger as men, so it could be surprising to uncover the fear and vulnerability. Life can become something that we are constantly learning from, rather than controlling. Rather than constantly testing ourselves against the tasks we set, we can begin to learn to recognize and name the needs of our bodies and spirits. We might also realize that we have fewer needs, as we have less need to displace them. This can slowly help to restore a sense of balance and harmony as we identify the need to express anxieties and frustrations that have been growing inside us. The language of release and discharge in early Freud goes some way in illuminating a need to express emotions we have been carrying.

As men it is easy to be haunted by a fear that we might lose control of our lives. Within modernity we do *not* recognize emotional needs as a source of fulfilment and nourishment. Supposedly it is through achievement and success that we will find happiness as men. This connects a dominant masculinity, the Protestant ethic and the spirit of capitalism as I have explored it in *Recreating Sexual Politics* (1991a). At some level we learn not to recognize our needs as men, for to have needs at all is 'not to be a man'. A society which began to recognize the goals of personal growth and fulfilment would have very different priorities. It would break the connection between a utilitarian vision of needs and wants and the capitalist ethic which treats work as an end in itself. This is difficult to talk about in a world where there is so much hunger, but it begins to question the consumerism that has become so dominant within the West. If people learn to appreciate a different relationship with themselves, they might be less likely to displace their unmet needs. But it can be misleading to view consumerism simply as a displacement, for it also meets needs of its own. Issues of social justice have to be argued out in their own terms. We certainly cannot assume that an awareness of emotional life has to go hand in hand with a political consciousness. They can often move in quite different directions.

A fear of contact can haunt men's relationships, especially if there is a fear of disintegration of our male identities as we allow ourselves to feel close to others. Often, in our growing up as boys, little prepares us for the demands of relationships. Traditionally relationships for men were a background against which they lived out their individual lives. Men expected their wives to put up with their demands because of the things they provided as 'good husbands'. It was only in the 1960s that we learnt a language of relationships, and it has been with the impact of feminism that women have asked more openly about what they get from their relationships with men. This is ground that Bly does not touch, for he takes refuge in a reworking of a traditional vision of masculinity in his concern to recover men's own gender ground, after a period in which it seemed as if feminism had set a false agenda for men. It might be important for men to recover this gender ground while acknowledging the feminist challenges to forms of male power. It might be that men cannot be exclusively identified with their social power and that we also have to recognize the power relations that divided different masculinities. But at the same time in the 1990s we can acknowledge a broad shift in many Western societies in the quality and demands of emotional and sexual relationships. This means coming to terms in diverse ways with the fear of intimacy that shadows many of our lives as men. It also means recognizing that men *can* change both in relation to ourselves but also in the ways we relate to others. But this will also involve giving up some of the power and control that we have traditionally taken for granted.

Love and Control

Withholding ourselves emotionally can be a form of control. This is something that men have been slow to recognize. As feminists encouraged women to challenge the way men are in relationships, so they also demanded that heterosexual men give more of themselves emotionally. This has not been easy to learn, and different forms of control have reasserted themselves. As men we have sometimes learnt to pay lip-service to feminism but have been slow to take greater responsibility for our emotional lives. Men across different generations *talk* more openly about gender equality and aspire for a more equal relationship with their partners. But at another level men often still fear commitment as they remain identified with a particular vision of freedom and independence. Men do not want to oppress women, but they do not want commitments either. Younger men want to be free to have multiple relationships but if you press them too hard they will sometimes leave. At the same time they remain proud of their new egalitarian values and will be ready to argue for them.

As Bly has it, a man often does not want to descend so that he can do 'ashes work'. He does not want to go down into his emotional life at all or recognize the complexities of his emotional inheritance which he brings into the relationship. He insists that this is his choice and has nothing to do with his present relationship, because as we have talked about it, the past is over. He might be clearer in his rights and his anger than men in the 1970s, who were often more deferential to feminism. He might be much clearer about what he wants from the relationship, finding it easier to declare his needs and go for them. You might say that he is much clearer about his *gender ground* as a man, but that at the same time he shares a fear of intimacy and commitment. You could think that he has read *Iron John*, though he has not understood what it is about. In some way he remains more attractive than the anti-sexist man who has overidentified with feminism, so much so that he does not feel entitled to his own feelings because he has learnt that these

can be oppressive to women. Both men have learnt in their own way to be
better listeners and more responsive to the pain of others than their fathers
were.

Often it is hard for men to trust that their partners can really be there for
them. It is as if we refuse to take the risk of ever finding out because it is
too threatening. If we are feeling needy and depressed it can be easier to
close down and withdraw into ourselves. We can feel that we will be *rejected*,
just as we were when we were young children. But if we are to grow into
our manhood it might be that we also have to learn to take risks in our
relationships, so giving our partners a chance to reach out to us in whatever
sexual relationship we have. For often, as men living diverse masculinities,
we can give to others and provide support but find it much harder to receive
the love and understanding that is available to us. It is this sense of reciprocity that is absent from Bly's account, and it can leave men in an isolated
and childlike position. But this learning involves showing our vulnerability
to our partners and taking the risk that they might not be able to meet us.
It is only if we take the risk that we can do the emotional learning and so
grow into ourselves.

Often men fear losing control because of the ways our male identities are
tied in with sustaining control. If things get too hot in our relationships we
might prefer to leave rather than to 'fight it out' properly. This is its own
form of control; our partners learn not to challenge us too personally, for
they sense that we might take flight. This is part of the 'refusal to descend'
that Bly illuminates so painfully. It can seem as if greener pastures lie elsewhere and it can be easier to blame our partners than to share responsibility
ourselves. In blaming we find ways of sustaining control for, if we can be
sure that it is the other person's responsibility, then we are blameless ourselves. Caught within the terms of a Protestant rationalism, it can be easy
to think that responsibility is a matter of assigning blame. It is time to put
the present behind us and to look towards a new relationship, for we think
that it might be quite different with someone else. We never think that we
take our issues with us. If we have grown up to blame others for our unhappiness it is a difficult pattern to break. It is far easier to carry on as we
were before, blaming others for our misery and unhappiness. It is part of
the power that we inherit as men to be able to fix the blame on others.

Women have often grown up to think that it is their responsibility to make
their partners happy. It is tempting to feel that part of their power lies in
being able to change the man they are with. They can replace misery with
happiness, or so they are often tempted to think. This makes it easy for men
to *shift* the responsibility for our emotional lives. We foster the notion that
if we loved someone then we would be happy. This can create a situation of
permanent insecurity, for our partners never really know where they are
with us. They are trained to watch our every mood and to respond as if it is
their fault somehow. As heterosexual men we often learn to expect that our
partners will be able to make us happy, and that if we are miserable or frustrated it must be that they are doing something wrong. But this also keeps

us in a childlike position as men, for we never learn how to take responsibility for our emotional lives. It is as if we hand ourselves over emotionally to our partners, often exhausted as our best energies have been used up at work. As far as we are concerned we have done our bit.

Emotions so often reflect a lack of control that we learn to fear them as men. This is part of the disconnection between the 'inner' and 'outer' that we inherit within a Protestant vision of modernity. What matters is how we present ourselves to others and behave with them, regardless of what might be happening in our inner emotional lives. We learn to disown our inner lives as shameful and as potentially capable of letting us down in front of others. Since emotions are 'irrational' they *cannot* be trusted or relied upon. We learn to swallow and conceal them before they surface and we live out the notion that if others do not see them then they do not really exist. So there is little to share with others, for we so often live as if our inner emotional lives have no existence at all. Once we have denied our emotions for so long, it can seem as if they do not exist and that we have perfected our control over our experience. This is integral to the identification of a dominant white heterosexual masculinity with self-control. We often learn to disdain others, especially women, who seem unable to sustain a similar form of control of their emotional lives. We find it hard to acknowledge that the ways we have suppressed our emotional lives connect to the tension and unease that so often surround us. This reflects a very different way of thinking about ourselves.

Notes

1 Some of the theoretical and practical consequences of the identification of a dominant masculinity with reason for the disdain of emotional life are explored in Victor J. Seidler, *Unreasonable Men: Masculinity and Social Theory* (1994).

2 The identification of masculinity with culture and the implications for the disdain and devaluation of women and nature is a central theme in Susan Griffin, *Pornography and Silence* (1980). For a sense of the development of her work see *Made From this Earth* (1982).

3 For discussions of the authority relations which are often treated as integral to the possibilities of transference within psychoanalysis see, for instance, Jessica Benjamin, *Bonds of Love* (1990); Steven Frosh and A. Elliot, *Psychoanalysis in Context* (1995); and James Hillman, *One Hundred Years of Psychoanalysis and Still the World Is No Better* (1993).

4 To think about the ways psychoanalysis can be understood as providing a challenge to the terms of modernity and its denigration of nature see, for instance, Freud, *Civilization and its Discontents* (1961). This is a theme that I explore in the closing chapters of *Unreasonable Men* (1994). It might also be useful to read in this context Marshall Berman, *The Reenchantment of the World* (1981).

5 Freud's relationship to Judaism and its possible influences on the shaping of psychoanalysis is explored in David Bakan, *Sigmund Freud and the Jewish Mystical Tradition* (1958). It is also a theme in Marthe Robert, *Freud: From Oedipus to Moses* (1977).

6 For some explorations in men's relationships to family and work see *Men, Work and Family*, edited by Jane C. Hood (1993).

7 An interesting study into the ways touch is devalued within the West in contrast to other cultures is Ashley Montagu, *Touching* (1971).

8 We need to explore what is involved in these processes of emotional learning, for they

challenge dominant cognitive models. Consciousness-raising as a process potentially enriched conceptions of learning, for it challenged the modernist distinction between reason and emotion. Unfortunately many of the ways we have conceived discourse have been set in rationalist terms.

9 Learning how to create more equal and loving relationships within unequal relationships of power is a central theme in the writings on respect and inequality in Victor J. Seidler, *The Moral Limits of Modernity: Love, Inequality and Oppression* (1991b). It was part of what drew me to Kierkegaard's work. It refuses to conceive of morality in impersonal terms alone.

10 The ways that as heterosexual men we often learn to go for sex because we have not learnt to differentiate our various needs are a theme in my *Rediscovering Masculinity* (1989). This can open up an exploration of the difference between needs and wants which are all too often identified with each other.

9

Language

Controlling Language

Often men grow up within the dominant white heterosexual masculinities which have been framed within modernity to use language as a means of self-protection. From early on in childhood men can learn to be careful about what they say because it can so easily be used against them, within the competitive terms that so often rule boys' relationships with each other. Anxious to prove that we are not 'wet' or 'weak' but that we *can* hold our own with other boys, we learn very early on to police and discipline our emotions and feelings. We have to be careful with what we say because we can so easily betray ourselves, showing some of the tears and vulnerability which have no place in boys' relationships with each other. We often learn to keep ourselves in check, and the control that we exercise in relation to language is a crucial part of this process.

Within the competitive relationships that govern so much of middle class boys' lives we often learn to use language as a weapon, especially if we do not feel very physically strong. We learn to hide what we feel inside, for to show our hurt and vulnerability would open us up to ridicule and rejection. As boys with diverse backgrounds we have learnt to cope with the pains of childhood as a way of proving our masculinities. It is not just that 'boys do not cry' but that very soon boys learn to disconnect from their inner lives.[1] Often we do not want to be reminded of painful hurts and rejections so we begin to talk to ourselves in a way that minimizes what we have been through. Safe in the knowledge that we have 'survived to tell the tale', we begin to tell ourselves that it was not so bad after all. So a gap opens up between our inner lives and our outer expression that becomes difficult to bridge. We learn to treat language instrumentally as a way of 'presenting ourselves' in acceptable ways to others. We rarely recognize that in denying our emotions we are also denying our experience and crucial aspects of ourselves. Rather as boys we learn to build a wall against our inner emotions and feelings. We learn *not* to know too much about them ourselves, lest they begin to threaten the image that we are creating for ourselves. At some level our inner life and experience cease to exist as a reality for us. We learn to judge ourselves according to external standards that are provided by the dominant masculinities.

Often it is difficult for men with different class, 'race' and ethnic identities to share ourselves in intimate relationships, even when we desperately want to. It is as if we no longer have access to our inner lives, and our partners may be left feeling that we are not accessible to them emotionally. It is not only that they do not know what is happening for us emotionally, but often do we not know ourselves. This sometimes goes along with the patriarchal notion that it is women's task to somehow interpret our emotional experience for us and that in some sense they are responsible for our emotions as men.[2] It is part of the power that we have as men that we can displace responsibility for our emotional lives in this way. Women often grow up feeling that it is somehow *their* job to make their partners happy and, if they are not, they are to blame themselves. It is no answer to this predicament to say that men do not have an emotional language with which to describe their experience within a rationalist culture. This can only be part of the problem, for men's relationships with language are crucially tied up with our relationships with ourselves as men.

If we are to trust enough to share more of ourselves then this involves a different relationship to our emotional histories that can no longer be so confidently denied. It means learning how to be less distant and impersonalized in our speech, as we learn to speak for ourselves more personally and so give up the automatic right to speak for others in the universal voice of reason. Language has to recover a connection with speech, having been so theoretically tied to the priority of written text, as we learn to be more honest with ourselves and our partners. This can be a difficult and scary path, since as men we are often so unused to a more personal voice, but it is a necessary one if we are to heal the gulf that separates our inner lives from our everyday expression.

Language and Experience

A middle class boy sent away to boarding school when he was eight years old might still say that 'it was the best thing that ever happened to him' and it might well have been preferable to the open warfare between his parents that he had experienced at home. But often there are other feelings around that can be more difficult to express. Sometimes there is a hidden feeling of abandonment that is hard to acknowledge, even to himself. If many of the boys that he knew had also been 'sent away', as it is still talked about in England, it might well have come to seem the 'normal' thing to happen. This can make it even harder *to connect* to hidden feelings of anger, for it can easily feel as if there must be 'something wrong with you' if you are feeling anger or unease about a situation that most boys seem able to handle without complaint. Some boys find it quite easy to say that 'my parents were doing the best for me' and at some level they obviously believe it. But it is also true that boys often learn to talk like an adult before they have learnt how to feel like a child.[3]

So it is that boys often learn language not to express their feelings or to give voice to their souls. Language so easily becomes disconnected as a form of self-assertion and self-protection. Boys often learn to use language as a place in which to hide themselves. Not only does it cease to exist as a form of expression through which we share our inner experience, emotions and dreams, but it fails to give us access to ourselves. We become estranged from our own emotions and feelings that are suppressed within the dominant culture. We fail to develop a relationship with our inner selves, since we assume that our emotions must be externally influencing our behaviour and distracting us from the goals and purposes we can set through reason alone. As middle class boys we learn to think as rational selves, learning to live in our heads.

Language becomes autonomous as it becomes disconnected from experience. As Wittgenstein (1958) expresses it in his later writings, it is like a part of a machine that does not connect to the main body of the machine. His task was to heal this split, so that language could be returned to its living context, where its meaning could be properly grasped.[4] As we grow up to adopt an instrumental relationship to language, so we often find ourselves *cut off* from our own experience, unable to share ourselves emotionally with others. As men we become comfortable with the instrumental language of work and the public sphere and we unwittingly attempt to frame our intimate and personal relationships in similar terms. We often feel easy as middle class men when we can organize our lives as a series of discrete projects and, growing up within the framework of a rationalistic culture, we can sense little wrong with this. It is 'others' who prove themselves to be 'irrational' if they refuse to see the reason in what we are offering. If others cannot accept that the best education is provided in boarding schools, then they are simply allowing their emotions to get in the way of their reason.

Often it is fathers, who have themselves been to boarding school, who insist that their children follow in their path. It serves to legitimate the ways they came to treat their own feelings of loss and abandonment, for it was supposedly all worth it in the end. They have survived the experience and supposedly made a 'success' of their lives, so it is only right that they should insist their children should go. If they suffered from loneliness or isolation it was all for a good cause. More than this, it was the 'making of them'. This resonates with broad cultural themes in a Protestant moral culture, especially for the ways boys are supposedly to learn how to become men. For masculinity is never anything that can be taken for granted. It has to be constantly affirmed and proved, so that from an early age boys learn that you *prove yourself* at the expense of other boys. You show that you are tough by showing that others are weak. This is the way boys learn to assuage the feelings of inadequacy that are so often structured into the character of a Protestant moral culture, as Weber (1930) grasps it.

It becomes crucial for boys to conceal what they are experiencing because vulnerability opens you to ridicule and rejection. So, as small boys, we learn in very different class, racial and ethnic backgrounds that we are 'strong' if we do not show what we feel, for emotions are a sign of weakness. If we feel anything we soon learn to keep it to ourselves. So it is that boys learn to create a sharp separation from their inner emotional lives. We often learn to deny the 'inner child' that we carry, or at least to silence it.[5] Somehow we learn to use language to sustain this suppression. Language becomes mechanical as it exists within the externalized realm of appearances. It is language that we use to defend ourselves, for what matters is how we 'present' ourselves to others. This creates its own rigidity and lack of movement, for often men are trapped, unable to give voice to emotions of love and tenderness even when they want to. We become scared of our own emotions, lest they reveal an aspect of ourselves that we do not want to know.

Often it is quite early, and in any case by the time boys are eight or nine, that this transition has taken place. It is a process of *closing down*, as boys learn to separate from their inner emotional lives. They often do not want to connect to the pains of childhood, choosing to see these as testing grounds on the way to manhood. As Bly also recognizes, there is a moment when boys seem to lose their sparkle and they can spend the rest of their lives trying to rediscover it. As boys learn to feel what is expected of them, they lose their spontaneity. Since they have to prove themselves to other boys, they have little sense of what they are being asked to give up. Since emotions and feelings are treated as 'soft' and 'feminine' it can be easy to give them up, for who would want them anyway 'as a boy'? But as boys split off from their vulnerability, they also separate from themselves. This can be difficult to recognize since the focus in diverse boyhoods is so often in being like everyone else. We want to be accepted and often we are more than prepared to pay the price. Boys can be cruel to those who would follow a different path.

I asked some five-year-old boys, with different class and ethnic identities, whether they would feel fear in front of a crocodile. The boys insisted that they 'don't get scared' and they were surprised when I acknowledged my own fear. So it is that boys learn to disown and cut off from their fear, so that in quite a short time they do not register the emotion of fear at all. It is as if they learn within the culture that it is better to live without the emotion at all, and so to dispense with the protection that fear can give. This reflects itself in language, for we lose the capacity to discern different emotions. As we suppress our fear so we *weaken* a connection with significant aspects of our experience. In time a transformation takes place. No longer do we choose not to express a fear that we keep to ourselves; we begin not to experience the fear itself because we do not want to be reminded of emotions which can compromise a sense of male identity. It might only be years later, after learning how to work on ourselves emotionally, that we can begin to recognize an experience of fear. This involves a somatic recognition that cannot be separated from a cognitive capacity.

Often boys who are left at boarding school will not allow themselves to feel abandoned. They learn to say, with a smile that does not quite ring true, that 'I felt fine and after the first couple of days I was OK.' But sometimes boys do not go downstairs to say goodbye to their parents when they leave them, or might refuse to talk to their parents when they visit. Often this is behaviour that the boys do not understand themselves. They do not know why they refuse, they 'just do not want to see them', or they feel that they 'do not have anything to say'. They have learnt to accept that their parents have made this decision 'for their own good' but they cannot help feeling rejected and abandoned; and often it is difficult to speak after being abandoned, for what is there to say? A gap opens up between parents and children that becomes difficult to bridge, though for many it might seem as if everything goes on as 'normal'. There are silences that enter the relationship at unexpected moments.

Unspoken Shame

At another level, middle class boys can be left with a deep and unspoken sense of shame. They can feel that 'if I was adequate then my parents would not have sent me away', while at the same time verbalizing quite a different reality. This helps feed the notion that 'there must be something wrong with me.' Some boys might withdraw, turning their feelings against themselves and so further withholding themselves. Others might be able to express their anger in a sullen silence whenever they are in their parents' company.[6] It might seem quite impossible for a young boy to challenge a father who is convinced that he is doing it 'for your own good', for this can further burden you with a sense of ingratitude. You might be told that you are being 'irrational' and 'emotional' in questioning the decision your parents have come to. It can feel as if there is no way out. There are few openings to communicate what you feel without a concern that you will be rejected further. It is as if you have reached a limit of language.

Freud's (1922) appeal to the unconscious can help us understand that our experience has different levels. At an unconscious level a boy might feel that 'my parents do not want me for otherwise they would not have sent me away', or that 'there must be something wrong with me.' Our experience might be shaped by these unconscious notions, but we might feel quite *unable* to articulate them in language. Freud recognizes that there are fears that we learn to carry which are deeply embedded within the moral culture. These truths are rarely spoken, even to ourselves, for they present something shameful that needs to be hidden. They are fears that attach to the cultures of diverse masculinities – the shame of not being 'man enough' – which are often carried in a tense silence. As boys we learn to separate and cut off from fears and inadequacies that we do not want to be reminded of. We can act angrily towards those who might remind us of emotions that we have long suppressed. But it remains a scar on the soul, for it leaves boys constantly feeling that we have to prove that we are good enough. Often we turn these judgements against ourselves, being unable to escape from the critical voice that rarely seems to rest.

Often it is easier to learn to say that you *liked* boarding school, for in this way you do not have to deal with your ambivalent feelings. With this defensive reaction, as Freud might grasp it, you never have to deal with the pain that is concealed. This is an example of the ways we learn to use language as a form of self-protection. It is a pattern that can pass down the generations, for when boys become fathers themselves they will often send children to the same school, secure in the knowledge that 'it makes you independent' and 'it teaches you how to stand on your own two feet.' So it is that fathers can protect themselves against having to deal with their own feelings when they were at school. If they carry any unexpressed pain and anger from those days, it is held firmly in check. Often it is *easier* to feel that 'if it made a man of me, then it can make a man out of my son.' Making a different choice for children can be difficult, for it brings all kinds of unresolved emotions to the surface that we are just not used to dealing with.

The boarding school stands as a powerful metaphor for masculinity in its dominant cultural form. It presents a classical Western conception of an initiation into manhood. It makes the kind of men who could run the empire that England sustained for so long. The kind of schooling that was developed in England was a powerful machine to produce men who could govern and rule.[7] As they had learnt to suppress their inner emotional lives, so they would learn to suppress others who dared to challenge their authority. As boys you learn to do what is expected of you, regardless of the emotional costs. As Kant (1959) has it, this is the way that moral characters are produced. As boys you learn to do your duty, and out of this selflessness grows a sense of *superiority* in relation to other 'lesser' beings who are less able to control their 'animal' natures. Women are deemed inferior because they exist closer to nature and so they are more influenced by their emotions and feelings. As a 'weaker sex' they need the protection of men who know how to rule within the public world of work. The father becomes the source of all authority within the family.

Within the culture of dominant white Christian heterosexual masculinities, men learn to curb and control their language. The stiff upper lip has taken generations to form and it lives on in subtle forms. Fathers teach their sons that 'it is a tough world out there so you might as well prepare for it when you are young.' Freud (1953) also sustains the place of the father as the source of authority who has the task of separating children – but especially sons – from their mother's emotional influence.[8] It is easy for fathers to feel that 'you've got to separate from your mother's apron strings sooner or later, so it might as well be sooner.' This is a realm in which fathers have traditionally had a particular responsibility. It is often said that if the father is not there to make the separation, then it might never happen. At some level this vision still lives on in Bly's telling of the tale of Iron John, even though he has more appreciation of the importance of timing and rhythm in the separation that has to take place.

Iron John carries the boy away on his shoulders into the forest but he does not talk to the boy about it. It is as if there is still an assumption that the boy would never want to leave of his own accord, for the relationship with his mother is always a form of entrapment. This is a way that Bly remains trapped in a vision of a return to a traditional, if rural, conception of manliness. As he has it, the boy has to be prepared to steal the key from under his mother's pillow, for she would never be prepared to give it to him of her own accord. If there are truths to be recovered from myths, there are also dangers in assuming that myths do not encode traditional male power and authority. It might be that many boys find it hard to make the separation from their mothers, especially if they have been intrusive and seductive in their relationships, looking to their sons for the kind of love and affirmation they were not getting from their partners. But it is wrong to generalize about women in this way and to suggest that there is no dialogue that can take place. It is traditionally fathers who say that boys will never be ready to make the break, so that they should be sent away to school, whether they are ready or not.

Listening and Validating

If we assume that as parents we know what is best for our children because we have reason on our side, then we never have to listen to them. We assume that we know what they want better than they can know themselves. This reflects the ways that childhood has been conceived within an Enlightenment vision of modernity. Children are regarded as animals who traditionally have to be trained and disciplined if they are to become human. It is because humanity is identified with rationality that children can so easily be regarded as 'less than human'. Along with women, Jews and people of colour they are regarded as existing closer to nature. As I argue in *Unreasonable Men* (1994), it is men alone who can take their reason for granted because the separation between reason and nature, which is crucial to modernity, guarantees that reason is formed in the image of the dominant white Christian heterosexual masculinity. If children can be thought of as *lacking* reason, so they are deemed as lacking humanity. It is said that children are selfish, and only have their own interests at heart, and that left to their own devices they will not discover any sense of morality.[9]

Only through the external intervention of parents do children supposedly learn what it means to behave morally. This is in line with Kant's (1960) vision. It is the father who is supposed to represent the moral law to the child and who stands as the figure of authority.[10] This legitimates a certain distance in the relationships between fathers and children because it means that if a father is too involved in the everyday care of children, he will not be able to exercise the impartiality and objectivity that supposedly goes along with being the source of authority. The point here is that children are understood as lacking reason, so it is only when they gain reason that they can have freedom, autonomy and morality. Since children lack reason they are also supposed to lack language and so to be *unable* to express themselves through language. If what children have to say can be judged in advance as 'irrational', then as adults we do not have to listen to them. It is a sad comment that on Daniel's first few days at secondary school one of his teachers shouted at the top of his voice for children to keep quiet and to stop the 'verbal diarrhoea' coming out of their mouths. Little seems to have changed since I was in secondary school in the mid 1950s. It is the teacher alone who is supposedly the source of knowledge and wisdom. Children have nothing to say because they are defined as lacking both reason and knowledge. Daniel fortunately knew better and wanted to report the teacher immediately to the authorities. He assumed that they would be on his side and that they would recognize that a teacher who talked in this way was not fit to teach at all.

Children often need to be listened to. When they tell us that they have had a difficult day at school and feel like giving up, they want it recognized and validated that this is the way they feel. But often parents think that it is their task to offer reassurance, to say that things cannot be that bad and that the child should not really be feeling this way. Even if we know better it can be difficult not to respond in this way. It reflects the difficulties we have in listening to what children have to say and validating their experience. We often say that the child is at the centre of our concerns, but the reality is very different, with parents often giving very little real time and attention. Again if you can assume that you know what your child is like, then you do not really have to listen to what they have to say. Often it is hard for us to listen, especially as men, if we have not learnt how to listen *to ourselves*. If we have suppressed so many of our emotions and learnt to dismiss and diminish our experience as 'childish', it is hardly surprising that we have not learnt how to listen to ourselves. This is reflected in the inner dialogues we have with ourselves and the language we use to illuminate what we are going through with ourselves. It makes it hard to recognize the wisdom that children so often express.

If parents do not listen to what children have to say, children very soon learn that there is no point in sharing themselves. They inhibit what they might otherwise say. Children go through a process of development within a particular cultural setting. Often there is a tension between what children need for themselves and the ways they are treated by others. If we do not listen to what children have to say we fail to respect them. This has consequences for the ways they grow up to think and feel about themselves. If the family and the school assume that they know what is best for the child, they will never learn to listen in a helpful way. From soon after birth parents are still often taught that they have to show a child 'who is in charge', though thankfully there are also counter-movements which encourage a far greater responsiveness to the needs of the child. But often there is a swing between authoritarian forms of child-rearing and a permissiveness that finds it hard to set boundaries. Sometimes parents feel that to set any kind of limits for their children is too legislative. But if there is widespread confusion about the nature of the authority which parents should exercise in giving boundaries to their children, it is partly because of the difficulties parents have in identifying their *own* needs and learning how to negotiate with their children so that the children will listen. It involves accepting the authority that we exercise as parents without becoming authoritarian. Not all forms of authority are authoritarian, though it can be difficult to discern difference within an egalitarian ethos.

It is still too easy to see childhood as a set of hurdles that children have to cross. This is a linear vision of development which is very much in line with how we have learnt to think about progress within modernity. Parents often push their children, thinking that the sooner they overcome the hurdles of crawling, walking, reading and writing the better. This puts them ahead of the game, or so they think. There is little sense of difference, so that we might more fully appreciate that different children have *different* timings and what is appropriate for one might be quite inappropriate for another. An abiding confusion between sameness and equality can make it difficult to appreciate the individuality of a child. We think that the sooner a child learns to surmount the hurdles that it faces, the better it will be for the child. It can be easy for parents to feel that their child's development somehow reflects upon their skills in parenting, so that they can begin to feel resentful if their child does not seem to be developing at the same pace as others. For mothers it seems easy to blame themselves for they learn to internalize responsibility within the dominant culture. Often it does not seem to affect fathers in the same way and they might more readily blame the child.

Possibly it is because we have so little understanding of the relationship between language and sensitivity that we often miss the significance of children learning to express themselves through language. This connects with the ways we learn to validate an infant's experience early in life. Often we do not want to hear what infants have to say, especially if we feel they are going to embarrass us in some way. A young boy child, for instance, is more likely to say that he hated a party he went to, only to hear his parent saying 'thank you very much, it was a lovely party.' For the child to say anything different is a sign of ingratitude. So children learn that they *cannot* express what they feel without risking rejection and negative judgement from their parents. Sometimes when a child feels unhappy or sad they can be told to 'cheer up' because they have nothing to be sad about. Or if a child feels angry, they can learn that anger is inappropriate, because it means that they are 'naughty' or 'disobedient'. As girls are often told that 'girls don't feel angry', so boys are told that 'boys do not cry.' So if children feel these emotions they can easily be persuaded that there must be something 'wrong' with them. This resonates with a deep feeling within a Protestant moral culture that there is something 'wrong' or 'inadequate' about us. So it is we begin to hide and conceal our emotions from others, for we do not want them to discover what 'we are really like'. We build a fence around our emotions and we learn only *to show* those emotions that are deemed appropriate within the dominant culture. We split from our inner emotional lives, learning only to show culturally acceptable aspects of ourselves.

Contact and Communication

We learn to speak within the context of a relationship. Often this has its source in the earliest contact between the mother and child in breastfeeding. There is a subtle and powerful process of communication established in which mother and child are learning to communicate. How the mother feels about her own primal needs, and the ways they were responded to within her own relationship with her mother, can influence the ways she responds to her baby. If she finds it hard to accept the baby's cry because of the unresolved emotions it triggers in herself, she might also use the breast as a way of silencing the child. She might think that she is responding to an expression of need, but something quite different might also be going on. It is in these very early patterns of relating that infants learn *how* to express their needs and learn whether 'others' will be there for them. It is in these early relationships that we learn to give and receive. The ways that we learnt to trust others in relationships are first set in these early encounters.

If fathers have a different role in the early weeks of life, it is equally crucial for them to establish a relationship of their own. This is something that Bly does not appreciate enough, for he is still caught in the traditional notion of the father as the person whose primary task is the separation of mother and child. This was also Freud's view. But it remains a patriarchal vision and it leaves us with a limited conception of the promises and pains of masculinity. I think it is important to recognize that, at least in the early months, the mother might have a primary relationship with a baby, but a crucial relationship is also being established between father and child.[11] This is why it can be so important for men to be fully involved in the process of pregnancy and birth, for it is in these early moments that forms of somatic resonance are established. The ways that men bond with their children is crucial. It is in these earliest moments that contact is established. Even if it is a father's task in the weeks after birth to support the relationship between mother and baby, it is also important for him to nourish his own developing relationship *even* if it is only much later that this comes into fuller focus.

Often men have found it hard to communicate with their children until they have felt able to do so in language. It has been easy for men to feel that small children are 'irrational' before this time and that you could not be expected to get any sense out of them. This vision has been powerful within a rationalist culture. It has tied reason, language and communication together in a tight knot. It has made it difficult for us to appreciate what is involved in learning a language and the role of preverbal communication. It has also made us insensitive to different modes of communication and the ways they relate to each other. There is a link, for instance, between voice and touch that is rarely recognized. Different realms of contact are established which draw upon intuition, sensitivity and feeling, which tend to be minimized within a rationalist culture that treats language as a feature of the left brain alone. We learn to value the mind and the organizing intellect but this only reflects half of the brain. Traditionally this has formed the 'unreasonable' form of reason, separated from feeling and intuition, that we have associated with dominant forms of masculinity. It has served to suppress other ways of knowing.[12]

Fathers who spend much time in the early weeks and months with their babies are often challenged in unexpected ways. It can be frustrating for men who have learnt to use their time quite differently. But it can also bring men into an appreciation of different forms of time as they learn to relate on 'baby time'. This involves tuning in to the baby's rhythms and learning to resonate with them. This is not easy, but if it happens it can bring men into quite another relationship with themselves. Possibly it is because we are often so out of touch with our own inner timing as heterosexual men, learning to suppress our emotions and feelings so that we can accord with what is expected of us from within the dominant culture, that it can be difficult to slow down and attune. Babies have quite different needs and rhythms and they operate at quite another pace. Often it is hard to slow down as men because this puts us in touch with our own unexpressed needs and the ways we were responded to ourselves as young children. It is too painful to be reminded.

As men we often speed up as a way of avoiding feelings. This is particularly true within modern Western urban settings where we can constantly feel that we have so much to do. It becomes difficult to value the time we have with babies, since it is easy to feel that so little happens. Often it can be uncomfortable since as we slow down a little it brings forward emotions from our own infancy that we have for so long suppressed. It is partly because we are so used to escaping ourselves, in order to focus upon the task at hand, that we end up with a very *externalized* notion of growth and development. As we have learnt to judge ourselves through applying externalized standards, so it becomes tempting to judge others. We inherit a linear vision of personal growth and development which has little sense of the different energies that are brought into play at different stages of development.

This means there is often a limited grasp of the significance of the different stages of growth and of the inner development taking place that expresses itself towards others. Often we are so much more focused within a Protestant moral culture on what people cannot do, on their failings, than upon the love and appreciation they *need* from us. Within modernity there is limited appreciation of the importance of love and emotional support. This is partly because we see development as a move from dependency towards autonomy and independence, so that dependency becomes a sign of weakness. It reflects a lack of character. It is because we traditionally see development upon the model of autonomy, established by Kant (1959), that we find it hard to make cultural space for mutuality, reciprocity and support. Outside psychotherapy and feminism there is little cultural sense of the importance of connection and relationship. It has been through these paths that we have begun to learn about ambivalence, care and concern. We have begun to find room for childhood experiences and to appreciate the resonance they continue to have in our adult lives. Rather than separate from our pasts, we have begun to appreciate the importance of building bridges with it. Rather than treating our emotional lives as a form of self-indulgence, we have begun to recognize them as a source of meaning and value. But these insights are yet to influence and take hold within the central institutions of late modernity.

Children learn to express themselves in different ways. It might be quite wrong to think that the sooner a child learns to read the better, for it is easy to force a process that has its own natural movement. Sometimes it is not appropriate for a child to learn to read because they are not ready to draw upon the mental energies required. It might be more important in their early education to draw upon their creative and intuitive energies through painting until they are ready to make some inner movement. If we insist on forcing children before they are ready then we will do harm to the balance of their energies.[13] It might show itself in the quality of attention they can give to their reading. But if we are so out of touch with when something is appropriate for us *as adults*, it can be hard to show this sensitivity to children. Often as men we have had to sacrifice our sensitivity in the process of growing up. As men we learn that we are not supposed to show our sensitivity because it can only reflect weakness and femininity. It is an aspect of ourselves that we learn to suppress.

If parents have learnt greater sensitivity to their infants over the last decade, often this disappears when it comes to schooling. Parents are constantly pushing their children, especially in the urban middle class. The idea of 'child-centredness', which sought to focus upon the developing child rather than upon the content of knowledge, came under attack in Thatcherite England. We have seen a reassertion in the late 1980s and the 1990s of a discourse of educational standards that addresses children in terms of what they lack. This places children into a situation of inferiority as they are constantly reminded of what they do *not* know or of what others have been able to achieve. All this leaves children with low self-esteem, feeling bad about themselves and unable to express themselves. Hopefully this current will eventually turn, but for the time being it has become difficult again to listen to what children have to say. Again it is easy for fathers to assume that they 'know best' what is good for their child, for in competitive times they are sometimes more anxious that their children might not be able to perform well in competitive relations.

Freedom and Expression

Bly's *Iron John* unwittingly reinforces some of the traditional patriarchal assumptions. It is easy for him to be carried away by the fairy tale that he shares. Though some children might be tied into a symbiotic relationship with their mothers long after this is appropriate, it is important to listen to what boys have to say before you carry them off. It is not always the father who 'knows best' and traditionally it is fathers who have carried off their children to boarding schools. There is much that boys can learn from contact with older men, but it is important to value what they have also learnt in their relations with their mothers. For it is the intuitive and feeling connection that is often most easily made in contact with the mother. The ability to care and connect is not easily valued within a patriarchal society. It is also something that men have still to learn in their contact with children, and that we can only teach if we have learnt it ourselves. This means facing some of the hurts of our own childhood. Bly appreciates this as 'ashes work'. But we need to be careful to specify what hurts men can share with each other and what feelings we have to learn to share with women or with our partners in intimate relationships.

It might only be in his thirties that a man allows himself to experience his anger and rage at the ways he was treated at school. This is something that can sometimes be poignantly shared with other men who have been through similar experiences. Often as men we have so much invested in sustaining the rationalism of the dominant culture that it is hard for us to *share* our experience without intellectualizing it, or feeling trapped in competitive ego games. Some of the techniques of the wildman movement, building upon the insights of encounter groups, and using drums and music, have helped men unlock aspects of their experience that were otherwise difficult to reach. Bly has helped with others to create and honour this emotional space that men can have with each other. He has helped men to recognize different forms of expression and so different ways of using language to tap into their inner experience.

Within a rationalist culture we learn that our thoughts and emotions are available to us and that if we choose to express them, then we are free to. But this is a limited vision of freedom, as Freud grasped. Often we feel excluded from our own lived experience, locked out of contact with ourselves. Even when we recognize our anger conceptually, it can be difficult to connect to the anger and give it expression. If it has been suppressed for a long time, there is often a controlling sense that if it is expressed it will be so enormous that it will surely destroy relationships it has taken years to construct. Men's groups have proved an invaluable place to *explore* such emotions and to provide a safe space for their expression. When we let some of these emotions go we are often struck by just how much energy has been taken up in suppressing them. If there is a clearance, as opposed simply to a movement of energy, we are often left with a greater sense of freedom. We can recognize just how much tension we have been carrying around and how this tension was also lived out in the ways we are often blocked in our intimate relationships.

If we are so used to splitting emotions from language, concealing the ways we feel in our expression out of a fear of rejection, then we will often communicate in a flat and unexpressive voice. Our speech will be strangely disconnected and it will lack feeling and tone. This is because we have learnt to speak in a way that conceals our inner experience. We did not want others to know what was going on inside, and in time we lost connection with this aspect of our emotional lives ourselves. Often we control the expression of our emotions, such as our anger, by saying for example that it is 'unreasonable' to feel angry because our parents were only doing what they thought was best for us. This is the way we can keep our emotional lives in check within a rationalist culture. As men we do not want to be thought of as 'unreasonable' or 'irrational', for this is to be thought of 'as a woman'. We learn to identify our masculinity with control as domination of our emotional lives. It is because we can control our emotions that we can know that we *are* men. This is a difficult taboo to break, for it challenges quite central cultural notions. To recognize, for instance, that we can feel angry at our schooling can sometimes be a great relief, as possibly for the first time we feel more honesty in our expression.

Expressive forms of therapy have been appealing to men partly because they have been direct enough to challenge the trap of rationalist culture, which insists that we can only allow ourselves our emotions if we know that they can be rationally justified in advance.[14] This builds a form of dishonesty into contemporary masculinities when we rarely share what we are feeling, often out of anxiety that we will give others grounds to reject us. The fear of rejection goes very deep within a Protestant moral culture. If we know that our emotions are 'rational', then we feel safe and protected. It is easy in contrast to express anger at someone who is a subordinate at work because they do not have the power to come back at us. Often they are forced to take their anger elsewhere. It is the same with children, who often get anger offloaded on them because people are unable to communicate more directly and honestly in their intimate relationships.

A boy, for example, might feel angry and outraged at having been hit by his father when he got back from work. He might have misbehaved but felt that the punishment was quite inappropriate. He felt that somehow he was getting the anger which had accumulated throughout the whole day at work. He felt instinctively that his father was 'taking it out' on him, though he could not express it. He knew that no one in the family would listen to what he had to say, so he had to swallow his emotions and turn them into himself. Literally it gave him a stomach ache. As far as his father was concerned, he had been disobedient and he was getting what he deserved. Part of him had heard this so much before that he believed it himself. It might have taken him years to name this treatment as physical abuse and to feel *entitled* to something better. It was only later that he realized some of the sadism with which his father was hitting him. This was a memory that was carried in the muscle tissue. When he explored some of these emotions in the context of psychotherapy he could also recognize the frustration that was being expressed in the ways his father hit him, but this understanding did not excuse the abuse. He knew that it was quite wrong for his father to use this level of violence against him. He carried the feelings of abandonment for many years, for he also knew that there was no one who would defend him when it happened.

Unless we are prepared to do this emotional work as men, we will often find ourselves behaving in similar ways when we are fathers ourselves. Even though we might be quite determined to have a different relationship with our own children from what we experienced with our own fathers, we might feel horrified to discover our own anger when it is released. It is only through awareness and emotional work that these cycles of abuse can be broken. They can be changed but only if we learn to take responsibility for our emotional lives. But as we inherit a cultural tendency *to flee* from our emotions and feelings, so we often flee from this kind of emotional work. Traditionally, as men in heterosexual relationships, we have left it to our partners, for it has been part of women's invisible work. Bly has reminded us of the importance of men's groups as a context in which some of this emotional work can be done. But they can also themselves be escapes, unless we are clear what learning we have to take back into our families and relationships. Some men have got trapped into a search for a lost male initiation, as if it is only when they have found their manhood that they can return to their intimate relationships. For it is also possible to get lost in these very same rituals and initiations, unless we keep in mind what their purpose is supposed to be.

It is striking how many men lose contact with their children once relationships have broken up. Sometimes this creates great pain and loss, especially when men are forced to give up contact they would otherwise wish to sustain. But in many cases it seems as if men do not want to sustain contact, partly perhaps because they do not want to be reminded of their past relationships. Seeking to turn over a new leaf, they do not want to be reminded of a history they are fleeing. It has not been uncommon for men to take flight from emotional involvements, even with children they were once close to. Sometimes men have taken flight into the men's movement as a way of escaping what was emotionally difficult to handle. We have to be careful not to read Bly, as some men have done, in a way that suggests that the move from the 'mother's house' to the 'father's house', as part of a process of initiation, leaves little space for relationships with women and children together. Often when we feel desperate or lost it is easier when we are on our own as men.

Minds and Hearts

Within a Western rationalist culture it can be difficult for men to maintain connection with their feelings. It is as if we are to know the world only through the right brain, through intellect and mental life. Our sensitivity and intuition are constantly devalued as 'subjective' and 'unreal'. Reason alone supposedly offers a path to wisdom and understanding. We seek compensation in our activities, learning often as men to identify ourselves with the achievements we can gain within the public realm. Often there is very little feeling of connection with what we are doing as men living out diverse masculinities, because we are wary of making ourselves vulnerable when others can so easily put us down or reject us. So as we grow into manhood we often build a wall around ourselves, unable to *connect* to the inner sources of feeling. We are used to suppressing our emotions because we have learnt that there is safety in living without them. This is often the way we can keep our male identity secure.

Iron John made a significant impact in helping men to recognize that through the path of myth, music and poetry they might forge a different relationship with themselves. They might take themselves by surprise, finding other forms of expression that yield a connection to an emotional life so long dispensed with. It might also be a context in which men could begin to draw support from each other and to trust that, if they shared themselves emotionally, then these emotions would be honoured, not ridiculed. This is a difficult step to take and many men have found it easier to make this inner movement within a ritualized situation. Other men have found a similar support within alternative forms of psychotherapy. In these different contexts men have learnt to take greater *responsibility* for their emotional lives and found ways of reaching out to other men. It has been a context in which men could begin to feel good about themselves as men, though sometimes it has also encouraged a blaming of feminism for the guilt and unease that men have come to feel about themselves in recent years. Sadly *Iron John* is not at all clear about its relationship to feminism, and Robert Bly has easily been misconstrued as anti-feminist.

I do not think it is adequate for Bly to claim that his interest was with men in their changing relationship to masculinity and that feminism had done its job for women. It is almost as if men have to find their masculinity and the individuality and self-worth that flows from it, in the ways that feminism had already helped women to do. But there is a blindness here to the place of relationships with women, as well as a vision of masculinity that needs to be questioned. Bly often seems to think of masculinity as something that men have lost, as a weakened inheritance from generation to generation of men since the industrial revolution. Men have supposedly lost connection with each other. If there is an important truth here about the ways men have lost a sense of what they can learn from each other, and how they can enrich each other's experience as men, it often does not help to think of reclaiming a masculinity that has been lost.

It has been easy to blame feminism for the ways that men are, because traditionally men have always had the power to blame women for the ways they were feeling. This has to do with the workings of emotional relationships of power. Feminism, on the contrary, has been crucially important in helping men to understand the relationship between love and power. It has also challenged men's position at the centre of the universe, for it has encouraged women to explore their own meanings and values rather than to live in a dependent relationship with men. This is something we will need to explore, but at the moment it is also important to honour what men can learn from women about emotion and feeling as sources of wisdom. Often men live with a disconnection between head, heart and sexuality as if they operate within discrete realms. This reflects itself in our relationship with language, for it often becomes difficult within Western traditions to speak honestly from the heart. Sometimes we can move into drumming and non-verbal modes of communication, which also need to be *valued* as a way of escaping the difficulties that we sometimes have in communicating in relationships. We have to be able to return to intimacy if we are to integrate understanding with expression.

Emotional work takes time and patience, for emotions have a movement of their own which needs to be respected. Within a rationalist culture we learn to subordinate emotions to the rule of reason and logic, as we learn that we have to be able to defend our emotions 'rationally' before we can allow them expression. This is a trap, for it fails to appreciate that emotions have a logic of their own. We might feel angry with someone, though we are not sure why. This is part of our experience, and it might be preferable to share our experience while acknowledging that we remain puzzled by it. Things can begin to change as we share our emotions and we might gain insight into what is happening. This is to learn how to respect our emotions, rather than to suppress them as 'unreal' or 'subjective'. It is to acknowledge the reality that they have in our lives at this moment. It is to recognize that they have a logic of their own.

But we can also be trapped by our emotions. We can be locked into an endless cycle of anger that does not bring us relief or nourishment. We can discover that we are caught in an endless loop that we cannot break from. So it is that our anger can become habitual, as we refuse to explore what other emotions it might be concealing. As men this is familiar, for anger is an emotion that can work to reinforce our masculinity. Often we resort to anger as a way of *pushing away* feelings of vulnerability, fear or uncertainty which we find much more uncomfortable because they threaten to bring our masculinity into question. It is as if the complexity of men's diverse emotional expression has been narrowed into what is culturally acceptable. Often it is useful to seek help to identify and explore these patterns, though this is hard for men to do because we learn that we 'should' be able to work things out for ourselves. To recognize that we *need* the help of others can itself be a breakthrough, for it can mean that we no longer think that we have to do everything ourselves. We begin to feel that it is all right to have at least some emotional needs. Again this can be hard to acknowledge, for as men we are not supposed to have needs at all. It is only 'others' who have emotional needs. As men we are supposed to be able to cope on our own.

Notes

1 The ways that boys often learn to disconnect from their inner emotional lives raise questions about the relationship of masculinity to psychoanalysis. For some helpful reflections see, for instance, D. Dinnerstein, *The Rocking of the Cradle and the Ruling of the World* (1976); N.

Chodorow, *The Reproduction of Mothering: Psychoanalysis and the Sociology of Gender* (1978); R.W. Connell, *Gender and Power* (1987); and Steven Frosh, *Sexual Difference: Masculinity and Psychoanalysis* (1995).

2 Jean Baker Miller, in *Towards a New Psychology of Women* (1976), did some of the pioneering work on the ways women were expected to do the emotional work for men. She shows how emotions are related to power. It is also a theme in L. Eichenbaum and S. Orbach, *What Do Women Want?* (1984) and *Understanding Women* (1983).

3 For some interesting reflections on the emotional development of men see, for instance, G. Corneau, *Absent Fathers, Lost Sons* (1991); R.J. Stoller, *Sex and Gender: On the Development of Masculinity and Femininity* (1968); Michael Kaufman, *Cracking the Armor: Power, Pain and the Lives of Men* (1993); and Lilian Rubin, *Intimate Strangers* (1983).

4 A helpful introduction to Wittgenstein's writings is given in Norman Malcolm, *Nothing is Hidden* (1986); and Stanley Cavell, *The Claims of Reason* (1979). In their different ways they give a sense of the development of Wittgenstein's work.

5 There have been different ways of conceiving of the 'inner child'. A useful way of thinking about some of these issues is given in Francis Wicks, *The Inner World of Childhood* (1977). Alice Miller draws on this notion in quite a different way in *For Your Own Good: Hidden Cruelty in Childrearing and the Roots of Violence* (1983).

6 Some helpful research on the ways that boys from different backgrounds learn to deal with their emotions is given in Myriam Miedzian, *Boys will be Boys* (1992). She brings together information from a range of different projects dealing with aspects of violence.

7 For some reflections upon masculinity and schooling, where traditionally it was the task of ruling class boarding schools to build characters and develop rulers for the empire, see, for instance, J. A. Mangan and J. Walvin (eds), *Manliness and Morality: Middle Class Masculinity in Britain and America 1800–1940* (1987); and M. Roper and J. Tosh (eds), *Manful Assertions* (1991).

8 For the ways Freud identifies the father's authority with the task of separating boys from their mother's emotional hold see Freud, 'Three Essays on the Theory of Sexuality', in *Sexuality* (1977); and the discussion in N. Chodorow, *The Reproduction of Mothering* (1978).

9 The moral lives of children are explored in G. Dennison, *The Lives of Children* (1971); and L. Kohlberg, *Essays on Moral Development* (1981). In showing the moral development of children they bring into question the traditional Kantian notion that they are selfish and only have their own interests at heart.

10 In *Education* (1960) Kant has it that the father represents the moral law to the child and so stands as the figure of authority. Alice Miller names this traditional vision a 'poisonous pedagogy' in her exploration of relationships between parents and children in *For Your Own Good: Hidden Cruelty in Childrearing and the Roots of Violence* (1983).

11 For some helpful insights into the early bonding between fathers and children and the changing conceptions of fatherhood see, for instance, *Fatherhood*, edited by Sean French (1992).

12 The ways that a dominant white heterosexual masculinity has been identified with a conception of reason separated from nature, and the ways this has served to suppress other ways of knowing, are a central theme in Victor J. Seidler, *Unreasonable Men: Masculinity and Social Theory* (1994). This is also a central theme in Sara Ruddick, *Maternal Thinking: Towards a Politics of Peace* (1990) which also contains some helpful bibliographical notes.

13 For some reflections upon the balance of energies in the growth and development of children see, for instance, Frances G. Wicks, *The Inner World of Childhood* (1977); and A.C. Harwood, *The Way of a Child* (1979).

14 Expressive forms of therapy, which are able to recognize that emotions have a logic and movement of their own so that they cannot be subsumed under the rule of reason alone, are helpfully introduced in *In Our Own Hands*, edited by Sheila Ernst and Lucy Goodison (1981). See also the more particular introductions to body related therapies in Ken Dychwald, *Bodymind* (1978); and Alexander Lowen, *Bioenergetics* (1963).

10
Emotions and Feelings

Levels of Experience

Within an Enlightenment vision of modernity, feelings are rarely concep-
tualized separately from emotions. They are often lumped together as 'inclinations', as in Kant's ethical writings, and set against reason. So it is that
with modernity centred around a particular identification between a dominant heterosexual masculinity and reason, we learn to talk about 'emotions
and feelings' as if they were the same thing. The point is that they are 'subjective' and 'unreal' because it is only reason that can be 'objective' and
'real'. In our modern Western philosophical culture, we grow up *unskilled*
in thinking about the relationship between emotions and feelings. We are
trapped into the idea that both lack reason and therefore should be limited
and suppressed, because they are deemed distractions that tempt us away
from the path of reason and knowledge. So we end up thinking that it is
pointless to draw any distinction between them.

But if there are important connections between emotions and feelings, it
is also helpful to distinguish between different levels of our experience.
Within a rationalist culture we conceive of identity in terms of reason and
mind. This is what encourages middle class men into a strong relationship
with mental life, for it places them at the centre of modernity. Emotions and
feelings fall outside our concerns with personal identity. In Cartesian terms
they are part of the body and, as we have seen, part of nature to be explained
through the external laws of science. Because we can only have an inner
relationship with mind and reason, it is as if only one half of the brain is
recognized in the moral culture of modernity. With reason identified with
morality in Kant (1959), and so defined as the primary source of human
dignity, integrity and self-worth, this becomes the aspect of ourselves that
we learn to respect. Reason alone is sovereign.

Within the rationalist culture of late modernity, it becomes difficult to discriminate between emotions and feelings. Often when we react emotionally
to a situation we can be aware that our responses are *not* appropriate to the
situation, but seem to be drawing upon different sources. Fathers who have
long thought of themselves as calm and controlled are surprised at the anger
they express at their children. Sometimes they regret the intensity of the
expression and end up feeling bad about themselves. Somehow they had
absorbed the message that it was 'wrong' to get angry, because it just
revealed a lack of control. They had prided themselves in the control they
had been able to achieve over their emotions. The dominant definitions of

masculinity often call for this suppression of emotions because we learn that as men we are supposed to be 'rational' and 'in control'. Sometimes fathers are shocked at the intensity of the anger they carry. If they have little relationship with their emotional lives, they will often treat anger as an 'episode' which does not reflect upon the kind of people they are. They resist the idea of thinking of themselves as an angry sort of person!

We may think for a moment about Dave, who has been shocked to discover the anger he expressed at his small child. He recognizes that though he was provoked by his son's behaviour there was something 'out of proportion' in his response. It does reflect a certain lack of control, but the rationalist assumptions that he has grown up to take for granted barely help to illuminate the situation. He is aware that it will not be enough for him to make a conscious decision not to do it again but to keep a tighter control of his emotions. He also needs more understanding of *how* the emotions that he has carried for so long have been triggered in the present situation. He is ready to admit that he has very little understanding and relationship with his emotions and feelings. He has always assumed that he could guide his life through reason alone, as long as he prevents his emotions from interfering with the goals and purposes he has set for himself. This is no longer working for him, but he has never learnt any different.

Dave feels bad because he recognizes that he has 'dumped' his emotions on his child. He can sense that they have a different source. He could not stand the vulnerability of his son, and part of the anger was to try and force him to be strong and stand up for himself. He knew that this was not the way to do it and he could also recognize that it has to do with how he had grown up to deny his own vulnerability. He had been sent away to boarding school when he was very young and he was forced to be 'grown up' before his time. He had not allowed himself to feel angry at his parents for having sent him away. He knew that he would not do it to his son and that he wanted to have a quite different relationship with his son. But this was why it was *so* shocking to recognize that in some ways he was behaving towards his son in exactly the same way as his father had acted towards him. It was an intensity of anger that he knew from his own childhood. Even though he had made a conscious decision to behave differently, it was as if he was being unwittingly controlled by an emotional history he had not come to terms with.

As boys we learn to leave our emotional histories behind us. If we give them no recognition they will not influence us, or so we learn. We can feel that it is 'pointless' to express anger at our parents, especially if we know that they were doing it because they thought it was 'best for us'. We might think that it is hopeless to express it to them directly, but it might be important for us to express these held emotions in a safe situation, for otherwise as we have learnt they leak out. It might only be with the expression of anger that we can move on and possibly come to some feeling of connection with our sense of abandonment. It is one thing to talk about it in abstract terms but it is quite another to come to *feel* what it was like at the time. This is a connection that we cannot make through will and determination alone. It comes in its own time, for it cannot be forced. It is part of a process of growth and development, and it takes time and patience before we are ripe to establish this kind of connection with ourselves. It restores a connection to the past which has often been severed. We can begin to integrate what we have denied.

As we make these kinds of connections with ourselves, we will recognize a different tone in our expression. Unlike a rationalist vision, a therapeutic vision assumes that it is only through *connection* with the past that we can leave it behind and so experience a fuller sense of freedom. It questions a Protestant tradition that would place mind over matter and would teach us that we must not dwell upon the pains and anguish of the past. We often learn to think of this in Christian terms as a form of self-indulgence. But within different traditions other ways of working on ourselves are recognized. Possibly Freud (Bakan, 1958) was drawing upon Jewish sources in his recognition that it is through reflecting and reliving the past that we can gain insight and freedom.[1] He was aware that we cannot suppress the past because it is bound to return to haunt our unconscious lives. We cannot turn our back to the past but we have to learn to face what happened to us in its detail. Again Freud recognizes that it is not a matter of talking with others because we also have to connect at a feeling level with what we say. It is so easy, especially as men, to intellectualize our experience. So often we talk about our experience in a way that establishes a *distance* with it. We do not want to make ourselves vulnerable for we fear rejection, especially from other men.

Often it is only through expressing anger at our parents and teachers that we can begin to reclaim some of our dignity and self-respect. Even though this might take place years later in the context of a therapy group, it offers us the possibility of reconnecting to what happened in a different way. Originally we might have been forced to swallow our feelings because there was no way that they would be safely expressed and validated. Often our fathers and teachers colluded with each other, for a child's word is traditionally never believed. If we have been mistreated and made to feel small, we soon learn whether we have to silence our own voices. It can take time to reconnect with our anger, even when we can recall the humiliation and the ways we were made to feel unworthy. Often we have learnt to keep these feelings to ourselves, for it can feel *shameful* to admit them to others, especially as adults. We hide them away.

As we reconnect to some of this anger it can bring an enormous sense of relief, as we feel that we are letting go of emotions that we have carried for so long. It restores a sense of justice, for as children we are often powerless to respond. Power is stacked against us and we learn to turn these feelings against ourselves as self-pity. If only we had behaved differently, we begin to think, then we might not have been punished. Often we learn to identify with those who are exercising power over us, as a way of not having to face and deal with our emotions. If we have grown up in the shadow of a very powerful and angry father, we can learn to accommodate or even to resist indirectly, but it might be very difficult to discover the sources of our own autonomy.[2] Even as adults it might be very scary to express some of this hidden anger so that we need to be in a supportive and skilled environment. Often it is a risk we have to take, for others cannot take it for us. We have to face our fear so that we can release some of our anger.

Only through exploring our anger can we discover what lies beneath it, or what emotions it gives way to. If Dave continually returns to his anger and its expression no longer brings relief, then we might sense a trap. We begin to recognize how emotions can form habitual patterns and we need to wonder how to move beyond them. This is the way that emotions can operate at a more superficial level, though it is important to keep in mind the righteous anger that we can feel against abuse and injustice. When a woman turns round in anger at a man who has been verbally abusing her on the street, this can have the deepest sources. Anger can emerge from the depths of our being and in this sense it can be misleading to treat anger as 'subjective' and 'emotional'. Rather the anger is quite appropriate to the situation, and it needs to be honoured and respected, in the ways it fails to be within a rationalist culture. It does not betray a 'lack of reason'. Far from it: it is an *appropriate* response to injustice.[3] The fact that it is emotional does not make it any the less rational. In *Unreasonable Men* (1994) I tried to show how this 'unreasonable' form of reason has become firmly institutionalized within modernity. It is tied up with a dominant notion of masculinity that prides itself in the detachment and impartiality of its reason.

When our understanding and our feelings connect with each other we can begin to 'let go' of what was a painful experience in our lives. It is when the anger gives way to a sense of abandonment that we can begin to hope for a release. Sometimes this only comes after years of emotional work; within a rationalist culture it becomes difficult to discern the differences involved, for often these are differences not of kind but of tone and quality of expression. It is as if we have to begin to acknowledge our own lack of relationship with our emotional lives. We have grown up learning to *suppress* emotions and feelings, especially as men, that somehow do not fit the image that we sustain of ourselves. So it is that emotions and feelings get confused, for they are equally suppressed. We learn that being located in our bodies, they have no connection with ourselves. Our identities are located in our minds alone.

Within modernity the split between mind and body reflects the division between reason and emotions. Inheriting a secularized form of Christianity, we learn to deny and disdain the body and emotional life.[4] This is reflected in the intellectual cultures of modernity which have found it hard to create space for emotions and feelings as sources of knowledge. There is no space for the heart and its wisdom and love. Since the mind alone is the source of knowledge, we lack understanding of the words from the Hebrew Psalm 90: 12: 'So show us how to spend our time and acquire a heart of wisdom.' This aspiration has become unintelligible within the secular terms of modernity.

We do not know how to spend our time within a materialistic culture which can only recognize the values of material wealth. The crisis that hetero-sexual men are feeling about what it means to be a man responsive to the challenges of feminism is tied up with a pervasive cultural crisis to do with meaning and value. Bly helps us some of the way, but he also blocks our understanding, for he wrongly insists that feminism has only taught men to be soft and unfocused. While these dangers remain and are vividly described in *Iron John*, it is too easy to fall into talk of reclaiming a 'lost' masculinity. This too easily feeds a backlash against feminism.

Grief and Integrity

Often it is only when boys have expressed the anger that they have carried for so long that they can begin to experience the grief at having been aban-doned by their parents when they were sent away to school. We can begin to *feel* the darkness of abandonment rather than just talk about it. We will be forging a deeper connection with ourselves, and this will be reflected in a different tone in our voice, for we will be coming from a different level within ourselves. Within current forms of social theory which recognize the ways that our identities are fragmented within a postmodern culture, it becomes difficult to talk about developing and sustaining a deeper connec-tion with the self. We have grown suspicious of this kind of language, assum-ing that it involves a coherence and integrity of self that has become an impossible dream within the complexities and shifting demands of a post-modern world.[5]

But often this misses Freud's (1961) insights into the ways that we learn, within late modernity, to intellectualize our experience as we present our-selves in culturally acceptable terms. Often this is an evasion which we pay for in a pervasive sense of unreality. In this way Freud challenges a subjec-tivism that would pretend that each person can construct their own reality. He insists that these 'realities' do not have an equal standing and that often they involve an avoidance of the pain and suffering that we carry from our childhood experience. There is a qualitative *shift* that can take place as we move from knowing in general terms that the distance we experience with our father, say, has its source in a distrust that began when we were sent away to boarding school and has grown into the direct expression of anger. This does not have to be an 'acting out' as traditional psychoanalytic theory often presents it. Rather it can be a way that a boy *can* reconnect to anger that he has always been scared of expressing before. It offers a different con-nection to self.

It might only be, for example, as John allows himself to express his held anger that he can begin to contact the sadness he also feels at not having had more contact with his father. Within the logic of emotions this makes perfect sense, though it is hard to say in advance how someone might come to feel. The notion that it is a contradiction in terms to feel both anger and sadness insists on evaluating our emotional life according to standards of logic which are not appropriate. Bly talks about this father loss as a deep hunger of the soul, and I think he is so right to draw attention to what has been going on in relationships between fathers and sons. It is as if we have not been able to thrive without this physical substance, as Bly describes it, that passes from fathers to sons. Somehow it touches our capacities to grow into manhood, for it is as if we always remain boys. But if manhood remains an illusive challenge, there are other sources which Bly fails to illuminate. For there is a pervasive feeling that men *want* to relate to their partners and their children quite differently from the ways we experienced our fathers relating. It is not simply that some 'essential' maleness has been diluted as it has been passed down the generations. Feminism has been important, in a way Bly totally fails to acknowledge, in helping men to rediscover and to rework inherited visions of masculinity. It is also important to recognize that daughters also feel this loss of contact with a father who has in many ways absented himself, though possibly they feel it in different ways.[6]

In my personal experience, after my father died in 1950 when I was barely five, it was hard for me to accept what older men might have had to offer. I do not think that I allowed my stepfather to give me the support and love that he might have been prepared to give. I preferred to live in a state of father hunger, thinking and praying in my dreams at night that, if only I was 'good enough' or 'loyal enough', my father might return from the land of the dead one day. He never did, but I kept on longing. Friends who were sent away to boarding school talk of a similar longing and the ease with which this longing is *confused with* love. Sometimes it is easier to long than to acknowledge that you have little love for a father who has just not been there for you. Often it is just confusing to think that 'underneath' all those feelings of anger and rejection, there are feelings of love waiting to be expressed. This is not always so and often it is healthier to acknowledge that we have little love for parents who gave so little real time, care and attention to us. Because we are told that 'you must love him because he is your father', it makes it difficult to break with this demand without feeling that we are being 'ungrateful' or 'bad' ourselves.

Michael tells the story of how his father refused to talk to him from the age of nine till he was 17 and managed to get a university place. His father thought that he was a 'rebel' and did not want to have anything to do with him. Not a word passed between them, just looks of disapproval through all these years. He can remember moments of attention, like when his father put him on his lap and allowed him to drive the car down the allotment they had. He ran over a watering can and, years later, was always proud to remember the moment whenever he saw the can. It held a warm memory of contact for him. The family was poor and never threw anything away, so that can was always around. Years later he reminded his father of the incident when he was visiting him in hospital. He did not have long to live and Michael wanted to remind him of easier days. But his father remained as rejecting as he had always been, blaming Michael again for having ruined the can so many years back. He held his grudges. Michael felt rejected yet again and it just reminded him not to hope for anything else from his father. He realized that he was not really trying to make contact for himself, but was just trying to make things easier for his father. He would still find it hard to say that he really loved his father after all those years of nonrecognition. But sometimes he *does* feel sad that he did not have a different relationship with him.

I feel it easier to say that I loved my father even if he was not around for me for very long. It took me years to also recognize the anger that I felt at his death. As a small boy I had learnt to live as if he was always about to come back. Sometimes I could feel him as some kind of protective spirit, but more often I felt that I had to prove myself to him. Somehow I had to prove myself worthy of his love, because at some level I felt that it was because I was not 'good enough' that he had died in the first place. I think many children feel responsible in this way, though adults often fail to recognize these feelings. But it also meant that I was closely identified with my father so that in some way I had to learn to live my own life rather than his. It was only many years later, as an adult, that I had to reenact the burial of my father in a psychotherapy group, so eventually going through the process of saying goodbye. It was a great relief to feel that he was settled rather than ever present in my aura somehow.

I was not really allowed to feel my rage at his death when I was young. It seemed such an unreasonable emotion to feel for someone who had died. If I had been told more directly then it might have been different, but I was left feeling that he was on a business trip to the States and that if I was good then he might come back. At least this was the way that I learnt to talk to myself about what was happening, because the adults around did not want to talk about death and they took refuge in the idea that as children we were 'too young to understand'. I still feel angry when I think about this because it says more about the difficulties that adults have with their feelings than it says about children. I think I was just shocked about what was going on around me and felt that I could only find safety if I withdrew into myself. It was as if my inner life and thoughts were the *only* things that I could trust. It felt as if I was constantly being lied to by the adults around. I was simply told that I had to be strong since there was no father around. As boys we were constantly told that we now had to look after our mother and that she needed us to be strong. As four boys left without a father in the early 1950s we felt scared of what might happen to us and very tense that something similar might happen to our mother. We learnt in different ways to grow up *before* we were ready. Our childhood had been tragically cut short. Since I was constantly told I looked like my father, I also felt a special responsibility.

I had not been able to attend my father's burial, and its reenactment within the context of a supportive therapy group helped to create some space and distance for myself. It allowed me to release emotions that I had carried for years. Whatever the weakness of a hydraulic conception of emotions, as Foucault (1980) has described it, it remains important to acknowledge the ways we can carry unexpressed emotions over many years.[7] They do not remain as they were in some kind of pristine form. As we give expression to some of our anger, for instance, we can begin to connect to a well of unexpressed emotion. I learnt that it was not appropriate to express anger at my father who had died, so that I suppressed these feelings as 'unreasonable'. Since I learnt that he could not help the heart condition that he developed, it was quite wrong for me to feel angry. I was allowed to feel sad, though this was not easy either, since it seemed to make the adults feel responsible and they made me feel that they had more than enough on their plate at the time. But as I learnt to block my anger, so I *also* found it difficult to connect to my grief.

Gradually as I was able to connect to more of the anger at my father's death I felt a little clearer in myself. This was not a mental process in that I could not simply decide to make a rational choice to express this anger, even when I carried a vague sense that it was something that I was going to have to 'go through'. I could not rush the process, and there were other emotions that I had to express *before* I was ready to explore the emotions that I had buried along with my father's death. It happened so many years back when I was a small child that for a long time it was difficult to imagine that I still had any emotions about it. But as I began to allow myself to express more of my emotions, rather than simply to understand them intellectually as I had learnt to do, I realized just how much I had been carrying around. Once I had allowed myself to express some of the anger, I could begin to allow myself to enter some of the grief and longing. I realized that I had long absorbed a dominant cultural notion of masculinity which made me feel that I had to be 'strong' in the face of emotions. This was the way that I had learnt to prove myself, as had other boys.

Emotions and Suppression

As I could go down into the grief and experience the loss at a feeling level, it helped create more of a connection with myself. It was a great relief to feel that I did not have to pretend in front of others, that everything was OK, and that I could 'cope' with whatever was going on for me. As men we often have very little sense of what is going on in our inner lives, for we are so used to proving ourselves in the competitive world of men. As far as I was concerned I could cope, and my father's death, having happened years back, didn't really matter to me. I had survived the experience, and even if I could have wished for greater truth and honesty at the time, it was something that was firmly placed in the past. I had learnt to leave the past behind me because supposedly it could not be changed. As we learnt it as children, 'there is no point in crying over spilled milk.' To allow ourselves to be affected by the emotions from the past was a sign of weakness, which reflected badly on our male identity. At some level it meant that we were 'not up to it'. As men we often learn to cope as best we can. We tacitly learn to focus upon the present demands at work and try to put everything else 'out of mind'.

But Freud (1961) has long helped us question this masculine vision of late modernity. We can learn that what we suppress just returns to haunt our dreams and unconscious life. We can only 'free' ourselves from the past if we are prepared to face what happened to us and learn to explore what we lived through with honesty and compassion. Often this is particularly scary for men to do because we have so much *invested* in sustaining an external-ized and culturally sanctioned image of ourselves. Often we leave our emo-tions and feelings behind as we identify with whatever is happening for us at work. This becomes the only arena that really matters, because it is here that we can listen to any praise being offered for our efforts. Often men within a Protestant work ethic have experienced their fathers making the same sacrifice of their lives for work, and at some level are still locked into proving themselves to their fathers. So it is work that still operates as the crucial arena for men, for it is here that male identities are sustained. Nothing else really matters very much, whatever lip-service is paid to notions of 'doing it all for the family'. Middle class men in managerial pos-itions, and also working class men, will often be working very long hours with very little contact with partners and children.

Even if, at some conscious level, men with diverse masculinities want to live a different life from the life they knew their fathers lived, it is easy to be sucked into a very similar relationship to work. The long hours become a way of affirming our virility and we can insist that we are sharper and more able to cope with the stress. In fact we often get off on the adrenalin and become dependent in a way that the term 'workaholic' suggests. We become dependent upon work to give our lives whatever meaning they have, and we fear the *void* that we might have to face if we stop working for a while. This is all part of 'making it' in a man's world. Whatever lip-service we might give to our partners and children it is easy for them to fall into the back-ground, for the demands they make simply cannot compete with the demands that we make on ourselves at work. It feels very easy for men to trap themselves in this way. In part it shows the strength of the continuing connection between the Protestant work ethic and dominant notions of masculinity. If there is less self-denial involved since the 1960s, it is partly because of the conspicuous consumption this often entails. Men in the 1990s learn to work hard and spend hard. There is little room for emotional con-tact or relationships because men, if they are fortunate to have work at all, are too busy all the time. We end up constantly promising what we cannot deliver, and contact in our relationships with partners, friends and children often becomes very thin. It can always be put off until tomorrow because there are always more urgent demands at work that have to be met today.

Iron John has been important partly because it has opened up the grief that so many men silently carry for their fathers. Often it is these feelings that are suppressed in the intensity of work. It is as if we are working hard to prove ourselves to fathers who we often did not know. Traditional forms of psychotherapy have focused upon the relationship between sons and mothers. Since Freud tended to be locked into a somewhat idealized relationship with his own father, especially after his death, he helped create a kind of protected space for fathers. In contrast, Bly has certainly helped men to focus upon the *unresolved* feelings they still carry for their fathers. Often there is an unspoken sense of disappointment and a yearning for a contact that rarely seems to come. Boys in different generations have had to learn that their fathers had to work so that the family could survive. So it is that boys from diverse class and ethnic backgrounds have had to learn to expect very little from their fathers. Often there is a smouldering resentment that sometimes breaks through the surface. At other times there is a resignation, as boys have learnt that it is 'pointless' to reach out for what never seems to come back. At some level there is also identification, for our fathers present us with all kinds of unspoken messages about what it means to be a man.

For many years I lived with an idealized image of my father that many times got in the way of relating to my stepfather after my mother remarried when I was seven. As far as I was concerned he was not my father, so that I needed to sustain a distance from him to stay loyal to my 'real' father. But as long as I idealized my father, it was hard for me to experience that anger that I also carried. I was locked into a certain relationship with him as part of an ambivalent relationship with myself. For a long time he was abstractly experienced as my 'father', for this helped to keep some of my emotions in check. It was harder to think about how I missed a 'daddy' because this term connected me to my emotions. Missing my daddy gave me a different connection with myself, as it brought forward different aspects of my experience. If I had stayed locked into my anger, repeated as an ever recurring pattern that was no longer nourishing or leaving me with a sense of release, I could have said I was trapped at an emotional level. A skilled therapist would have detected this and helped me to find ways of moving on in my process. In the very repetition of the pattern I might have found a certain kind of security, fearful of exploring other, less familiar emotions.

In time I had to face that my father was not really there for me, even when he was alive and around in my life. As I learnt to express anger at the disappointment that I felt, I found that the idealizations began to give way. I began also to appreciate some of the complexities of his own life. Whether I loved him or not, or whether I was confusing love with longing, became an issue open for exploration. The point is that these matters cannot be decided through will alone, for our emotion and feelings cannot be so easily controlled. We have to learn in therapy to be open to *discovering* what it is that we feel, and it might come as quite a surprise to us. A strength of humanistic forms of psychotherapy is that they have relatively little confidence in established patterns or norms of relating. Traditional psychoanalysis is often still too keen for people to be judged as 'pathological'. People have to be open, to discover for themselves what emotions are coming forward, for they cannot judge in advance.

So it is, for instance, that mourning is a process that we have to go through, and one that has its own rhythm and movement. It has its own sense of timing, which different religious traditions have learnt to recognize but to which we have often become blind within secularized visions of modernity. We learn that it is 'pointless' to mourn because you cannot bring people back. Learning to think in utilitarian terms brings little sense of the emotional dimensions of our experience and the needs we have to let those who have died go.[8] Often when people have learnt to be 'strong' in the face of death, it has made it much harder for them to complete a process of mourning. It may be years later that they recognize from their dreams that they have considerable unfinished work to do. But it is hard for people to acknowledge that a period of mourning allows a process to take place that has its own pace and timing and that to cut it short can create emotional difficulties years later. Again this was a powerful insight which Freud (1961) was able to share in his challenge to utilitarian conceptions of modernity. He knew the costs of blocking emotions and recognized the need for certain rituals of mourning. But for Freud this was still within a secular framework, for he was less ready to acknowledge the spiritual connection that people can sustain with those who have died. This made it hard for him to fully honour the wisdom of different spiritual traditions and their understanding of mourning as a process which takes time.[9]

Psychoanalysis as a predominantly secular tradition also fails to appreciate the ways a dialogue can sometimes continue between someone who has died and those who were close. I realized that the relationship I had with my father did not end when he died. Rather my dialogue remained significant to me in all kinds of ways. It took me time to appreciate that I could still draw on this relationship for understanding and support, that I could still allow it to nourish me. Within the dominant culture there is little language in which to make sense of spirituality, for it is still much easier just to think of death as an ending. At least Freud recognizes that we continue to have emotions and feelings for people long after they have died, and that they can remain significant people in our lives. In my own learning it took me time to accept that my father had died and even longer to recognize the different ways that I was *still* living under his shadow. For years I was locked into a pattern of proving myself to him in everything that I did, for at some unconscious level it still remained paramount for me to vindicate myself in his eyes. It was only when I could begin to identify and name this pattern that I could begin to live in my own light. I was gradually beginning to learn to live my own life, which was not easy after so many years of living in his shadow.

Even as adults we can be haunted by a sense that we are *not* living our own lives. This is an unsettling thought and it can take time to identify such feelings. For instance, we can begin to recognize the ways we are living out the expectations that our parents have had of us, rather than what we want for ourselves. Even though we take ourselves to be 'free' and 'autonomous' we can still be living out the dreams that our parents long held for us, partly because we have not dared to recognize or name our own dreams. Unless we can begin to identify our own feelings, as much as our own ideas and beliefs, we are bound to be accommodating and lacking definition in ourselves. Often we take refuge in a false sense of security, learning to become what others want us to be, especially our parents and later possibly our partners. In blocking our emotions, especially if we fear that they are not acceptable, we are blocking the possibility of developing a deeper *contact* with ourselves. If we do not really exist for ourselves, it becomes difficult for us to thrive in relationships with others. For heterosexual men this issues takes on a particular form, because in identifying so much with work we often drift in other areas of our lives.

Notes

1 For some explorations into the relationship of Freud to a Jewish tradition see, for instance, David Bakan, *Sigmund Freud and the Jewish Mystical Tradition* (1958); and Marthe Robert, *Freud: From Oedipus to Moses* (1977).

2 Kafka's *Letter to My Father* (1954) shows the influence of a powerful and dominating father in the life of a child.

3 The ways that anger can be a rational response to abuse are explored in much of the feminist literature on rape. See, for instance, Susan Griffin, *Rape: The Power of Consciousness* (1979).

4 For some insights into the ways bodies are disdained as sources of knowledge within modernity see, for instance, Sara Ruddick's comment that 'In the post-Cartesian world, Plato's controlled body becomes fundamentally abstract, a characterless, colorless, sexless extension of matter in space', in *Maternal Thinking* (1990, p. 196). See also the explorations in Elizabeth Grosz, *Volatile Bodies: Towards a Corporeal Feminism* (1994).

5 The fragmentation of identities which is taken to be a feature of postmodernism can make it difficult to sustain notions of the self. But the difficulties reach back into some of the structuralist writings that were critical in the 1970s, as I have explored it in *Recovering the Self: Morality and Social Theory* (1995). Some of these issues are also explored in Z. Bauman, *Postmodern Ethics* (1995) and more recently in *Life in Fragments* (1995).

6 For some reflections on the relationships between fathers and daughters see, for instance, *Fathers and Daughters*, edited by Ursula Owen (1984); and Sue Sharpe, *Fathers and Daughters* (1994).

7 For a discussion of some of the weaknesses in Foucault's hydraulic conception of emotions see Victor J. Seidler, 'Reason, Desire and Male Sexuality', in *The Cultural Construction of Sexuality*, edited by Pat Caplan (1987).

8 The difficulties of mourning within a Western utilitarian culture are explored by A. Mitscherlich, *The Difficulties of Mourning*. See also Philip Aries, *Western Attitudes towards Death* (1974); E. Kubler-Ross, *On Death and Dying* (1970); and Steven Levine, *Healing into Life and Death* (1987).

9 For a sense of how different spiritual traditions have dealt with issues of death, dying and mourning see, for instance, Sogyal Rimpoche, *The Tibetan Book of Living and Dying* (1995).

11
Relationships

The Inner Child

As young children growing up in different families we are often very sensitive to feelings and atmosphere, for this is how we are anchored in the world before we come into language. Our early relationships are established on a feeling level and it is only if we feel unwanted, hurt or rejected that we learn to withdraw. We learn to protect ourselves against contact. From our earliest moments we respond to the ways in which our mothers and fathers look and hold us. As we reach out to others we live in the hope that we will be seen for who we are, rather than what others would want us to be. So from our earliest years we learn to *resonate* with different forms of communication. If our expectations are dashed and we feel unmet in our reaching out, we soon learn that the adults around us are not to be trusted. We learn to withdraw into ourselves and to seek the nourishment from within that does not seem to be forthcoming in our contact with others.[1]

Within the West we do not learn to recognize a new-born child as a blessing, especially within a dominant Christian culture that carries a tradition of original sin. From a very early age children begin to feel that there is something wrong with them and that they are not acceptable as they are. As boys we learn a message that we have to prove ourselves and become 'other' than our 'animal' natures might dictate. For as boys we are often made to feel 'unacceptable' or 'unloveable' within the dominant Protestant culture. As boys we soon learn that we are not supposed to be soft or loving for it is wrong to have needs. We soon get the message that we have to be independent and be able to manage on our own. This is reinforced as we learn to separate from our mothers and identify the 'feminine' as what we have to define our masculinity against. We have to prove that we are not soft or weak or 'sissies' – that we are *not* girls. This sustains a deep fear of gayness, a homophobia that is rarely far beneath the surface of many straight boys' experience. It exists as a constant anxiety, for at some level it represents an ultimate 'failure' in our masculinity.[2]

As we learn to treat emotions and feelings as 'childish', we learn to separate from them as part of a process of 'growing up'. But Freud (1953) teaches us that we cannot leave our childhoods behind. Rather we have to be ready to face what we have lived through as children, if we are to free ourselves from some of its hurts. But within the larger culture it becomes difficult to reclaim such a sensitivity, for there are few ways of appreciating as men what it means to be sensitive. As boys it becomes something to feel ashamed of. So it is that we learn to silence the cries of the 'inner child'. We do not want to be reminded of the pain that he or she carries, for we fear it might interrupt what we have managed to achieve as adults. As men we have a lot invested in not getting to know ourselves any better, especially as it seems to threaten the efficiency with which we can operate in our work lives.

But I think the notion of giving voice to an inner child can be very helpful, for it can help us reconnect to a sensitivity that has long been forsaken. It can help us recognize emotional needs that we might otherwise overlook, as long as we recognize there is also a responsible adult part that needs to be addressed openly and honestly. We can begin to develop a language to express our emotions, even if these do not fit the ways we think we ought to be. This 'inner child' is always with us, often as a reminder of aspects of ourselves we have too easily forsaken. If we find it hard to *acknowledge* the emotional needs for contact, recognition and affection we carry as adults, we might at least hear them as the voice of an inner child. Importantly it also faces us with the issue of how we have learnt to look after ourselves. Often as men we have learnt that we do not have needs so that we have no need for nourishment. It is only 'others' who have needs, while we have learnt to manage very well on our own, or so we like to think. The idea that we as men also have emotional needs which need to be nourished has become quite strange to contemporary ears. It is easy to think that having needs is a sign of inadequacy and reflects some kind of lack. It seems always far better to prove that we can do without the help of others. Often as heterosexual men it is as hard for us to receive from others as it is to give, sometimes harder.

As we learn as boys to share ourselves according to the expectations of adults around us, we think that this is the way to win approval and love. Within the middle class, boys soon learn that love is not a blessing that flows freely but is something that has to be earned through proving ourselves. We do not want to accept our anger, disappointment or fear if these mean rejection. It seems easier to split from these emotions and to live as if they do not exist as part of our experience. We often learn to shape our experience so that it fits with what is culturally expected of us. But as we learn to win the approval of those around us, we often *lose* an inner connection with ourselves. We forsake our own integrity as we seek the approval of others. As boys this seems to be a deal worth making, for little value is placed culturally upon those aspects of our inner emotional lives which we are forsaking. We do not think that we are selling an important birthright, for we rarely learn that, in forsaking our emotions and suppressing those feelings which are deemed 'unacceptable', we are forsaking aspects of ourselves.

Of course boys react to this predicament in many different ways according to class, 'race', ethnicity and sexuality. Some react with hostility and anger, for this is the only way they know of winning attention from adults. It may be negative attention, but it is often preferable to no attention at all. Other boys become adaptive and ill-defined. Rather than risk the rejection that might come from sharing what they feel, they learn to feel in a way that is expected of them. They do not want to discover their own emotions, because this might bring them into conflict with the authorities they have identified with. Unfortunately a rationalist culture does *not* teach us to respect our own emotions as part of a process of self-respect. Since we learn to suppress emotions, we expect other boys to do the same. Boys who have been brought up to acknowledge and respect their emotions can become a target for the hostility of other boys. They can seem 'soft' and so appear as easy targets. This is one of the conflicts for parents who are seeking to bring up boys in anti-sexist ways. They might encourage boys to share more of their feelings, but this can create its own difficulties when boys get to school.[3]

Lost Childhood

Since boys are often encouraged to be independent and self-sufficient from an early age, they learn to separate from their inner emotional lives. Within late modernity, emotions become a sign of dependency and reflect a lack of self-control which is particularly threatening to sustaining dominant notions of male identity. I knew this from my own experience because I was forced to be 'grown up' before it was really appropriate, when my father died. I had to learn to cater for my own needs. Very quickly I learnt that I was supposed to manage everything emotionally on my own and that I was not supposed to make demands on adults who were already weighed down with responsibilities. My mother had to go out to work and she had more than enough on her plate without having to worry about us. If we were sad or unhappy we learnt to keep these feelings very much to ourselves. In time we had so separated from these emotions that we did not detect their signs. It is as if we learnt to live *without* emotions at all. We lost the capacity to register what we were experiencing emotionally. Rather we learnt to content ourselves with whatever was going on, unless it was obviously disastrous. We 'put up' with things, but often we were so used to doing it that we did not recognize the self-denial involved.

I had an older brother but, because I was supposed to be the 'clever' one who looked like my father, I was required to be responsible beyond the calling of my years. Like the rest of my brothers I lived in fear that something might happen to my mother and we would be left orphaned. As part of a family that had been refugees from Hitler's rule in Austria, we did not have much extended family and even less that we were on talking terms with. It felt as if as a family we were very much alone, though we learnt to call some special friends of my mother 'auntie', as if to make up for this gap in familial life. It was part of a more general pretence to normality that was very common growing up as Jewish in the 1950s in England. We were to be 'like everyone else' and we picked up that our security was to lie in becoming invisible. We were to aspire to being 'English', indistinguishable at least in public from everyone else. At the same time somehow we were to feel proud of being Jewish. This was not easy to achieve and meant that there was a very sharp split between family and school, between private and public life. We learnt to behave differently in the different contexts of our lives and to minimize whatever differences might arise. This made me very sensitive to what others were feeling and what they might expect from me. It was as if security lay in becoming what others wanted us to be, for 'they' knew the 'correct' ways of behaving. I have since rebelled against this in different ways, but there is still part of me that tends to be quite adaptive. Then I do not want to know what I am feeling, partly because it might not be appropriate to the dominant culture. This is something that many refugee groups are used to, particularly in the first generation of settle-ment.[4]

I desperately wanted to be 'accepted' by the other boys at school and was prepared to pay the price in my sensitivity, though when I was about 10 the tensions began to show as some kind of illness through various skin aller-gies. Often the suppression of emotions shows itself on the skin, especially the suppression of sensitivity. I worked hard to be accepted but this meant an estrangement from my own emotions. I was keen to have the same emotions as all the other boys. I wanted to adjust and fit in. In this process I learnt to *minimize* my Jewishness because this threatened to draw atten-tion to a difference. It could give other boys a reason to reject me. So I had to learn to be Jewish in a way that did not draw any attention to difference. This was a matter almost of squeezing my experience into a shape that was not of my own making. I used to police the boundaries between school and home and in many ways I think I was a different person in the two contexts. I was more uncertain at school, so I was a little stiff and reserved. I did not know what was going to come to me next, so I was constantly on my guard. It was as if I lived in a constant state of *alert*, not knowing what harmless comment might contain a barbed attack. My body was in a state of readi-ness that I can still experience in moments of stress. The tension became part of my muscle structure and I did not know that an easier and more relaxed body was possible. I soon learnt that life was something I had to 'get through'.

I can feel grief for a 'lost childhood', in the sense that when my father died I had to become more serious and responsible than was appropriate for a child of five. I had to learn to look after others when I really needed looking after myself. I learnt to suppress my own emotional needs in order to be strong for others. Psychotherapies recognize that it is not so unusual for children to feel, for a variety of different reasons, that they had to look after their parents and so to give the support that they really needed for themselves. More generally it is not uncommon for us to give to others what we really need for ourselves emotionally. These reversals need to be acknowledged in understandings of how identities get shaped. Sometimes we can find precious spaces in which we can play and relive some of the childhood that we did not have. This can help us be less serious than we need to be. It can also help to bring pleasure and humour into our lives. It can be a relief for children who have somehow accepted responsibility for their parents' distress, whether this be due to divorce, alcoholism or death. Often children make an inner promise to do their best to rescue their parents, even feeling responsible somehow for what has befallen them.[5]

It becomes important, if healing is to take place, for people to discover ways of giving themselves the childhoods that they might never have had, or in another idiom, nourishing the 'inner child' who is hungry for the recognition, love, support, pleasure and fun they never had enough of. Often it is when we have children of our own that we are given a second chance, so to speak, to repair some of the deprivations and emotional hurts which we carry from our own childhoods. Spending time with our children can give us a chance to recover *lost* aspects of ourselves and to build contact with qualities we have never been allowed to express. I know how fortunate I have been to be able to spend so much time with Daniel and Lily when they were still young. It is a sadness that many fathers carry with them, especially if they feel they have been so identified with work that they have 'missed' their children growing up. Distances are created that are difficult to dissolve. But we have also lost important opportunities as men with diverse masculinities to heal some of the hurts we carry from having been forced to be more independent as boys than was really appropriate for us.

Unless we find ways of acknowledging theoretically the ways we grew up before we were ready, and so of giving ourselves some of the pleasures and joys we missed first time round, we will be constantly seeking indirect means to meet these unmet desires. As we become more aware of the ways our 'inner child' has long been ignored and neglected, we can begin to listen and respond. Rather than feel ashamed of these 'childish' needs, and so discount them theoretically in notions of identity, it is far more helpful to recognize them. Sometimes we need to find a *space* within our intimate relationships in which we can safely exercise some of the fantasies and playfulness that we rarely allow ourselves. It is partly because we grow up, especially as middle class men, with such a strong self-critical voice that we are often very hard on ourselves. Because we have learnt to treat ourselves critically in this way, we are often deaf to the cries of an inner child. Rather we can find ourselves becoming punitive, especially with our own children. It is as if as fathers we unconsciously feel jealous of the pleasure and fun that we were never allowed to enjoy in our own childhoods. But we may remain quite unaware of these unconscious drives, thinking that we are doing 'what is best' for them, very much echoing what our parents felt about us.

Men often feel threatened by the voice of an inner child, for it can seem to challenge transitions to manhood, however we come to understand this. It is easy to feel that we have never really 'grown up' and the impulses of the inner child seem to confirm this. So it is that we learn to *silence* these stirrings as a way of affirming our manhood. It might only be in the setting of an intimate sexual relationship that we allow some of these desires to be more openly expressed. Here we might allow a playfulness that is quite foreign in other parts of our lives. But often, especially in long-term relationships, it is possible for our sexual contact to become routinized as we lose contact with a sense of pleasure. The ways we separate from a relationship with an inner child may leave us with less contact with ourselves. We lose contact with some of the sources of our emotional well-being as we silence the stirrings of the inner child. We dampen our spontaneity and we can become so identified with what others expect of us that we lose connection with our own needs.

Pleasure and Guilt

Within a vision of modernity shaped by a secularized notion of a Protestant ethic we learn to avoid not only grief but also pleasure. We learn to suppress emotions which we take to be 'unacceptable', for it is only work that can supposedly really give meaning to men's lives. Often we have learnt that it is only if you have worked hard that you can deserve pleasure, and then only in small measure. From early in our boyhoods, especially in middle class families, we learn that happiness comes as a reward for effort and that if you have not worked for something then it is not worth having. This is a way in which we are embedded within an achievement ethic which haunts our adult experience as men. Often we can feel that we are *concealing* a hidden sense that we are not 'good enough' and that only if we work harder can we become deserving. Even though we live in more permissive times, it is striking how hard men can be on themselves. The inner critical voice that was called by Fritz Perls (1971) in the early days of Gestalt therapy the 'top dog' never seems to rest.[6] It seems as if we could always be doing that bit more, trying that bit harder.

Robert Bly is also aware of how men have lost a sense of spontaneity within the corporate cultures that rule Western societies. He is also aware of how this connects with the loss of an *inner* sense of self. It is as if we have become adaptive, shaping ourselves according to what is expected of us. It becomes threatening to have too clear a sense of your own needs and desires, for this can easily bring you into conflict with those in authority. It becomes preferable for men to have few firm beliefs and values of their own. If alternative psychotherapies have proved attractive to men in this predicament, they often operate within their own individualistic assumptions. Often therapy sustains the idea that people create their own reality and are responsible for the lives they live. If we are unhappy or distressed, then it can seem as if we only have ourselves to blame. If we are ready to work on our relationships and the patterns that are constantly defeating us, then we might find our way through. Often the growth movement and psychotherapies have limited insight into the workings of class, 'race' and ethnic relations of power and subordination. Structured relations of power are too easily dissolved into personal relationships.

Psychotherapies can certainly help people to reconsider the ways they are responsible for the patterns they live out in their everyday lives, rather than simply to blame 'others' for their misery and unhappiness. This can help us reclaim a freedom which we too often deny, learning to blame others constantly for what we feel. In this regard at least, a revitalized individualism can help us to accept greater responsibility for the ways we live in our everyday lives. For example, we might assume that we are 'too busy' to give an hour to ourselves each day, only to recognize ways we trap ourselves. Similarly, therapy can help us become aware that we might constantly tell ourselves that we have too much on our plate at the moment to share what is going on for us with our partners. We can be shocked to realize that though we spend a lot of time in each other's company we spend very little time making contact with each other.[7] Again, it can be helpful to recognize that this is something we *can* do something about.

Often as men it takes time to become aware that we have very little relationship established with our inner child. If we are to open up a dialogue then we have to learn how to hear what the inner child has to say. This means giving time and attention which we might not be used to, because we are so used to filling the time available. Often as men it is hard to make time for our partners, friends and children unless we have learnt how to make time for ourselves. At some level this can be difficult to do because we remain haunted by a sense that we are 'unworthy'. We do not want to face the abyss within and we assuage these unsettling feelings by keeping ourselves busy. It is striking how men from very different backgrounds can find it hard to spend time with themselves. Often they feel bored and anxious and they cannot wait to be 'doing something'. Within a Protestant moral culture we learn that time is *not* to be wasted, and spending time with ourselves can feel like self-indulgence. This is partly related to the difficulties we often have as men in acknowledging that we have needs at all, for, as I've tried to show, to have needs is a sign of weakness and so a potential threat to male identities. At some level we seem to be constantly pushing ourselves, as if we prove ourselves by showing that we can cope with the endless pressures and demands. Sometimes our backs give way for we have so little personal support ourselves. This is a need we are often slow to recognize.

As men we are often scared of acknowledging our 'childish' feelings and desires. It is as if we are men because we have learnt to *split* from the stirrings of the inner child we carry. We learn to put the past behind us because it is only the future that really matters to us. We are identified with the plans and goals that we set ourselves, for this is the way we affirm our masculinities. It is because we have to constantly prove ourselves as men that we can never take our manhood for granted. It has to be defended and we have to be on guard against threats. This partly explains why we inherit such an impoverished notion of childhood within modernity. Childhood exists as some kind of 'irrational' time which serves as a preparation for our movement towards being 'rational selves'. Within a rationalist culture children do not have to be listened to, for they cannot be expected to reason logically. Childhood has no intrinsic value in itself. So it is hardly surprising if we never learn to honour the voice of our inner child, for at best it is a distraction. Like emotions, it serves as an interference with the path towards freedom and autonomy, which can be reached through reason alone.

Boys often learn to make a more radical break with their 'childish' emotions, for they soon learn to identify emotions with the 'feminine'. But they are rarely aware that in suppressing their emotions they are left with less contact with their inner selves. Boys learn that to be emotional is to be 'childish', and though this might be all right for girls, it is certainly not all right if you want to make it as a boy. We rarely appreciate the injuries that we do to ourselves in the process, for not only do we abandon our inner child but we lose connection with our inner selves. We also become less clear and defined in relation to our emotions and feelings and this affects the ways we are in relationships. If we are to restore this inner connection with self, then more is involved for men than a return to traditional notions of masculinity. We have also to come to terms with the *diverse* ways dominant masculinities have been shaped within modernity. Traditionally there has been little space and recognition of love, care and tenderness in men's lives or the importance of developing a feeling of connection with what we do. All this has seemed marginal to male identities largely cast within the terms of war and work.

Fear and Rejection

Why do men in modern Western societies so often feel haunted by an unspoken fear that we are not lovable and that at some level we are not capable of loving others? Not only do we find it hard to love, but we also find it difficult to accept the love that comes to us. Somehow this relates to how masculinities have been conceived within the dominant cultures of modernity, even if it is played out in the specific terms of personal histories. Some of this goes back to early childhood when boys often get the message that there is some deep flaw in their makeup, for as boys we are 'animals' that need to be trained if we are ever to become 'human'. Sometimes we absorb an unconscious feeling that if we were adequate then our parents would be willing to spend more time with us and would not, for instance, have abandoned us to boarding school. Often it is the case that fathers are just too busy to spend much time with their sons, but boys internalize this as a *rejection* that somehow proves that deep down there is something 'wrong' or 'inadequate' with them.

Often boys carry this hidden sense of rejection. They do not want to reach out towards others for they do not want to risk more rejection. It feels easier to turn in on yourself and learn that it is preferable to live without others. We often learn to hide our vulnerability because we interpret this as a sign of weakness that gives others grounds to reject us. So it is that we harden up. We close our hearts for we no longer want to feel vulnerable. It is a risk that we cannot take. We learn, especially in the individualistic ethos of the middle class, that we do *not* need the love and support of others because we can manage all right on our own. Often we want relationships because we do not want to feel isolated and lonely, but at the same time it is too scary to face what might be involved in giving and receiving love and support. It is easy to feel that if we can survive on our own, so others should be able to do so too. Often as men we withdraw into ourselves.

If we are not available to ourselves emotionally as men it is difficult to be available in our relationships. Sometimes we feel that we can only be ourselves and exist as individuals in our own right if we do not get too sucked into a relationship. Often we feel uncomfortable, especially as heterosexual men, with the emotional demands that our partners increasingly make. This is not something that our fathers had to put up with. Until the 1960s there was a general expectation that men and women wanted different things out of life and would be happier in each other's company. Women did not expect to receive much emotional support from their partners, but there was often a network of other women that they could draw on. It was the breakdown of the extended family and the emergence of new forms of housing after the Second World War that left couples in a much more isolated situation in the late 1960s. There was also the early stirrings of feminism that encouraged women to think in new ways about what they could expect from relationships. With working class women also having more access to clerical work there was more income around, which served to challenge the traditional division of labour within the working class family. Women did not see why they should be solely responsible for domestic work and childcare if they were contributing more equally to the income coming into the house. There was a different, more egalitarian vision of relationships that seemed to work well as long as both partners were working and did not have to confront issues around children. The easiest solution was to *put off* these questions till women were much older.

At some level men often carry a fear of intimacy that can have its roots in their early possessive relationship with mothers. Men can feel that if they get 'too close' they will begin to disintegrate. It is also that dominant notions of masculinity are organized around ideas of independence and self-sufficiency. This can make people feel that they should not need contact and that intimacy somehow serves as a threat to masculinity. *Iron John* does not do enough to challenge this traditional vision or to show where these feelings might come from. Sometimes Bly's work can foster a vision of an isolated man who, though he can draw upon the support of other men emotionally, still has to make it on his own in the world.

The competitive institutions of advanced capitalist societies mean that men are locked into competitive relationships with each other. Often we can only feel good about ourselves at the expense of other men. It is partly because we have such a weak connection with our inner selves that we are constantly comparing ourselves with what other men are doing. This serves to undermine the possibility of male friendships because it becomes difficult to *trust*. Sometimes we feel competitive with those we are closest to, because they provide a standard against which we evaluate our own lives. Because masculinity, especially in a middle class professional world, has so much to do with being 'successful' and 'achieving', it can serve as a pressure in whatever domain we might have chosen. Ambition and initiative have their place in our lives, but for many men they become the sources of meaning and value. Sometimes we can feel as if we do not exist outside of our work and the success we have made of it. We acknowledge the importance of emotional relationships but at some level we also feel that what matters happens elsewhere in the realm of work.[8]

Within a Protestant moral culture, men are haunted by a fear of rejection. It becomes hard to reach out to admit that we need help as men. We are constantly learning that we have to make it on our own. But this can leave many men feeling isolated and alone, even within relationships. Rather than helping us identify what we can change, there is too much in *Iron John* that still suggests that men are 'naturally' competitive and aggressive. Bly seems to fall back into thinking that these are aspects of our masculine biology that simply have to be accepted. Bly does not help us identify how men can change when he seems concerned that men should stop trying to believe that they can be like women. If it is important for men to redefine their masculinities, Bly often leaves us with misleading messages, since sometimes what seems to be the matter is that men are refusing to accept their masculinity. He has more usefully been an important voice in encouraging men to share themselves emotionally with each other, so learning to trust other men where formerly there was mere suspicion. But sometimes his messages are confused because he seems to be pushing in different directions at once.

Often men can feel locked into a lonely isolation that feels hard to break. Some men defend themselves against the risks of contact through feeling superior to others in a group. They stay on the periphery, wondering why they should share themselves with others who are 'not worth it' or who 'won't understand'. Other men feel trapped into a silence in a victim position, feeling that they are not entitled to a voice because others will discover what inadequacies they are hiding. They often feel that others will not listen to what they have to say, since what they might say will not be interesting enough. These different patterns can each work to make it hard to share ourselves with other men. Along with this goes an abiding sense of homophobia. We fear as heterosexual men that if we get too close to other men or share our feelings with them, others might think that we are gay. But it is also that we are scared of discovering our own emotions. We do not feel in control of the situation because we have suppressed our emotions for so long that we are left with little relationship with them. Since male identities are so often tied to notions of self-control we fear any situation that we might not be able to control. It often feels preferable to remain a stranger to our own emotions.

Part of the appeal of *Iron John*, as I have already argued, is in the guarantee that it can seem to give to men in advance that they will not turn into wimps, which was what supposedly happened to men who were influenced by women in the early anti-sexist movements. Bly's promise that hetero-sexual men will *not* find out they are gay, or put themselves at a disadvan-tage in relation to other men, drew many men who would have been suspicious of sharing themselves emotionally with other men. This third route which Bly promises, which allows you to avoid the charges of macho man on the one hand and wimp on the other, was very appealing. It could also draw men who felt antagonistic to feminism, even though this was not Bly's purpose. The idea that it is 'time for men to be men', with the hidden inference that women will be shown their place, was also part of the rhetoric for some.

Competition and Pressure

Within a Protestant moral culture, boys often grow up with an abiding feeling that there is something rotten in their natures. It is through hard work that we are supposedly able to assuage these feelings, but it is hard to silence the fear that someday others will find out what we are 'really like'. This can make it difficult to feel entitled in groups of men, where we might sometimes feel on the edge or the 'odd one out'. It is often through the power that men exercise in relation to women that they feel entitled. Also it is a feature of relations of power between men, as young boys learn to make anti-gay remarks as a way of dealing with their own insecurities. Often there is a *fear* of exposure when heterosexual men get together in groups which can make it hard for men to trust each other. For some men this was cracked in the early consciousness-raising groups, but sometimes these were hard to sustain because of difficulties men had in sharing their experience rather than talking about it.[9] It is this tendency to rationalize our experience as men that the wildman movement has been able to sidestep through its use of drums, music and dance. This has provided different ways for men to be together and gain trust and confidence in each other's company.

But in these contexts it does not really help to say that men are 'naturally' competitive or aggressive, for this can work to make it harder for men to trust each other. But it can seem that the rhetoric of men together can provide the guarantees that many men seem to need before they will share themselves emotionally. This is an instance of Bly pulling in different direc-tions. For all the insight that is contained in the story of Iron John, Bly can suggest that there is a single path with its different stages that men have to pass through. It can feel important for men to begin to acknowledge what they can receive from their relationships with other men that they might not be able to receive from women. Partly it has been because men have learnt to expect everything emotionally from women that men have learnt to take such little responsibility for themselves emotionally. This is what puts such a strain on heterosexual relationships. Also when men grow up to think of themselves as 'independent' and 'self-sufficient', they can find it hard to

acknowledge the ways they remain emotionally dependent upon their partners.[10]

If Bly's vision of the warrior acknowledges that the warrior can share his
vulnerability and hurt, it might be one thing to learn to do this with men
and quite another to reveal ourselves in the intimacy of heterosexual
relationships. It is often with intimacy that we have difficulties in our
relationships with women, but these are not faced. Too often the warrior
goes his own way. He must take the lonely path of self-discovery, though he
comes across people on the way. This might be a traditional male archetype,
but it is something we might also be wary of reintroducing. It takes humility for men to acknowledge our need for others, for it threatens the notions
of 'independence' and 'self-sufficiency' in a way that the language of the
warrior often fails to illuminate. In the vision of romantic love this is given
its own form, for 'if the relationship is good' then supposedly you should
not be in need of anything else. Sexual politics have helped us question this
ideal and so explore some of the hidden relationships of power at work.

Acknowledging that we have emotional needs is to admit to a vulnerability that can be scary. This is why it is often so hard for men to allow themselves to be looked after in heterosexual relationships. We do not want to
risk our control, and this is what we do when we make ourselves vulnerable.
Often we reject what our partners have to offer because the notion that we
have to do without is so deep seated. In the process our partners can feel
rejected and soon learn not to offer, and so it is that a distance is created
within a relationship. Partners learn not to expect too much and we, as
heterosexual men, are often so used to not having contact that we barely
recognize what has happened. It is as if we have learnt that we only need to
put energy into a relationship when things are going wrong. Otherwise we
learn that a good relationship is a relationship that you *can* take for granted.
Often men feel that they have more than enough to cope with at work, so
when their partners start making demands they can experience it as a
betrayal. Heterosexual men may respond with irritation as it can be safely
assumed that the well-being of personal relationships is the concern and
responsibility of women. Even if this is never said openly, it is still often
unconsciously felt.

It is harder for heterosexual men to feel secure in the notion that they are
working hard for the family, if they also feel at some level that they want to
be more involved with their partners and children than their fathers were
in a previous generation. At the same time the intensification of work in the
1980s and 1990s has meant that many men work very long hours and spend
very little time with their families. It can be hard to live with this contradiction, and often men can only deal with the inner pressure they carry by
drinking a great deal after work. Feeling locked out of their relationships at
home, it can be hard to reach out. Work often seems to bring the only recognition and validation they know. Men lock themselves away as they
surround themselves with enormous tension which they cannot release.
Sometimes if they feel that there must be more to life than this, they can

blame their partners for the frustration and unhappiness they carry. Men can begin to look to other relationships for an excitement that has left their intimate relationship with their partners. Marriages may come to an end soon after. But work holds so many middle class men in such a tight grip that the pattern is soon repeated in the new relationship, as people drift apart and have little sense of how to revitalize the contact between them.

Even when men feel silently desperate, it can feel very difficult to reach out for support and help. It is easy to feel that this will only make matters worse, for it will bring masculinity into question if we cannot sustain our self-sufficiency, the sense that we do not need others. For a generation in their thirties and forties it can be especially hard to share themselves emotionally with other men, partly out of a fear of homosexuality. We can drink 'with the boys', but this partly depends upon us being able to feel better through putting our emotions aside. Often where there are strong bonds between men, these are built around doing things with each other.[11] In a crisis things might change as men recognize that they *need* to talk to someone. Somewhat paradoxically, it is common for men to say that 'they can only really talk to a woman' and sometimes there is a woman friend around who they can share with more easily.

Consciousness-raising groups have been important for men as a means of learning that we can receive love and support from other men. It can be very significant for men to learn that they can be with each other and share themselves emotionally, for often it is scary to think of connecting to a group of men, especially if we still carry the scars of humiliation at the hands of other boys. This is not simply an exercise in men reclaiming lost power but can involve sharing a vulnerability that is often buried. Men have resisted joining these groups, saying that they were unnecessary for them because they *already* knew how to talk to women. But this was not the point. It has been comforting for men to think that anti-sexism has to do with helping women out in their struggles against institutionalized oppression. But often the best first step is for men to sort themselves out as men. The white knight needs to look at himself before he mounts his charger in support of women. Times have changed and it is crucial to start with ourselves. If we are unprepared to face the difficulties of change in our own lives, what insight can we bring to others?[12]

The point is that if men with diverse masculinities learn to take more responsibility for their emotional lives, this will take a great strain off relationships. The difficulties that we have in sharing ourselves emotionally with other men are reflected in difficulties we have in connecting to our inner emotional lives. This creates an imbalance and lack of equilibrium. In a talk in London in the early 1990s, Robert Bly shared the fact that a woman had refused to talk to her husband about an emotional problem he was having until he had already talked to one other man about it. This seems like a helpful rule. Often as heterosexual men we find it much harder to reach out to other men when we are feeling down. We might hover around the phone but it seems much harder to make the contact than when we are feeling up. It is shameful to have needs, especially in front of other men. We prefer to work things out for ourselves, for it feels much easier to share things when we have sorted out some solution. It is when we are unsure, and so out of control of a situation, that it feels hard to share. For it is when we feel vulnerable that we most fear that other men will take advantage and put us down.

If our heterosexual relationship is good we can easily feel as men that we should not need anything else. To go outside a relationship, as a man might experience it, can feel like an admission of defeat. Often there is a tight boundary that is drawn around an intimate relationship, as if it is a matter of the partnership against the rest of the world. Both partners can invest a great deal in presenting a 'good face' to the rest of the world, even to other heterosexual couples they are close to. This has to do with competition between couples but it also has to do with an *ethic* that issues should be worked out within the confines of the relationship. Men can feel bitterly betrayed if they think their partners have been talking about them. This might make it even harder for them to trust and they might just withdraw further. It is supposedly one thing to acknowledge that there are issues that need to be faced in a relationship, but quite another to talk about this with others. This creates a lonely space for many heterosexual couples. It becomes impossible to learn from the experience of others and easy to project either that everyone else has it much easier, or that 'talking about problems' can only make them worse.

Men often feel that talking about things can only make things worse. It is partly because we grow up with the power to think that we can create our own realities as men, and that we can invest our experience with whatever meanings we wish to assign, that it is easy to confuse language with reality. It has even become fashionable to think of 'reality' as an effect of language or discourse, which only affirms, as I have tried to argue in *Unreasonable Men* (1994), the power that men maintain in the theoretical realm to shape understandings within the terms of a dominant white heterosexual masculinity. So it becomes easy for different men to feel that if they do not talk about 'problems' in their intimate relationships then they do *not* exist, or else that they might disappear with time. Talking about them is what makes them 'real', and in some sense inescapable. This means that men often refuse to talk about what is happening for them. We think that things are 'more or less OK', for we learn to put up with relatively few expectations and expect others to do likewise.

Intimacy and Relationship

Even if at some level we are haunted by a fear that we are 'unlovable' as men, it seems to make it only harder to acknowledge difficulties that we have in relating. Often we withdraw and act defensively at the notion that we have difficulties we might need help to deal with. But if we find it hard to receive, because as middle class men we have learnt that to have needs is a sign of weakness, then it is hard to find a balance between giving and receiving in intimate relationships. If we have never learnt *how* to nourish our inner child, then it can be difficult to accept the nourishment others might be ready to offer. We will find it hard to take in emotionally, without feeling that our masculinity is somehow being compromised. With so little sense of self-nourishment it can be hard to identify the needs of our bodies and spirits. We become so used to refusing what is being offered that we have little sense of what nourishment contact might bring. As men we have so long learnt to live without, that we are often unaware of our own emotional hunger.

Within a capitalist culture it becomes easy to identify happiness with material success. As middle class men we become so focused upon achievement at work that it becomes difficult to identify what we have given up. Sex and love are so easily identified within a performance ethic that we often have little sense of what a nourishing contact can bring. Within modernity, as it has been defined in the West, there is little *recognition* of the body and emotional life. We become so used to living without contact in our relationships that we do not miss it. As boys we are often so split from our emotional lives at an early age that we become identified with the mental. There is little recognition of the heart and of the importance of establishing a deeper contact with ourselves. Within visions of postmodernity we have become even more suspicious of notions of 'depth', as we learn to accept the realm of appearances as the only 'reality'.[13] We can become mesmerized by the surfaces of a consumer culture, accepting that goods alone can be trusted to bring happiness. This is what we learn to sacrifice our working lives for, for we have lost a sense of other sources of value and meaning.

As sex becomes a commodity like any other on the market that can be bought and sold, it becomes difficult for men to disentangle the relationship between sex and love. If sex becomes a matter of performance it is a way of proving ourselves as men. Often there is a disconnection between the heart and the genitals. This is reflected in modernity in ways the connection between mind and body is conceived. The body becomes an *instrument* that is at the service of the mind. It is remarked that women often need to make emotional contact before they can relate sexually. Sexuality seems to have more to do with contact and expression than it does for men, who have often learnt to treat sex as a separate activity. As men we learn to think of sex as a 'bodily need', and often we do not like talking about what we want because this supposedly takes the magic out of the contact. Passion exists in an antagonistic relation to language. For men it is often simply a matter of what turns you on.

As men we learn very little about how to sustain sexual excitement within a long-term relationship. Partly because we can think of sex as discrete encounters we can find it difficult to place sex within a developing relationship. As it is, men may look elsewhere for sex once their partners become mothers. In part this has to do with what happens with sexual energy when there is a small baby around. Men can feel displaced as the attention of their partners seems to shift irrevocably towards the new baby. Men can feel dispensable, having previously felt at the centre of things. This can be a difficult transition for men to make, especially if they do not establish their own bonding with the new baby. Sometimes they can feel pushed out of the house because they cannot accept this transition in their partner's affections. Many marriages seem to break soon after the birth of a first child, for there is so little that prepares young couples for what to expect. It can be difficult to share some of the unconscious emotions that emerge in this difficult time. As far as some men are concerned their partners have simply become more demanding and less available to them. They begin to look around for other relationships, not knowing how else to cope.

If women close up emotionally because they no longer feel appreciated within the relationship, they often withdraw sexually. Heterosexual men may make matters worse by blaming their partners, because they assume that this is a process over which they have conscious control. Because we think of responsibility as something that can be *shifted* between individuals, we find it hard to think creatively about how distances are created. If women have an easier connection with their hearts, this is partly what makes them mysterious to men who seem to work in different ways. It is easy for men to feel rejected and so to act with hostility. Rather than making efforts to recreate contact within the relationship, men often withdraw further. It is partly because we grow up to assume that there must be something that we can do to make them feel better that we become so impatient so quickly. When we make efforts but they seem to make little difference, then we easily give up.

If women feel unrecognized in the relationship or taken for granted then they can find it hard to respond sexually. This can be difficult for heterosexual men to appreciate because we readily assume that we have control over our experience and emotions. But often this is a control built around suppression. It takes us time to realize what difference it makes for us to have feelings for our partners when we make love. Often this is scary for it leaves us too vulnerable and we withdraw. Feminism has helped to open up a language of love, vulnerability and power. It has helped women at least to understand how undermined they can feel if they do not have a means of expression within the public realm of work. Certainly it is because men are *so* focused upon work to sustain male identity that it is easy to take our partners for granted, whatever we might say. It is as if we learn to place our attention elsewhere, and they can be left feeling part of the wallpaper. Often women will blame themselves for what is happening, as if it reflects a personal inadequacy. But feminism has taught otherwise, as it has helped women to reflect upon the workings of power and subordination within relationships. It is not a question of sustaining an attitude of respect towards a partner for, as Simone Weil (1988) grasped, if respect is to be real it has to be *realized* in the everyday organization of institutions and practices.[14]

A feature of power is that middle class heterosexual men often find it easier to find *fault* with rather than to appreciate what their partners have done. We seem to sustain our position by finding the one thing that is not quite right, rather than affirming and praising all the things they have done. This partly reflects the self-critical voice that we use against ourselves constantly, but it has also to do with the ways we learn to sustain control within the relationship. If we think about it for a moment, we might be aware of how rarely we give appreciation to others and how readily we seem to blame. It isn't simply that we are applying the same high standards to others that we are applying to ourselves. It is also that an undermining tone begins to characterize the relationship, so people become wary of making themselves vulnerable to each other. Partners begin to expect to be criticized, so they *withdraw* their energy in subtle ways. People learn to put up with it because it has become habitual. Some of these patterns can be interrupted if we learn to offer appreciation and if we are also careful to make recommendations for how things can be changed whenever we have a complaint to make. This helps to separate the behaviour that we might be objecting to, for instance clothes being left on the floor rather than tidied away, from the person who no longer has to feel it so personally.[15]

Disdain is such a feature of dominant masculinities that it casts a shadow over intimate relationships. As men we often lack confidence to use other means of communication. Even if we do not want to put people down and make them feel small, this is often the effect. This is especially true within a middle class culture in which men have learnt to use language very much as a weapon. This is difficult to shift, because it is often rooted in the ways that men learn to bury their own pain and harden themselves against it. Sometimes even when we can feel supportive of the sadness or depression that our partners are going through, there is something that *despises* this weakness at the same time. As men we learn that being strong means giving support to others, but it becomes hard for others to accept this loving support if it always flows in one direction. In the end they begin to feel weakened because an imbalance is created that seems to get larger.

Since as men we learn to despise our own emotions as signs of weakness that threaten to bring our male identities into question, it is difficult to feel fully supportive of the emotional pain of others. Often it has to do with a hidden feeling of male superiority, for in a somewhat patronizing way we learn to expect different behaviour 'from women'. The ways that women allow themselves to express their emotions so easily serve as a confirmation of male superiority. Because we often remain trapped in these traditional notions of masculinity it is difficult to feel different about it. Bly's discussion in *Iron John* does not really help us with this, because in many ways he remains trapped in quite traditional notions of masculinity. He might help men to share their vulnerability with each other and even give evidence of tribes where this is common practice, but this remains something different because it is taking place between men. It does little to change our relationships to women, or really to help us to reflect upon the ways male superiority is sustained in the ways we continue to despise women's emotional 'weakness', even if we would rarely voice it.

This is particularly true of a younger generation of heterosexual men who have grown up since the dawn of feminism. They might feel much easier in their relationships with women, and many feel much easier and open with their gay men friends, but often there is a learning of appropriate behaviours. This can leave young men feeling confused: they internalize the notion that it is wrong to feel angry or resentful at their partners because this is an exercise of power, but then they feel forced to swallow these emotions which they do not know how to handle. Different generations of men can learn from each other in their responses to feminism. The issues of what it means to have a more equal and loving contact with your partner might be different, but there are similar struggles with the legacies of dominant masculinities. It is only as men learn to put the critical voice aside, so that they can *accept* more of their emotional lives and honour their vulnerability, that they will begin to love more openly and honestly. In part this involves learning *how* to love ourselves more, if we are also to be more loving with others.

Notes

1 A sense of the early bonding between mother and child is explored in the introduction to the theories of Margaret Mahler provided by Louise Kaplan, *Oneness and Separateness: From Infancy to Individual* (1978).

2 For some argument that homophobia, men's fear of other men, is the animating condition of the dominant definition of masculinity in America, see Michael Kimmel, 'Masculinity as Homophobia', in *Theorizing Maculinities*, edited by H. Brod and M. Kaufman (1995, pp. 119–41).

3 As things change in the sexual politics of schooling, so it becomes easier for boys who have been brought up to respect their emotions to feel less exposed and isolated and more able to draw support from other boys. For a helpful investigation of the different masculinities contesting with each other in school see M. Mac An Ghail, *The Making of Men* (1994).

4 A sense of the conflicts of growing up to be English coming from a background of Jewish refugees is given by Ursula Owen, *Fathers and Daughters* (1984); and in Marion Berghahn, *Continental Britons: German–Jewish Refugees from Nazi Germany* (1988).

5 The ways that children often feel responsible for what has befallen their parents are a theme in D. Winnicott, *Playing and Reality* (1974).

6 For some explorations of Gestalt therapy see, for instance, *Gestalt Therapy Now*, edited by Joel Fagan and Irma Lee Shepherd (1972).

7 To think about the contact and withdrawal that is so often a feature of intimate relations see, for instance, Lillian Rubin, *Intimate Strangers* (1983).

8 The difficulties of balancing the competitive demands of the public world of work with the cares of intimacy within personal relationships are a theme in Arthur Brittan, *Masculinity and Power* (1989); and Michael Kaufman, *Cracking the Armor: Power, Pain and the Lives of Men* (1993).

9 For a sense of how diverse men coped with the hopes and frustrations of consciousness-raising groups see *The Achilles' Heel Reader*, edited by Victor J. Seidler (1991c), which brings together writings from this period.

10 The ways that men are often dependent within heterosexual relationships are explored by Louise Eichenbaum and Susie Orbach in *What do Women Want?* (1984) and also in their

Understanding Women (1983). Often it is difficult for men to become aware of these dependencies because they have learnt to think of themselves as being self-sufficient and independent. Traditionally it is women who need the support of men.

11 We still need to explore the ways that men from diverse backgrounds learn to support each other. It is important not to devalue these forms of support, though it can be hard for men to draw upon them when they get into emotional difficulties they are not used to handling. For some reflections upon men's relationships with each other see *Men's Friendships*, edited by P. Nardi (1992).

12 Sometimes it is difficult for men to give time and attention to themselves without thinking that this is a form of self-indulgence. This is part of a moralism that blighted the sexual politics of the 1970s, as I have explored it in *Recreating Sexual Politics: Men, Feminism and Politics* (1991a).

13 The difficulties of recognizing different levels of experience within a postmodern culture which is closely identified with consumerist identities are a theme in Z. Bauman, *Intimations of Postmodernity* (1994). There is a growing awareness of these issues as we come to feel the absence of a discourse of value within a post-communist world.

14 Simone Weil talks about respect needing to be institutionalized in the organization of social life in the early pages of *The Need for Roots* (1988). I have explored these writings in *The Moral Limits of Modernity: Love, Inequality and Oppression* (1991b), where I link respect to power in a discussion of Kant, Kierkegaard and Simone Weil.

15 An awareness of the importance of changing everyday patterns of behaviour which are too often trivialized and devalued is crucial to Virginia Satir's *Peoplemaking* (1985).

12
Sexualities

Mind and Body

How we relate to others sexually partly reflects how we relate to ourselves sexually, for if we have grown up to despise our sexualities, how can we expect to respect the sexualities of others? Within an Enlightenment vision of modernity we often inherit a secularized form of the Christian *disdain* for the body and sexual life. The body is related to as a source of sin and temptation. This prepares the ground for the Cartesian tradition which largely defined the dominant terms of modernity. As white heterosexual men we learn to treat our bodies as objects which are separate and estranged from our 'selves' which within a Cartesian tradition are identified with independent and autonomous minds. The particular identification of a dominant white masculinity with a notion of reason separated from nature means that this relationship to our bodies is gendered. It is also racialized. It is hardly surprising that as white middle class men we learn to live in our heads.

Within modernity we learn to take for granted a dualism between mind and body, as I have already mentioned. Emotions are attached to the body and within the dominant tradition, largely shaped by Kant, they are 'inclinations' which interfere and distract from the path of freedom, autonomy and dignity that is set out by reason alone. There is little place for the heart and for recognizing the importance of establishing feelings as a source of meanings and value. Rather we learn that beliefs are concerned with reason and interests alone. As white middle class men we learn that the mind has to exercise a tight control over the body and its troublesome emotions. This prepares the ground for sexuality *as* performance for men and it establishes a link between the head and the genitals with little connection to the heart. So it is that sexuality is often for heterosexual men to do with conquest, performance and self-assertion. It has little to do with the vulnerability or the heart.[1]

Within an Enlightenment vision of modernity we also grow up accepting a sharp distinction between sexuality and spirituality. This is part of a Christian inheritance which in a secularized form continues to shape modernity. At some level we are still haunted by a sense of sexuality as dirty and evil. It has to do with our 'animal natures' and with the temptations of the flesh. It has to do with a sinful earth that can have few connections with the spirituality of the heavens. For Kant (1959) it is reason that exists as an autonomous faculty because it can have no connection with our natures, our 'empirical selves'. Reason alone is the source of our human dignity, morality, autonomy and freedom. We learn to disdain our natures as a sign of weakness, without appreciating the cultural and historical sources for feelings we take to be 'personal', and so feel uneasy and embarrassed about our sexualities. It becomes difficult to speak openly of our sexual needs, for speech is supposedly a rational activity separated from the movements of the body. But it is also difficult to allow the spontaneous movements of our bodies, for we have learnt in different ways that bodies as part of nature need to be controlled by minds.

Feminism has helped provide a new geography of desire when it is not interpreted in moralistic terms, for it has reminded women that they have their own sexual desires and that these are to be celebrated. This was quite foreign to an earlier generation that had learnt of sexuality as a duty which was owed by women to men. As women have become more active in their sexualities, so men have felt threatened in new ways. It has heightened an anxiety in relation to sex as performance, and often heterosexual men's sexuality becomes focused upon giving women an orgasm, as if their virility is to be measured by whether a woman has come or not. But men have been slower to recognize a need to share their *own* sexual needs more openly and to gain more contact with their own bodies. This is linked to the disdain of nature. Often we have little contact with our bodies as men, having learnt to treat them as machines at our disposal. This makes it hard to identify what kind of touch brings us nourishment and to appreciate sexuality as a form of communication. Often if we have little contact with our hearts then orgasm, as Reich (1974) appreciated, becomes a matter of ejaculation. Rarely does it involve a meeting of souls, for we just do not have this contact with ourselves. But again it is hard to acknowledge where we are emotionally as men; it is far easier to pretend that we are already where we want to be.

Sexuality often serves to conceal a whole range of different needs for contact, touch and affection. But it is hard to acknowledge such needs without feeling that our masculinity is somehow being compromised. It becomes easier to 'go for sex' in the vague hope that other needs will be satisfied on the way. Because acknowledging our vulnerability is often so scary, as men we tighten up so much around sexual contact. It is as if we want the sex *without* the contact because this threatens to bring to the surface a deep seated fear of rejection. Since traditionally it has been up to heterosexual men to take initiatives sexually but at the same time to suppress their fear and vulnerability, men often learn to ask without really asking. In different generations and different class and ethnic backgrounds men have learnt diverse strategies which work to keep their sense of male identity intact. Sometimes we are quick with our own rejections, saying, for instance, that 'I wasn't really interested in the first place.'

Often the abiding fear of intimacy that men feel is connected to the potential threats it offers to their male identities.[2] It is as if so little in the culture really prepares boys to grow up ready for intimate relationships. Often heterosexual men grow up so identified with the control they are supposed to sustain as men that it is difficult to allow themselves to be vulnerable. Being in control of a relationship acts as a security for men for it allows them to deal with the rejection if it comes. Sometimes this means making sure that heterosexual partners like us *more* than we are ready to admit liking them. Being cool fits into this nicely for it means that boys learn to sustain a distance. Sometimes they assume a cool self-confidence which they have not earned through the experience of life. This is learnt behaviour that often comes from imitating other boys at school, for the popularity stakes are high at school and boys cannot afford to make a mistake. As they grow up into heterosexual relationships they often feel isolated because they have had to sustain an image of themselves. Since they pretend to already know, it is hard to listen and to learn about intimacy and love.

Men's Bodies

As men we often grow up with an instrumental attitude towards our bodies. Our bodies are things that we *do* things with in order to prove both to ourselves and to others that our masculinity is intact. Testing ourselves against our bodies, say through sport, becomes a crucial way in which men can feel good about themselves. Sometimes if a man is feeling angry or sad, but unable to express it, he will tighten against his emotions and prove himself through some activity. He will take his anger out on the football or on the windsurfing sail. This is a way men deal with their frustration. As men we might not even be consciously aware of *how* we feel because, for instance, we failed to say something we had in mind. All we might know is that we feel rigid and tense as we tighten up. Often it is at moments like this that people's backs go. But within the culture we learn to treat the body as discrete and separate. If we deny the existence of the psyche and inner emotional life, as so many modern and postmodern forms of social theory have tended to do, we are often unable to see any connections with the way we have been living.

   Within modernity we have learnt to treat the body as a machine that functions according to its own laws and principles. We learn to treat it something like a car. If it breaks down it needs to be taken to the garage. Similarly it is doctors who have professional knowledge about male bodies. This sustains an *external* relationship with our bodies that allows us to continue using our bodies as instruments for proving ourselves as men. For instance, men will resist going to the doctor unless they have to because to admit help, even in situations of illness, can be felt as some kind of threat to male identities. It seems as if almost double the number of women to men 'present' to their doctors as depressed, although there is some evidence, especially in the United States, that men are starting to become less alcoholic and more depressed.[3]

   Often as heterosexual men we never learn about our bodies in different ways, or for that matter what might be involved in establishing more contact with our bodies. We never learn to *listen* to what our bodies have to say or to recognize how to nourish our bodies with care and attention. One of the striking features of basic sexuality groups run for men is how hard men find it to give an hour a day for themselves.[4] We seem to do everything to avoid establishing more contact with our bodies, since there seem to be always things that get in the way. Not only does it seem that we know very little about how our bodies work, having left so much of this up to the doctor, but we are often unused to touching and making contact with different parts of our bodies. This is why touch and massage can be so rewarding for men. We can feel that we have never really been touched in a nourishing way before and our bodies are hungry for contact. This resonates with ways we were touched when we were very small children. Often within the West there is a fear of contact through touch.[5] We feel embarrassed about reaching out physically towards others and fear our touch will be misinterpreted. This means that we are relatively unskilled in being able to differentiate between different kinds of touch. Psychoanalytic forms of therapy remain limited partly because of this taboo on touch which is deemed to be automatically invasive. It does not have to be this way.[6]

The men's movements have been important in providing the possibility for closer physical contact and support between men. This is something that gay men have long appreciated, but heterosexual men have often been homophobic about touch, fearing that wrong messages will be transmitted or that they will discover pleasures that feel too hot to handle for them. But many men have learnt about how to give and receive support from each other. There is nothing like a good hug from a close friend when you are feeling down. But as men we have learnt for so long to take pride in living *without* the support of others, especially other men. For too long we have learnt that standing alone without the support and understanding of other men is a proof of our masculinity. *Iron John* is ambivalent about this and can be confusing because it pulls in different directions at once. The initiations into manhood it describes can help us accept the love and support of other men, but traditionally they have too often been an exercise in teaching men to survive on their own, even if it is with other men. We can learn that we have to be as tough and self-contained as others. We do not learn *how* to share our vulnerability and need with other men. It is a slow process for men to learn to trust each other, especially with our histories of competitive relations in which we are often put down and made to feel small.

With Durkheim (1961), we have learnt to treat the body symbolically as if it reflects and expresses mythical and societal relations. We assimilate the body to cognitive modes of representation and so fail to appreciate that the body has a life of its own and that this is mediated through relations of gender, 'race', class, ethnicity and sexual orientation. We have different bodies and they assume different shapes, reflecting how we have learnt to experience life. Often within the West we learn to conform and fit in, as we squeeze our bodies into acceptable moulds.[7] We treat the body as disobedient if it fails to conform to what we expect of it, for it is supposedly an

instrument that has to obey the dictates of the mind. Within a Christian tradition the body has long been distrusted for it tempts us into sin and transgression.[8] We learn to despise the body and to silence its desires. As the
body becomes a machine within the terms of late modernity it is equally
denied a voice of its own. The body is to be trained and it is to be com-
manded. It is to become an instrument of our will. This is especially so for
men. Women can sometimes develop a different relationship to their bodies
because of the cycles of menstruation which can call for a more intimate
response to the movements of the body. But this has been largely hidden
within the dominant patriarchal culture.

Bodies and Emotional Life

Wilhelm Reich's (1974) work still remains crucial in helping us understand
the emotional life of the body. Within a structuralist tradition his work has
been too easily dismissed as 'biologistic'. This has been a pity since it has
held back our learning and has largely reflected an ambivalence and disdain
for the body and emotional life which has haunted modernity. Meaning was
firmly situated in the mind and the body became *disenchanted* along with
the rest of nature. It was to be grasped according to the external laws of
science. It was through language that we were supposedly to 'know' the
world as 'socially and historically constructed'. But this stubbornly repro-
duced the modern distinction between nature and culture with the idea that
nature was 'given' and existed outside the boundaries of history and
meaning. Supposedly it was only within the realm of culture that we could
talk about 'meaning'. This was to sustain the humanist vision that it was
human beings alone, through their minds, who were the source of meaning
and value.

Though Reich remained trapped in a positivist vision of science his sensitivity to the body as a source of knowledge represents, as Myron Sharaf
recognizes in *Fury on Earth: A Biography of Wilhelm Reich* (1985), a crucial
challenge to the Cartesian paradigm that has shaped dominant visions of
modernity. It opens up a tension between our thoughts and our feelings and
emotions, our minds and our bodies. There is a dialogue that needs to be
reinstated as we *learn* to respect both our emotions and our somatic experience. Too often we have regarded them as 'irrational' and 'subjective' and
so as interferences and interruptions in the flow of knowledge that has its
source in reason alone. In helping to reinstate the body and emotional life
Reich makes us aware that our bodies have a history and that they exist as
part of culture as well as part of nature. The dualistic boundaries which
structure late modernity begin to dissolve as we learn to appreciate how our
emotions are inextricably tied up with the histories and structure of our
bodies. We learn to disconnect from our bones as men through identifying
a dominant white heterosexual masculinity with reason alone.

Reich recognizes ways that as men we learn to tighten ourselves *against* emotions and feelings. This is a process of armouring that shows itself in the tone and structure of muscles, giving a particular shape to our bodies. Our bodies reflect our experiences growing up into manhood. Initiation into manhood has long involved a process of splitting, for we had to learn to swallow our tears and tenderness. We learnt these qualities to be 'unmasculine' so they had to be suppressed. In so doing we *cut off* from our hearts, unable to feel even when we want to. As we harden our hearts as men it becomes difficult to feel a connection with what we experience. We learn to disdain experience and treat it as a sign of masculinity. Often as middle class men we are very hard on ourselves, always pushing ourselves forward against bodily limits so that we can prove ourselves. Men take different paths into manhood, for there are different masculinities, but often they involve a hardening against particular emotions and feelings.

Heterosexual men learn to sustain a sense of masculine identity through feeling superior within relationships. It is as if men have to prove themselves constantly in relation to partners. Often this connects to the control that men insist on sustaining, though paradoxically they deny the control they wield, thinking it is somehow in the interests of all. Partly because we can grow up within competitive relations feeling that we have to be the best, we can only feel good about ourselves at the expense of others, often those we are closest to. Such structures of superiority and inferiority take many different forms. Often there is a smouldering resentment that breaks the surface when least expected. Sometimes a sense of superiority goes back to the ways boys were treated by their mothers, constantly expecting things to be done for them, never really having to make efforts themselves. Sometimes this is encoded in religious traditions. I know from my own experience how easy it is for Jewish men to feel superior in relation to women because of the centrality of men's relationship with God in the tradition. An emotional softness might be allowed, but this is often tied up with an abiding sense of superiority.

Within the terms of late modernity men can easily feel superior to women because of their emotionality. It is because women are more emotional that they supposedly need a support from men that men do not need from them. This gives men from various backgrounds even more incentive to suppress their emotions. Often we hold on to our emotions for years, learning to *tighten* up against them. This can also be true of our anger, which comes out in all kinds of indirect ways, especially for middle class men identified with their 'reasonableness' and 'rationality'. We can grow to be scared of expressing anger because we have so little relationship with it that we fear being overwhelmed. Traditional forms of psychoanalytic therapy have relatively little experience with anger work since they treat it as a form of 'acting out'. Again this reflects a failure to discriminate, for there are very different forms of expression of anger. But the removed stance that is so much a part of training for analysts can make it difficult for them working with their own anger, let alone with others.[9] They have much more to offer for men who need emotional containment and possibly a detailed working through of early childhood experiences.

As we hold anger bodily in the jaw and in the shoulders, so grief and sadness are held in the chest area. If we have locked away our grief or have learnt, in Bly's useful term, to 'ascend' over it, we will often experience a deadness and lack of movement in our chest area. We have to be careful to be flexible in the ways we interpret this emotional geography of the body, for it is a matter of processes of change that we are linking into. We have learnt particular patterns as young children which involve both the ways that we learn to hold our bodies and also the ways we respond to situations emotionally. Often these are so habitual that they are difficult to identify. Unlocking and becoming aware of emotional patterns involves a process of exploration that can take us back into emotional histories as we learn to 'let go' of emotions we have held for so long. This means that the pasts we have lived, often unconsciously, are literally *embodied* in the ways that we organize our bodies, emotions, feelings and thoughts. Often our attitudes are tied up with our emotions, in a way a dominant rationalist culture has found it hard to acknowledge and theorize.

Weakness and Strength

As men growing up within the terms of late modernity we often remain fearful of weakness. We do not like being considered 'weak' for this is a threat to our very masculinity. A weak man is not a man at all, or so we learn. This fear is played out differently within different masculinities, but often men respond harshly to an accusation of weakness, experiencing this as an attempt to humiliate them. Somehow emotions have been identified with *weakness* so that we learn that to be 'strong' means being 'in control' of your emotions. This attitude makes it difficult to share our vulnerability and tenderness, without first knowing that we are in control of the situation. This is a form of self-protection which means that we minimize the risks we might otherwise take with ourselves. It involves a shift of attitude to recognize, perhaps surprisingly, the courage that it takes to share our emotions with others. This is risky, especially if we do not know how we are going to be heard.

Bly learns in different ways from Freud, Reich and Jung that it is only when we have come to terms with our emotional histories that we can make a proper transition to manhood. But like them he remains trapped by traditional notions of masculinity at the same time. Freud (1953) tends to treat the feminine as an 'enigma' because he sees sexuality in masculine terms and tends to judge women by the terms set by men.[10] This leaves women's sexuality defined as a lack and it becomes difficult to develop an autonomous vision of women's sexuality in the terms defined by Freud. Often people turn to Jung (1986) because his language seems to create space for both the 'masculine' and the 'feminine'. He recognizes the importance of men coming to acknowledge their 'anima' aspects and the ways this helps them integrate aspects of themselves that remain hidden and unappreciated. But there remains a strong strand of masculine superiority within Jung's writing, even if there is more appreciation of the 'feminine'.[11]

Bly also seems haunted by a fear of men who have become 'feminized', and this is part of a suspicion of feminism in its relation to men. He recognizes the importance of men sharing their vulnerability, especially with other men, but remains uneasy, at least in *Iron John*, about the importance of relationships with women and children. It is as if a threat to our masculinity lies dormant here so that it is difficult to acknowledge how our tenderness and vulnerability might be important aspects of our masculinity. These are qualities that we might well be able to learn in our relationships with women, if we can find ways of letting go of our controlling superiority. This is an issue of power and control that Bly avoids, finding it easier to say that feminism has allowed women to define themselves much more clearly than men. So now it is the time for men to regain their masculinity. But one cannot help feeling that this is a masculinity that has been *threatened* by women. This echoes a traditional fear that it is women, especially in their sexuality, who are a threat to men. Rousseau's fear has been given a new form in the threatened 'feminization' of men.

Iron John sets the transition to manhood in such symbolic terms that it can be difficult to discern what is at issue. Bly's talk of the inner warrior can be helpful in identifying the difficulties that some men have in standing their ground and knowing what they want and need for themselves. This is an issue for men who easily accommodate to the wishes of others. If we have grown up to be 'good boys' then we often do not want to disturb the peace and we want to fit in with others. This is an issue that also emerges quite strongly for women who have more clearly grown up to put the interests of others before themselves. But it has also become an issue for men, especially in relation to feminism, and Bly helps to identify it. But the language of 'warrior' is not very fitting in this context for it suggests that it is a particular issue for men. I doubt this. Rather it relates within postmodernity to larger social processes of identity formation which no doubt are also gendered and sexualized. It relates to a pervasive corporate culture, as Bly also identified. Somehow in a corporate culture it has become threatening for men and women to have strong beliefs and desires, for this can bring us into conflict with those in authority. We learn to play the game and become *adaptive*, shaping ourselves according to the expectations of others. A weak sense of identity in the 1990s seems to offer a secure way of 'getting on'. It has also to do with a loss of vitality and spontaneity that affects men in corporations and bureaucratic institutions who have learnt to evaluate themselves according to external rules and expectations and who have to deal with women in managerial positions.

Again we can be confused because Bly pulls in different directions at

once. He talks about the warrior but he is clearly anti-militaristic in his
stance. Sometimes the argument wobbles when he talks of contemporary
leaders, though his individual insights can still be withering:

> If you have any doubts that patriarchy has damaged men, look at George Bush.
> He epitomizes that theory in which business and success is everything, feeling and
> grief are nothing, dominating other men is everything, having friendships with
> other men is nothing. You have to realize that Bush is like a ten year old boy. He
> hasn't had any initiation. He's not a man. Lincoln was a man. During the Civil
> War he felt the suffering of the other side deeply. Bush, after they'd finished killing
> 150,000 Iraqis, first thing he says is 'Great, that'll get rid of the Vietnam thing.' No
> compassion at all. This is a dangerous boy here. (*I-D*, 'Identity' issue, November
> 1991)

I'm not sure whether it helps to say that Bush was not a man. He is a very
dangerous kind of man and there are lots like him in leadership positions.
He represents a particular kind of masculinity that needs to be carefully
located. It is a masculinity which does not feel the sufferings of others. But
it is possible to feel the grief and also continue with the killing. We have to
be careful how we think about this. Bly might be right that drumming 'helps
take people out of that academic setting, helps them drop down out of their
heads and into their stomachs. Drumming is a good way of forming a bond
between men. Something happens when groups of men drum together' (*I-
D*, 'Identity' issue, November 1991). This is all very well, but sometimes this
bonding can *submerge* crucial differences that exist between men that also
need to be explored. For we need both our heads and our stomachs.

We can learn from this bonding between men but it can also sustain a false
sense of community which could show itself in quite different attitudes
towards the war with Iraq, say. It is important not to suppress these differences between men, whilst also learning to celebrate what we can share
together as men. It was an abiding strength of feminism to recognize that
consciousness has both personal *and* political aspects. You can grow in your
sensitivity as a man but still lack in political awareness about the ways patriarchy and capitalism have operated over long periods of time.

But it is still important to value what men can give to each other through
contact. There is an important initiation that can take place within same-
sex groups. There are also important initiations that require the participation of different sexes. These are different ways that can help men to
deepen the contact they have with themselves. They can help men to
identify their physical and emotional needs and so to define themselves
more clearly. This is part of a process of *individuation* that needs to take
place in different spheres of our lives. For it is only when we are clearly
grounded in our own experience that we can negotiate more equally with
our partners. This is equally true of heterosexual and gay relationships.
Sometimes we have learnt to give up what we need or want for ourselves,
either because we do not feel entitled to be nourished and satisfied, or
because we have identified ourselves with an ethic of self-denial. Often we
do this as men because we have inherited a sense that it is quite wrong for

us to have needs at all. We have learnt that to be 'strong' means to be able to do without. So we become fearful of discerning our own desires. We do not want to know them lest they show us in a compromising light. But often this means that we end up feeling silently resentful, doing what we do not want to do with the aim of pleasing others.

Sexuality and Control

In sexual contact this often means that as heterosexual men we can push for orgasm because we feel so uncomfortable in our bodies and deaf to our own sexual needs. Feeling embarrassed of talking about sex, we take refuge in the notion that if sex is to be passionate then it is to be unspoken. But often this reflects the cultural unease we feel with sexuality, feeling at some level that it is still dirty and 'animal'. This is part of what makes it so *difficult* for us to begin to listen and respond to the movements of our bodily desire. Often we feel trapped as observers of our own experience, watching ourselves from a safe distance, not feeling too involved with what is going on. Since we learn to identify with our minds, it is as if the sex is happening to someone else – for our bodies seem to be 'persons'/objects in their own right. This is part of the confusion that men can still feel in relation to heterosexual sex. It feeds an uneasy sense that we cannot really take time over contact but that somehow we should 'get it over with as quickly as possible'. It becomes difficult to *enjoy* sexual contact in its fullness if we are still trapped within an instrumental relationship with our bodies. Since we have so little relationship with our bodies it can be difficult to enjoy the contact with others. Sex remains an issue of performance for so many men. We learn very little that might teach us different.

Even though there is much more cultural talk in the 1990s of bodies and of sexuality, this often remains strangely disconnected, as if bodies interact with each other in a sphere of their own. Often the theoretical language is empty and rhetorical because we have so little in experience that would help ground this language and make it meaningful. Since sexuality is so readily commercialized and objectified within the dominant postmodern culture, it is hardly surprising if we *shrink* from language that promises us deeper contact with ourselves. This can feel like a romantic withdrawal, as if we are saying there is a space that remains untouched by relations of power. Foucault (1980) dispels such false consolations but in the end gives up the notion that sexuality is an exercise of power alone. He recognizes how sexuality easily becomes boring.[12] He is seeking a different ethical relationship to the self. He is looking for ways of caring for the self that do not involve conforming to external rules of behaviour. Attempting to escape from the limitations of a discourse analysis that refused to recognize anything beyond language, Foucault is attempting to care for himself in different ways. This seems to involve developing an ethics of sexuality that can respect bodily emotions and desires. It rejects a Kantian moralism which would legislate

for particular acts and behaviours. Rather people have to learn to relate
with tact and kindness towards each other. They also have to acknowledge
and respect the feelings and emotions of others. This is a path Foucault
seemed to be treading in his last years, but it is very much at odds with the
general project he had earlier conceived for himself. Possibly this was a
response to his own developing illness.

Within late modernity so many of our intellectual traditions serve to
sustain the control that a dominant masculinity seeks over experience. At
some level we fear losing control as a sign of weakness. This is part of what
has *devalued* the notion of 'experience' within rationalist traditions. We
have little respect for learning from experience. Rather, experience is something that we are committed to controlling, either through meaning and consciousness in the tradition of Weber and phenomenology, or through
language and discourse within structuralist and poststructuralist traditions.
The point is that life is there to be controlled, not to be lived. Once we recognize that we cannot control life, as Spinoza, Bergson and Deleuze seem to
appreciate, but that we can learn to respond creatively and with feeling to
it, we begin to appreciate that we are involved in a meaningful process of
living. In part it means learning *how* to sustain a clear sense of self while
being able to respond to others and the wider political world. This is not
something to be solved through reason alone. It involves forming a deeper
connection with aspects of ourselves so that we do not have to 'cut off' and
'separate' from what is happening for us. This involves appreciating how to
live a just and fulfilling life that we cannot control.[13]

Bly tempts heterosexual men into thinking that they can turn away from
women, and all the difficult issues that arise in intimate and sexual relationships, to find each other 'as men'. This seems like a return to a traditional
vision of masculinity that is no longer viable. In part it is a refusal to face
the difficulties of what it means to be a man after the challenges of feminism. This involves a different kind of emotional work than Bly seems able
to recognize. This is not to minimize Bly's contribution and the very real
insights offered in *Iron John*, but it is to place his struggles in a larger
context. Bly is also responsible for unwittingly giving support to men who
want revenge on feminism, who wish to return to a power they could once
take for granted. Bly does not say enough about these difficult questions of
sexuality. Where he helps is in identifying issues that have to do with men's
unease and loss of vitality in their bodies. He also reminds heterosexual men
of what they can learn from each other if they are prepared to make themselves emotionally vulnerable with each other. But Bly does not really help
men to illuminate confusions they feel in relation to women or to think
clearly about their relationship to feminism.

Iron John has been important in helping men to explore their own gender
ground and to gain crucial insights into a particular process of growing from
boyhood to manhood. But if he does not recognize the *diversity* of paths
boys can take but focuses upon a single line of development which can too
easily be normalized, he at least helps men identify the dark spaces they too

easily want to avoid. But too little is said about relationships with women and the impact of the women's movement which we need to explore to clarify the predicaments that men face in the contemporary postfeminist world. It becomes too easy to blame feminism for the ways men have lost their 'gender ground', and even for making men feel that they have to placate and accommodate because women have morality and virtue on their side. This is the backlash against feminism we can find in the men's rights movements. If Bly helps to restore a balance in relationships by helping men to a clearer sense of their own identity, he does not go far enough in illuminating issues men and women face in creating more equal relationships.

Notes

1 For some discussion of heterosexual male sexualities and the ways they can be connected to performance see, for instance, *Men, Sex and Relationships: Writings from Achilles' Heel*, edited by Victor J. Seidler (1992); *Male Order: Unwrapping Masculinity*, edited by R. Chapman and J. Rutherford (1988); and R.W. Connell, *Masculinities* (1996).

2 I have explored the links between fear and intimacy in heterosexual relationships in *Rediscovering Masculinity: Reason, Language and Sexuality* (1989).

3 For some interesting work on the ways that men present themselves in terms of alcohol and depression see *Men's Health and Illness*, edited by Donald Sabo and David Frederick Gordon (1995).

4 Some of the ideas that have informed the basic sexuality groups that have been organized with men from diverse cultural backgrounds are explored in Bernie Zilbergeld, *Male Sexuality* (1980) and Linda Levine and Lonnie Barbach, *The Intimate Man* (1983).

5 An interesting exploration of the place of touch within different cultures is provided by Ashley Montagu, *Touching* (1971). This taboo on touch was continued within classical psychoanalytic work where it was deemed to interfere with transference.

6 Body oriented forms of psychotherapy have more openly explored the respectful use of touch. Of course it is possible for the relationships of power between therapist and client to be abused, so careful ethical guidelines need to be in place.

7 Stanley Kellerman has done important work on the relationship between mind and bodies and ways we learn to organize our bodies so that they conform to what is culturally expected. See, for instance, *Your Body Speaks its Mind* (1975), *Somatic Reality* (1986) and *Living Your Dying* (1979).

8 An exploration of the renunciation of the body and sexuality within a Christian tradition is provided by P. Brown, *The Body and Society: Men, Women and Renunciation of Sexuality in Early Christianity* (1989). This work influenced Foucault in his influential writings on sexuality, particularly in relation to the later volumes of *A History of Sexuality* (1980), *The Use of Pleasure* (1985) and *The Care of the Self* (1986).

9 An appreciation of the importance of therapists continually working emotionally on their own issues, rather than thinking this is completed with the end of their training analysis, as well as a recognition of the dangers of the detachment so often encouraged within traditional psychoanalytic encounters, is present in James Hillman's recent work. See, for instance, *One Hundred Years of Psychoanalysis and Still the World Is No Better* (1993).

10 For some discussion of Freud's views on female sexuality see, for instance, Jessica Benjamin, *Bonds of Love* (1990); Nancy Chodorow, *Feminism and Psychoanalysis* (1992); C. Bernheimer and C. Kahane, *In Dora's Case: Freud–Hysteria–Feminism* (1985); and Janet Sayers, *Mothering Psychoanalysis* (1991).

11 For some interesting engagements with Jung's writings on sexuality see, for instance, Andrew Samuels's *Jung and the Post-Jungians* (1986) and his more recent *The Political Psyche* (1995); R. Stevens, *Jung* (1994); and James Hillman, *Revisioning Psychology* (1975).

12 Foucault gives an interesting account of how he sees the development of his work in relation to sexuality in 'Technologies of the Self', in *Technologies of the Self*, edited by L. Martin, H. Gutman and P. Hutton (1988). There seems to be a theoretical rupture since he cannot explore issues of identity, self and ethics in terms of the framework of knowledge/power that he was formerly working with.

13 The change in Foucault's concern is clearest in *The Care of the Self* (1990) where he recognizes that this is a matter not of putting certain principles into practice but of developing a different, more attuned and sensitive relation to self. This calls for a different kind of moral education from what we can know within modernity.

13
Responsibilities

Power and Control

Myths have their own sense of time, and if they carry important lessons for us as men about lost or neglected aspects of our masculinities, it is important not to lose a sense of historical and cultural time. For our lives, as men growing into different masculinities, need different kinds of grounding. Bly recognizes the ease with which contemporary masculinities encourage men to 'ascend' over their experience. It is because we are often tied in knots of self-rejection that we feel a pressing need to prove as men that we are other than what we are. Within the secularized forms of Christianity which persist in shaping so much of liberal moral culture within modernity, we learn as men to despise our bodies and emotional lives. We learn to train our bodies as if they were machines and to suppress our emotions as if they only exist as reminders of an aggressive 'animal' nature and as interferences to our rational selves. We also learn to treat the earth as 'feminine' so it becomes easy to insist that progress within modernity involves the control and domination of nature.[1]

If we have experienced close and protective relationships with our mothers we can spend many years in a process of separation. At some level we can learn to despise our mothers who are unconsciously identified with the emotions we cannot allow ourselves as men, unless we threaten our sense of male identity. But as we separate from our mothers we can also be escaping from ourselves, for we have often lost control with our denied emotions and feelings in the process.[2] We have hardened our hearts in the process and lost an inner connection with ourselves, as we learn to *prove* ourselves against other men. Rather than accept our diverse experiences as men we learn to devalue experience within an intellectualist culture and so inherit difficulties in sharing our pains as well as our joys. We learn to ascend over pains as we minimize their impact on our lives, learning to speak to ourselves in a language which says, 'It wasn't all that bad', 'I survived so it could not have hurt that much.' These become ways, as I have stressed before, of testing our male identities against our bodies and so of affirming our masculinities and proving ourselves as men.

Within modernity there is an identification between a dominant white heterosexual masculinity and reason, for men learn to think of themselves as the rational sex. This connects to the power and control men often insist on sustaining over their lives. With the disenchanting of nature that characterizes an Enlightenment vision of modernity, there are no values or meanings to be discovered in nature. Rather human beings, which meant white European men, were supposed to assign meaning to a nature which was bereft of value. As men were to learn to control their experience through suppressing their emotions and feelings, they also learnt to control outer nature. Control became intimately tied up with masculinity, so much so that to lose control of oneself was deemed to be a threat to one's male identity. As the mind was to control the body, so reason was to control the emotions and control was understood as a form of domination. It was not through developing a relationship with our emotions that we were supposed to exercise control, but through suppression. This is what helped to produce an abiding fear of emotions, for they were deemed to be a prelude to a lack of self-control.

So it is hardly surprising that as men, particularly middle class white heterosexual men, we learn to live in our heads and we learn to construct 'reality' according to our wishes. It is an aspect of the power that we grow up to take for granted within modernity that we can give meanings to our experience as men and have the power to negate anything that might threaten the meanings we assign. So it is that as men we insist, in a Weber-ian tradition, that we have control over our experience through controlling the meanings it carries. This is part of the temptation of a rationalist tra-dition within modernity which insists that experience is ordered through the categories of the mind. In this way we silence the conflict and tension that might otherwise arise between our thoughts and our emotions, for we insist on shaping emotions accordingly. We only allow ourselves, as I have been trying to argue, those emotions which we *know* we can rationally defend in advance. This also relates to the devaluation of experience as a category within the intellectual cultures of late modernity. But already within an empiricist tradition we only knew experience as something external, rather than something we can enjoy an inner relationship with.[3]

This connects to the issue of power and control within relationships, for it becomes important for men to be able to silence women who might be challenging meanings heterosexual men assign to their experience. So it is crucial for men to be able to diminish women's challenges as 'emotional' or 'subjective'. It is men alone who can take for granted their 'objectivity' and 'rationality'. Somehow this control over experience and relationships, to which men hold tight, is tied to the difficulties men often have in accepting experience and learning from it. We are so focused as men upon what we *should* be feeling and thinking that it is hard to acknowledge what we are experiencing. We are wary of this contact with our experience because it might shame or embarrass us in front of others. We are encouraged to split from our emotions which might otherwise work as sources of knowledge about experience. We learn to disdain our natures as 'animal' within a Kantian framework and so identify with reason alone as the source of freedom and autonomy.

Similarly our class, ethnic and gender experience are treated as forms of determination and unfreedom. In their different ways they reflect a weakness of the will, for they show within a Kantian tradition that behaviour is being influenced by external forces and is not operating under our control as free and autonomous rational selves. So it becomes difficult to ground our experience either in our emotional lives and histories or in our class or ethnic backgrounds. We learn within the dominant framework prepared by Kant (1959) to separate from these aspects of our experience. We are left divided against ourselves, often in a stance of self-rejection, for we learn to live up to standards not of our own making and to evaluate experience according to external norms. In ourselves we are sinful beings who require salvation. Put in more secular terms, we are failures who need to prove our adequacy through showing that we are more able or competent than others. We are left with a very thin conception of personal identity, for it is only as rational selves that we can know ourselves as free and autonomous. Often we take our blessings for granted, for we are aware of what we have not achieved in a struggle to constantly prove ourselves. Even if we know different it can be difficult to adopt a different attitude to ourselves, for it is harder to change attitudes than we conventionally imagine.

Identities and Histories

As we learn to identify ourselves as rational selves within an Enlightenment vision of modernity, we learn to abstract from our emotional histories and from the social relations of power and subordination within which we live. It is as if we are constantly pulling away and ascending from our experience, so finding it hard to acknowledge *what* we are living through, even to ourselves as men. Learning to live in our minds it is easy to feel distracted and withdrawn, especially in intimate relationships. We are constantly looking away from ourselves into the future, for it is there that we will eventually prove our adequacy. We become identified with the aims and goals we have set ourselves through reason alone and we are constantly assessing and comparing where we are in relation to them. As middle class heterosexual men it can seem as if we have no bodies and no emotional life, for we are constantly testing ourselves against the limits of our bodies and suppressing our emotions as interferences that can only threaten the goals we have set for ourselves. Put crudely, we live in an externalized relationship to ourselves. We should be hardly surprised if every so often we wake up to the recognition that life is passing us by. For at some level we are not living our own lives, but living lives others have prepared for us.

If middle class life only has meaning because of the goals we have reached, we can feel constantly under pressure, for there is always more we can achieve. There is always room to feel disappointed and that we should have done more. Often what we lack is an inner connection with ourselves which might at least help us appreciate our achievements. This is a vision quite at odds with a capitalist ethic which always leaves open the vista of what we *should* be doing with ourselves. This is what makes it difficult to *ground* our experience as men either in our histories or in our emotional lives. If we have learnt within a liberal moral culture that to know ourselves is a psychological task, somehow separated from our class, ethnic and gender histories and, sexual relationships, we will be constantly denying and abstracting from what might give our lives more meaning. For we learn that it is only when we leave our pasts behind that we can discover freedom and autonomy as individuals in our own right. We rarely learn that we have to come back to work through these diverse histories if personal identities are not to be thin and attenuated and if we are also to recognize solidarities and shared experience with others.

We have to be ready to do this emotional and cultural/historical work *if* we are to grasp where cultural visions and expectations of manhood come from. For it is hard to change as men unless we also understand what has helped make us who we are as men. This is to broaden the vision of psycho-therapies too often trapped within individualistic and familial assumptions, as if experience can be adequately grasped by understanding hurts and suf-ferings endured within the family. It helps us if we can realize that we are never simply the 'products' of our background and that there is always an interaction and dialogue taking place as we shape ourselves in relation to the expectations of others as well as what we strive for ourselves. It is impor-tant not to lose sight of a growing individuality and the risks we have to take to assert it, as we come into deeper contact with different aspects of our-selves. But if it is true that to know *who* we are, we have to know *where* we have come from, then the links between emotions and power, therapy and politics become indispensable, even if they remain hard to disentangle and work with.

But it is only if we have learnt how to ground ourselves in the earth and the social world that we can begin to draw from the heavens and so find spiritual grounding. For we begin to learn that we cannot do without others as men. This is a painful lesson when we realize how hard we have strug-gled to live *without* the loving support of others. We can also begin to recognize that there is a reality beyond ourselves and our individual needs and fulfilment. As we break through the isolation and aloneness we so often feel as men, learning to share experience with others, we can some-times experience a sense of love and support quite new to us. As we learn that growing into manhood involves relationships and responsibilities, we can begin to trust that others will also be there for us, so that we do not need to be so self-sufficient and independent. Since men are so used to dis-counting their emotional needs it can take time to discern the different needs we so often conflate. Within a rationalist modernity that has suppressed the existence of spiritual traditions separate from the insti-tutions of religion, it also takes time to recover a sense of spirituality as men. Again where there are so few spiritual and political models around we can often feel that we are literally groping in the dark. But sometimes we find our way to a light that reminds us of a sensitivity long forsaken in boyhood.

Power and Ethics

With the challenges of feminism many heterosexual men from different backgrounds have become confused about what it means to be a man. Often we have lost a sense of our gender ground, as it has been easy to feel that because men have power we are *not* entitled to have our own pain or sufferings. Since it is women who have so long been oppressed by the institutions of patriarchy, and suffered rape, violence and harassment at the hands of men, it is easy for men to feel that there is no way that we might begin to celebrate the conditions of manhood. When we are aware of the violence that is exercised against women and the ways their experience is devalued and their bodies abused, it can seem almost immoral to complain about the conditions of heterosexual men. *Iron John* has helped men to realize how destructive it can be for them to feel demeaned in their own eyes, to feel that there are no ways in which masculinities can be redeemed. But it has also encouraged men in men's rights movements to feel that they have little to apologize for, since as they can only be responsible for themselves they have not been personally responsible for this oppression of women. It has tempted men into thinking that they can only be held responsible for their own abusive behaviour towards women, not in any way for the mistreatment and oppression women have suffered over time.

But history leaves a moral legacy and the ways we grow up to inherit masculinities as men reflect the powers men have traditionally exercised in families. Often, as boys growing up in the 1950s and 1960s, we have been treated quite differently from our sisters. We enjoyed different freedoms and privileges: we were not expected to do the washing up, for instance. If times have changed at all with the impact of feminism and ideas of gender equality, and parents are more concerned to treat their children more equally, boys still often have a much easier time in getting attention and space for themselves. But it is quite wrong to think that boys are always the problem, for this blinds us to the issues and the deprivations and humiliations they are silently expected to put up with in their own lives. It is not simply that we benefit from the power men have exercised over women in the past, but that our sense of ourselves as white middle class heterosexual men has largely been shaped through these histories and experiences. A sense of male superiority is often not far from the surface.

There is a widespread recognition that as heterosexual men it is crucial for us to *change* our attitudes and behaviour both towards ourselves and towards women, gay men and lesbians. As we begin to accept emotional vulnerability it might make us more aware of what others are going through and more tolerant of ourselves. As we find a less defining place for reason in our lives, so that our lives no longer consist of an endless argument in which as middle class men we are having to constantly prove that we are right, we will hopefully communicate more equally with others. As a dominant reason is no longer so firmly and categorically set against nature, we can begin to accept more of our inner 'natures'. Emotions, needs and desires no longer have to be suppressed to confirm our identities as rational selves. This hardness in relation to inner nature reflects a callous and utilitarian attitude towards nature generally. For in different ways we have become suspicious and distrustful of nature. Often we can only trust our inner natures if we are already firmly in control. This means learning to listen to ourselves in different ways *if* we are to begin to trust our inner natures.

As we begin to appreciate ecology and so recognize that our humanity does not have to be defined as a relationship of superiority towards the 'animal' world, we can acknowledge that in important respects we are part of nature. This can help us begin to feel a little more accepting and tolerant of ourselves. When we feel threatened we police boundaries very sharply and as long as we experience our natures – emotions, feelings and desires – as a threat to our masculinity, we suppress them before they have a chance to show themselves. There might be some kind of dialectic which means that as we become a little easier and less judgemental with ourselves as men, so we can also appreciate nature around us with its seasonal rhythms in different ways. If we are less tied to a Eurocentric modern vision that nature has to be tightly controlled because it is a measure of our 'civilization' and 'progress', so we become more open to developing a relationship with nature. We are more ready to listen and to attune. This is why we cannot sharply separate the attitudes we have towards ourselves as men and the ways we learn to regard nature. As we allow more balance between reason and emotions, treating the latter in their own ways as sources of knowledge, we can also sometimes feel more open and responsive in relationship to nature. In this regard at least, ecology is inseparable from ethics.[4]

Blame and Responsibility

Men have often felt defensive in the face of feminism, and especially the notions that have been around for the last 20 years that 'all men are shits' or that 'all men are insensitive' or possibly that 'all men are unemotional.' Feeling unrecognized, men often protect themselves through hiding, withdrawing or withholding within relationships. This has been less destructive as heterosexual men have learnt to adapt to what women want, but often this has been wounding to men's own sense of self-esteem. It has been easier for men to forsake the region of personal and intimate relationships, thinking that here at least women know best. But this signals a withdrawal as men seek satisfaction and recognition at work when it is available, and try to minimize the conflicts at home. But this does not help in developing more open and equal relationships between the sexes. Rather men learn to *withhold* what they think and feel because they want to avoid conflict. Sometimes this withdrawal is legitimated through the idea that because women have been oppressed for so long they have virtue on their side. But at some level men often do not believe this is at all, for they remain secure in the notion that as possessors of reason they 'know best'. Rather it can be a new form of the old idealization of women, which works as yet another way of not having to take their experience and values seriously.

Sometimes men think that through living their identities in the public world of work and leaving women to take responsibility for social and intimate life, they are giving to women the power they are demanding. This is another form of the idea that feminism should be left to women and that it has nothing to do with the lives of men. But women have also made demands upon men to change, so that men begin to take more responsibility for their emotional lives, leaving women freer to live their own autonomous lives, rather than having to concern themselves with making sure their partners are happy. Bly readily blames older men for not having taken more responsibility for the upbringing of younger men in families, but he misses that this is connected to ways heterosexual men have absented themselves from relationships with women. Often women have looked for the love and support from their sons because of what they are not receiving emotionally from their partners. This creates imbalances in a relationship, helping to produce the very emotional structure which Freud universalizes as the Oedipal complex. As women make emotional demands on their partners, so men often withdraw into themselves.

As women feel that they are not being met in their partnerships, they become frustrated and angry. Often it turns out that women are carrying the anger for both partners, which is why it feels they are constantly bad tempered. It is because men refuse to acknowledge their own anger that it is left to women to carry it. Men can sometimes feel self-righteous as if their refusal to show their anger is a mark of superiority. It proves that as men we have a *self-control* that women lack. But this notion is not well grounded, for it reflects a difficulty of heterosexual partners meeting on equal ground. Sometimes it reflects a difficulty that men can have in defining themselves emotionally so that they do not recognize what they need for themselves. Often they 'go along' with what their partner wants in personal life, thereby thinking that she is more likely to be happy and that in any case she will have no grounds to complain. But this accommodating behaviour does little good, because in the end both partners remain unrecognized and unfulfilled.

This does not always reflect a personal choice on the part of white middle class men to withhold themselves emotionally within intimate relationships. Rather this is connected to the ways male identities are structured elsewhere within the public world of work. It is not that men are not emotional but that they are often emotionally tied to their work and to how they feel at work. This is what causes friction and unease in relationships, as women feel that they are not met emotionally within their intimate relationships. These somehow remain central to the sense of well-being they can feel as women, while middle class men can feel that in their detachment they are behaving perfectly reasonably. There is a way in which women's lives, even when they are climbing a career ladder, remain more centred on what is going on in their intimate and sexual relationship. If this is going well they often feel they can cope with the world. In contrast, men seem to feel that what matters, at least as regards sustaining their male identities, happens at work. Men can feel that they are there to support their partners and to be listened to when there is trouble at work. Often different things seem to matter in life and this creates difficulties in communication across gender, though obviously this is mediated by class, 'race', ethnicity and sexual orientation.

Often as men we learn that there is always something that we can do to make things better. But things do not work this way in intimate relationships, when quite a small incident might eventually work to finish a relationship. Then it is often impossible to retrieve the love that has gone. We can find this hard to accept and can feel bitter that our gestures of reconciliation seem to do no good. Often then we turn to blame someone, perhaps our partners, for what went wrong. Growing up within a Protestant moral culture, we think of responsibility as something that can be located specifically, and this allows us to disclaim any responsibility ourselves. It makes it harder to recognize that *both* partners are involved in what goes on in a straight or gay relationship. Sometimes patterns get established, especially in long-term heterosexual relationships, which we find hard to recognize. If our partners feel that they are being taken for granted and gradually give up hope of making changes in the relationship, then it can be quite a small incident that ends the relationship for one partner. As men it can feel unreasonable to put such emphasis upon a single incident as a cause for ending the relationship, but this is often because we have failed to appreciate how distances have been created over a long period.

If we can convince ourselves as heterosexual men that it was really our partner's fault that the relationship ended and that, for instance, if they had not shown an interest in other men we would still be together, then it is easy to feel that things might be very different with a new partner. It is only when we have had a series of relationships that seem to reproduce similar patterns that we are more likely to acknowledge our part in what is going on. Sometimes this happens to men in their early thirties, and they then sometimes become interested in therapy. It is as if as men we learn either to be adept at placing responsibility on to others, or to believe that there is no point in dwelling upon the past. We look to the future and we learn to 'turn over a new leaf'. But this means that we rarely learn from our experience. Within the postmodern intellectual culture there is little that helps us reinstate experience as a source of knowledge, and since this partly reflects our experience as men, we learn to discount experience as 'subjective' or 'personal' and so as easily put aside.

Listening and Appreciating

Because as middle class heterosexual men we so often learn to control our emotions, we are wary of getting into emotional spaces within relationships. Sometimes we cut our partners off because we can sense what is coming and we do not want to deal with it. We have little sense that some issues have to be worked through emotionally before they can be resolved. We can feel that our partners are being intrusive when they fail to appreciate the difficulties we have with intimacy. But sharing how hard we can feel when they want to make eye contact, or sit closer to us than we feel is comfortable, is a way of being more honest and intimate, rather than putting up some kind of pretence that we feel comfortable when we do not.[5] In part it has to do with both partners learning how to respect each other emotionally and to recognize that personal change involves a process that takes time. As heterosexual men become more confident in sharing their emotional position, it becomes more possible to *listen* to what partners have to say. Often it is easy to feel that they do not want to be absorbed by their emotions so they prefer to keep them to themselves, because they are having a hard enough time maintaining control of themselves.[6]

But it is hard to listen to others unless we have learnt how to listen to ourselves emotionally as men. It is easier to think that our partners are being 'irrational' or 'unreasonable' because we have learnt as men to listen for the truth-value of what someone says. We learn to evaluate what they are saying in terms of reason and logic. But often this means being removed and detached from what it means emotionally for them. This involves quite a different relationship to ourselves for it means *tuning in* at levels we are not used to responding to. This is a source of misunderstanding within relationships for it means that men are listening for different things, often assuming that it is our task to provide solutions for 'problems'. This is the way we learn as men to give support. But often all our partners want is to be listened to for this is the way they feel affirmed and validated. But we miss this, for we assume that they will want to rid themselves of their sadness or depression, since this might be what we would want. They eventually withdraw as they feel frustrated in the contact.

If our partners share with us that they are feeling sad or that they are feeling uncomfortable with their bodies, often they just want to be heard. This is part of validating and affirming their experience. But if we find it hard to listen because of what it touches emotionally in ourselves, we might give them suggestions for the way they might feel happier, or exercises they might think of doing to shift the ways they feel about their bodies. Not only is this advice not wanted, but it can make our partners feel wiped out and unheard. They can feel criticized, as if we are yet again finding fault with who they are and what they do. Often in heterosexual relationships women complain of not being heard. It is partly that as men we fail to appreciate what they want from the contact and assume it must be the same thing we are looking for as men. This can make them feel so little appreciated and cared for in the relationship.

This ties in with the difficulties that men, but also women growing up within the competitive terms of late modernity, have in appreciating what they do. It is as if we begin the next project before we give ourselves time to appreciate the fruits of our labours. Sometimes we fear the revenge of the gods if we stop to appreciate the efforts we have made. We do not want to bring misfortune onto ourselves so we learn to avoid anything that smacks of 'self-indulgence'. Rather we are haunted by a sense that whatever we do we could have done better. Within a Protestant moral culture we easily feel that we are never good enough. This attitude pervades the educational system so that as children we are used to teachers telling us what we have done *wrong* rather than appreciating what we have managed to do. They are constantly finding fault, and this shapes the ways we learn to talk to ourselves. It would involve a revolution in attitudes for children to feel recognized and appreciated for what they do. Often this is the only way that children can learn to build their self-esteem and sense of self-worth. As white middle class men and women we often grow up to be too hard on ourselves, never learning how to feel good about ourselves or how to build self-esteem. Bereft within late modernity of any inner relationship to ourselves we are at the mercy of others, constantly looking to others to compare ourselves with. There is little sense of the uniqueness of our individualities, even within a liberal culture which supposedly takes pride in them.

We need visions of initiation which do more to appreciate the importance of men reconnecting with their emotional lives. If Robert Bly has helped men recognize their vulnerability, especially in relation to their fathers, he still leaves us with a slightly terrifying and unyielding vision of masculinity. When men are not together in groups they are still often left isolated and alone, unable to reach out towards others, especially when they feel down. As Terry Cooper has talked of this in a men's group he was leading at Spectrum North London, it was easy for his son Jody to identify with him when what he did was exciting, going out into the world of sport or doing windsurfing. But unless he was careful this served to separate Jody from his mother and to diminish what she tended to do with him in the house. It involved a subtle rejection and devaluation of the female and the domestic sphere. This is something that Bly misses in his demarcation of the mother's house from the father's house. It leaves us with too traditional a conception of masculinity still identified with the public realm.

Not only was it crucial for Terry to learn to be more involved within the domestic sphere and to recognize this as equally a sphere for men, so validating domestic work and childcare, but he could do this because in Jody's early years he had been able to arrange to spend half-days with him. This had created a bond of intimacy and understanding that he can still draw upon and develop. While there might be a difficulty if we think of childcare exclusively as a set of discrete activities that can be shared equally, it is also important to negotiate a fair division of labour. Men and women might have different facilities and different levels of tolerance, but it is difficult to generalize. At the same time I think it is important to break with the 1970s notions of sexual equality that failed to appreciate gender difference.[7] It might well be that fathers have something *distinct* to offer to their children and that parenting also has to be appreciated as a gendered activity. Different energies are brought into relationships with babies and small children, and distinct personalities are involved. This is something that parents recognize who know how different are the personalities of their children and how this cannot be accounted for by theories of socialization alone. We need new ways of thinking about gender differences in childhood without forsaking aspirations towards equality which take on new forms.

As fathers we can offer something particular to our sons, which does not mean that we are not equally involved with our daughters. But it might be that we also have to recognize differences that we have not wanted to acknowledge because they seem to threaten visions of equality.[8] But it was a mistake of libertarian politics in the 1970s to construe equality as sameness. *Iron John* has helped to question some of this, but at the cost of shifting to another extreme which serves to reinforce gender differences, especially when Bly is tempted into saying 'Men are really tired of being told they should be women' and when he seems to identify maleness with aggression. For all the insights in *Iron John* there is still, as I have shown, a traditional vision of masculinity that holds to an essentialist vision of gender. At some level there is a sense that men have been the way they are for too long to think that they can change. Again there is inconsistency, for there is a lot of insight in the particular that is betrayed in the general argument. Men do not have to be macho, but nor do they have to be 'feminized'. If this is to be acknowledged we need a different vision of *how* men can be with each other as well as be in relationships.

Terry had to carefully reintroduce Jody to his mother, through helping him to appreciate the different things that she did. He had to appreciate that the mother's house was the father's house too. This was to go against the grain of a patriarchal culture which would tacitly diminish and devalue what takes place within the home. Excitement was what went on when you left home, or so boys often learn. This was a way of creating greater harmony within the relationship and a way of helping Jody to find more balance between male and female. Again there is a process of growth and development here that takes time. It is in no sense a matter of conforming to some pregiven ideal, but is one of recognizing that we all need different things at different moments in our lives. As we grow, experience takes on a different shape. Here we can still learn from the wisdom of nature, for as a seed grows into a plant the petals express their beauty and then give way, falling to the ground. In part it involves learning how to respect a *process* that also has an inner rhythm and timing which it shows in its outer expression. As our children grow we have to learn what freedom is appropriate for them, as they learn how to earn the trust and responsibility it also involves.

Notes

1 The ways that the earth is treated as 'feminine' and progress is identified with the control and domination of nature is a theme in Susan Griffin's *Women and Nature* (1981) and *Made from this Earth* (1982). See also M. McCormack and M. Strathern, *Nature, Culture and Gender* (1980); and E. Fox Keller, *Reflections on Gender and Science* (1984).

2 For some helpful reflections on mothering and the separation that boys make from their mothers see, for instance, Nancy Chodorow, *The Reproduction of Mothering* (1978); Dorothy Dinnerstein, *The Rocking of the Cradle and the Ruling of the World* (1976); and J. Treblicot, *Mothering: Essays in Feminist Theory* (1984).

3 For some discussion on the devaluation of experience within the intellectual cultures of modernity see, for instance, Iris Murdoch, *The Sovereignty of Good* (1970); Simone Weil, 'Human Personality', in *The Simone Weil Reader*, edited by George A. Panichas (1977); Jean Grimshaw, *Feminist Philosophers* (1986); Sara Ruddick, *Maternal Thinking: Towards a Politics of Peace* (1990); and Victor J. Seidler, *Unreasonable Men: Masculinity and Social Theory* (1994).

4 To explore the relationships between ecology and ethics see, for instance, Brian Easlea, *Fathering the Unthinkable: Masculinity, Science and the Nuclear Arms Race* (1983); Marshall Berman, *The Reenchantment of the World* (1981); and E. Benton, *Natural Relations: Ecology, Animal Rights and Social Justice* (1993).

5 Men from diverse cultural and sexual backgrounds can learn to be more open and honest in their intimate relationships in the context of men's consciousness-raising and therapy groups. Some of the difficulties that men often have in emotional expression are explored in Victor J. Seidler, *Recreating Sexual Politics: Men, Feminism and Politics* (1991a).

6 The relationship of dominant masculinities to notions of control is explored by R.W. Connell, *Gender and Power* (1987); Arthur Brittan, *Masculinity and Power* (1989); K. Solomon and N. Levy (eds), *Men in Transition: Theory and Therapy* (1982); and V.J. Seidler, *Rediscovering Masculinity: Reason, Language and Sexuality* (1989).

7 For some reflections upon shared parenting see, for instance, Virginia Held, 'The Obligations of Mothers and Fathers'; Diane Ehrensaft, 'When Women and Men Mother'; and Susan Rae Peterson, 'Against Parenting', which all appear in Joyce Treblicot (ed.), *Mothering: Essays in Feminist Theory* (1984).

8 To think about ways fatherhood can be reworked see, for instance, Samuel Osherson, *Finding our Fathers* (1987); John Hoyland, *Fathers and Sons* (1992); and *Fatherhood*, edited by Sean French (1992); bell hooks, *Feminist Theory: From the Margin to the Centre* (1984); and Carolyn Steedman, *Landscape for a Good Woman* (1995).

14
Spiritual Groundings

Self-Rejection and Empowerment

In recent years feminism, psychotherapy and ecology have helped us to rethink the relationship between 'inner' and 'outer', for they have shared a sense of the need for people to change themselves individually as part of a larger process of social and political change. They have helped restore empowerment as people begin to sense how individual change is vital if the world is to be transformed and the planet redeemed. The feminist notion that 'the personal is political' has helped to reinstate the importance of sexuality and personal relationships, so that love cannot be separated from power nor reason separated from emotion. Ecology has also challenged the modernist distinction between 'private' and 'public' for it has made people more aware of being responsible in their individual actions. How we think and how we behave as individuals *matter* if our world is to survive. We also begin to see ourselves as part of nature and so refuse the categorical distinction between 'culture' and 'nature' that has been internalized as a relationship of superiority within modernity. In the West we learn to take superiority for granted because we supposedly have 'culture' and 'science' as part of our birthright while 'others' have 'nature' and 'spirits'. Often a pervasive sense of superiority is tacitly communicated within our schooling without us being aware of the attitudes taken on, for at another level we can pride ourselves in a liberal tolerance.

Within the dominant Christian traditions in the West we have learnt to disdain the body and sexuality as 'dirty' and 'sinful'. In many ways this has served to poison the springs of our creativity, for so many people seem trapped in patterns of self-rejection and self-blame, making it hard to trust and value their ideas and emotions. It is as if, for instance, the fact that 'I' have thought of something means that it cannot be any good, so that we are always looking beyond ourselves for a validation that rarely comes. A Protestant moral culture has powerfully shaped subjective experience in the West, teaching people to put the needs of others before their own and making it hard for some people to *recognize* the needs and desires they carry. In this way we are constantly learning to discount ourselves with the idea that it is 'good' to be 'selfless'. We are very hard on ourselves, constantly pointing the judgemental finger at ourselves, unable to value anything that we produce. This is something that women often feel acutely, though feminism has gone some way to question these cultural assumptions.

Often as men we can only feel good about ourselves if we put others down.

We can feel constantly trapped in competitive comparisons with other men, and relationships with men become unbalanced because we always have 'to be right', 'to know what is best'. Since within a Protestant moral culture we inherit a notion that our natures are 'evil', we are always struggling to prove that we are 'other' than we are. Haunted by fears of *inadequacy*, we can seem trapped into continually proving ourselves man enough. This creates enormous pressure that men learn to carry as a sign of honour. The pressure somehow feeds us, for it allows us to feel that we are affirming our masculinities. But often we are doing too much and the resentments are building under the surface. Unless we become more aware as men of some of these processes, our backs give way or we get ill, for we have never learnt how to listen to our bodies. Rather, they are despised and often punished for letting us down when we need them most. For our bodies as machines have become property that is at our disposal. Our freedom supposedly lies in being able to do with them whatever we will. If they let us down we can feel they deserve to be punished. But the body has its own way of getting its revenge.

Within modernity we inherit a sharp distinction between the earthly and the spiritual. It is as if we have constantly to leave our bodies behind, as part of a disenchanted nature, if we are to ascend to the spiritual. These notions live on in secularized forms. It is only because we can leave nature behind that we can be secure that we are 'civilized' and 'modern'. Bly draws upon different spiritual traditions as he helps us to reinstate the spiritual qualities of the body as part of nature. He recognizes how the escape from the body into reason and the head, and the escape from sexuality into a disembodied vision of knowledge and spirituality, can leave us ungrounded. Escape does not bring us *back* to ourselves or give us ways of working on the emotional histories we carry. Rather modernity can give new form to the traditional notion, which men so easily identify with, that there is no point dwelling upon the past. In this way we learn to separate from our experience in the present and past and we look to a future that can be controlled by reason alone. Too often this is a form of *escape*, though it is attractive within a culture that for so long has denigrated nature, sexuality and the body. If nature is sinful, we learn to leave it behind, to ascend to a spiritual realm.

Within a Christian tradition that is built around notions of sin and transgression we are often left aware of our failings and inadequacies, as if we are constantly struggling to live up to ideals that are not of our own making. We feel resentful because, as men, we are left with so little time and space for ourselves. We can feel guilty in taking time for ourselves, especially if our partners are busily engaged in the house or homework with children. It is as if we have to justify taking time for ourselves since it always has to be 'earned' or 'deserved'. This leaves many middle class men with an abiding culture of self-rejection in which, as I have argued, it becomes hard to even acknowledge our personal needs and desires. Many men take pride in not having any emotional needs for they are a sign of weakness and inadequacy. But then they are left to pile on the pressure for themselves, barely recognizing how low they are feeling or how frustrated. This is hard for middle class men who so easily accommodate to the needs of others, finding it hard to define their own needs and desires more clearly. Often there is a layer of resentment smouldering just beneath the surface. It can find expression in snidey attacks and in putdowns that are rarely owned, for often we can defend what we have said when challenged.

Heaven and Earth

Visions of a creation based spirituality have helped us to discover a different relationship between Christianity, Judaism and Islam.[1] In reclaiming the Jewish sources of Christianity we can begin to learn a different relationship to nature, the body and sexuality. The land is fruitful and is a place of milk and honey. The abundance of nature is to be celebrated. We begin to learn that we can only draw from the heavens if we have begun to do our work on earth, for the task, at least within a Hebraic tradition, is to recover the spiritual *within* the earthly. The earthly is not sinful but exists as a source of spiritual work, and the covenant is a process of sharing a task of creation that has not been completed. We are involved in a partnership in the processes of creation, for we are all born in the image of God. This is a theme of original blessings as opposed to original sin which Mathew Fox (1983) has done so much to recover within lost traditions of Christianity. It is also related to a recovery of the feminine, for the devaluation of nature has gone together with the denigration of the female within modern Western culture.

Ecology helps us understand that the earth has to be redeemed as a source of spiritual value. This has to go along with transforming understandings of ourselves as part of nature and so questioning a humanist tradition that has too readily identified humanity as a relationship of superiority to nature and the 'animal'. This relationship of superiority is too often echoed in a gendered relationship of superiority and inferiority between men and women, for men learn to identify women with emotions that have no place in masculinist identities as rational selves. But if we are to reinstate emotional lives as sources of meaning and knowledge we have to rework Western conceptions of personal identity. As men we have to be ready to face ourselves in different ways in exploring the self, which means facing emotional histories that have long been suppressed. This takes courage and humility, for we have to begin to acknowledge how *little* relationship we have with our emotional selves. Rather than turning away from our histories we have to face them. Only if we can open up communication with our inner emotional lives can we learn to communicate more openly and honestly with others.

But this reflects a break with an Enlightenment tradition of modernity which has seen nature as disenchanted and dead. As nature was reduced to matter, so our bodies were reduced to machines. We were left with an external relationship to our emotional lives which, as I have argued, were deemed to be forms of unfreedom and determination. But if we are to find

ways of acknowledging emotions and feelings as sources of knowledge we
have to begin to listen to our bodies in new ways. They silently carry the
experiences of our past. As the Sufis have it, 'the body is the temple', and
it has to be cherished and honoured as such. We have to discover ways of
listening to its wisdom as we learn to connect more to our hearts.[2] At some
level men remain fearful of establishing a deeper contact with themselves,
for they have not learnt to trust themselves in this way. Rather as men we
learn to harden our hearts as a way of affirming our masculinity. But in
losing contact with our hearts we are losing the possibility of establishing a
deeper contact with ourselves. This is something that various spiritual traditions have recognized. The Psalms talk of the importance of gaining a
heart of wisdom. But if we have been ready to challenge the terms of
modernity in the discussions around postmodernism, we have been slow to
recognize the wisdom of diverse Eastern and Western spiritual traditions it
so cruelly displaced.

We have found it easier theoretically to challenge the terms of modernity
and the vision of the unified rational self it proclaims in the name of a postmodernity which speaks in Eurocentric terms of the fragmentation of identities. Often we are left with a provisional sense of identities as if freedom
lies in their continual reconstruction out of what is culturally available. We
become suspicious of the integrity of different spiritual traditions, thinking
that it is only through the mixing of hybrid traditions that we can recognize
and articulate the issues we face in a postmodern society.[3] But if it is valuable to honour the different notions that can be borrowed from different
traditions and the fact that many people seem to feel uneasy within the
terms offered by any particular tradition, we have also to *value* the integrity
of particular spiritual traditions and what they have offered to the world.
This is yet to happen in the discussions around postmodernity, which too
often leave us with a sense of the relativity of human values, as if they exist
as individual choices alone.[4]

But there is a danger of missing the depths of particular spiritual traditions, and their complex relation with diverse Western philosophical
writing, if they are too easily related to each other. We can be left with a
very superficial grip of diverse histories and cultures that have grown over
long periods. We can only meaningfully talk of tolerance *if* we are also prepared to validate difference. Often we still find this difficult, for despite critiques we are trapped within a modernist notion that implicitly holds that
differences are superficial and that underlying the surface there is a shared
humanity. Postmodern writings have wanted to talk of differences but they
have often cast them in individualist terms, or else in terms of the unsettled
categories, of 'race', class, gender and ethnicity. We have been slow in contrast to acknowledge the integrity of different spiritual traditions, partly
because we have also wanted to engage with them critically, say for their
visions of nature, their treatment of women, their conceptions of homosexuality, disablement or authority relations. But in postmodern writing we
are in danger of sustaining the very Eurocentric superiority and arrogance

that has been part of a modernist tradition. We assume, especially as men from diverse backgrounds, that we know best and that somehow we can still feel secure of the postmodern positions from which we critique and evaluate these traditions. But this is simplistic and reflects a failure to listen to what these traditions offer.

Writings around postmodernity have also been cast within the secular terms of Western modernity, even if they have wanted to break with the sovereignty of reason which modernity sustained. If we are left with a plurality of different spiritual traditions we find it hard to recognize the values they carry, for these can be undermined by the familiar postmodern notion that 'anything goes'. We have yet, as the later Wittgenstein grasps (1980), to rethink the distinctions that were so firmly established within modernity between 'reason' and 'faith', 'spirit' and 'matter', 'mind' and 'body', for at some level contrasting theorists of modernity share different kinds of secular materialism. But as Simone Weil recognized in her later writing in *The Need for Roots* (1988), the distinction that was drawn between the humanities and the sciences within modernity left no space for spirituality. What is more the identification of spirituality with religion meant that it was difficult to engage critically with different religious traditions and the authority relations they so often embody. It was hard, she argues, to recognize the integrity and diversity of spiritual needs which were too often dismissed as false expressions of unmet material needs. In an orthodox Marxist vision they would supposedly wither along with the state.

But Weil refuses to contrast the 'material' with the 'spiritual', and though she gets trapped into a Christian ethic of self-denial, wishing to reduce even herself to matter in the hands of God, she does open ways for recognizing spirituality as part of a revisioned material process of growth and development.[5] It is a slow and difficult process that involves discipline and honesty as we learn to face ourselves in ways that are often uncomfortable. We have to recognize feelings and experiences in relationships, even if they are painful. In learning to be more open and honest with ourselves we have to be more honest with others. Different spiritual traditions have recognized the importance of learning to speak from the heart, but this *cannot* be achieved as a matter of will and determination. We do not have the kind of control of our experience that modernity suggests. Rather there is a whole process of personal growth and development that Eastern spiritual traditions have often been more aware of. Since for years, especially as men in the West, we have systematically learnt to harden our hearts, this cannot easily be undone. Rationalist traditions, which have been dominant in the West as Wittgenstein and Weil both acknowledge, have left us with impoverished conceptions of personal growth.

Inner Work and Outer Work

For men growing into different masculinities it can be particularly challenging to ask from where in our lives we get our nourishment, from what particular relationships and activities. As we grow up within late modernity *not* to need, and to identify masculinity with being independent and self-sufficient, it can be helpful to wonder when and how we get our needs met. This is particularly significant since identities as men are still so often established within the public realm of work. Even though heterosexual men are more prepared to acknowledge the importance of their relationships, often these are unwittingly taken for granted as forming the background against which we learn to live out our individual lives as men.

At some level many heterosexual men seem to live as if they do not need relationships at all, especially if most of their energies go into work. So often men become dependent upon work as a habit that is difficult to break. It is only when marriages fail and separations take place that men begin to *value* what they have lost. Again this is structured into ways male identities are established and sustained within Western cultures, so that men are shaken when they realize what they have so easily put at risk. I remember how hard it was for me when my partner said that she was ready to leave because she just was not getting enough for herself from the relationship. It was a terrible shock, but what was most shocking was how unaware I was of what she was feeling. I found it hard to sustain a balance between the demands of work and family life and seemed to constantly drift into giving priority to work and losing connection with my partner and children. Of course there are always particular issues that come into play, but for me they had to do with a difficulty in sustaining a feeling connection in everyday life. I would move from one activity to another, one demand to another, but somehow found it hard to sustain an everyday connection. It was as if my energy was elsewhere, trapped in a mental space, so that it was easy for her to feel that she was simply not getting enough from the relationship.

Creating more harmony within a long-term relationship with children does not just involve inner work, as some Jungians have it, but also crucially involves who does what, and how a whole series of emotions, activities and practices are validated. As children grow up with more contact with their fathers a different sense of balance can be created within relationships. As women's lives in the 1990s are less limited and prescribed than they traditionally were, they face similar issues of how to balance their different activities in private and public life. Again there are few ideal patterns, and there is a compromise when partners have different levels of earning power. This involves careful negotiation if paid work is not to take precedence and if people's different times are to be equally respected. Again it has to do with the quality and quantity of *contact* that is sustained between partners. If issues remain unresolved between adults they often reflect themselves in what is going on for children. As both men and women are exploring different ways of being, finding ways of defining themselves more clearly and more equally, even if this challenges the dominant culture, they need to develop means of open and honest communication. This does not dissolve relationships of power and subordination to personal relations but involves finding ways of mediating different forms of power within relationships.

There is no way that a relationship can be isolated from the pressures and demands of the larger society which work to influence and organize the ways people can be with each other. Relationships do not exist in an autonomous private realm of their own. Rather there is a crucial dialectic between 'public' and 'private' emotions and power as people explore ways of living more truthfully and equally with each other.

In intimate relationships we have to work to bring inner lives into harmony with outer expression. The ways we care for others have to be shown in our behaviour towards others. Attitudes cannot be neatly separated from behaviour. As we learn to listen and respond to our inner lives as heterosexual men, it should become easier to listen to our partners. Unless we learn to involve ourselves more equally in housework and childcare we will not value these activities and relationships properly, but continue to pay lip-service to an equality we do not live.[6] It isn't easy to make changes and we also need to imagine new images which can help to support men through these changes.

It is not easy to sustain a balance between work and family life, and within relationships it can be hard to maintain contact with partners and children. I know how easy it is for me still to think that I have to solve things on my own and that it is somehow better to do so. But then if I share so little of my own feelings this makes it difficult for my partner to share what is going on with her, without feeling she is making undue demands. Often heterosexual men feel that they only have to give attention to a relationship when things are going wrong, but then it is too late. It is striking if we think as men that to sustain contact in an intimate relationship we might have to spend at least an hour a day communicating and sharing with each other, appreciating, giving new information and also possibly giving complaints with recommendations. It is only if we are ready to structure time with each other that we can remain open and communicating. Otherwise it feels so easy as men to close down or else to find ourselves constantly arguing and fighting in unhelpful ways. Taking time to share appreciations of each other, and also taking time not to forget our dreams for the relationship, even if they mean remembering that it would be good to go to a movie, can sustain a connection that is so easily lost.[7]

Learning to be self-sufficient involves learning to do without the support of others. For men this means that we learn to live as if we do *not* need a relationship. It is hardly surprising then that heterosexual boys feel so confused about how to relate to girls, for so little prepares them for this transition in life. Often boys learn very little from their fathers, who are either absent emotionally or sustaining an image of self-sufficiency themselves. Unless I learn, for example, how to share some of my fears with my son Daniel, then he easily learns that there must be something wrong with him if he feels scared of some of the boys in the playground. It is a matter of discerning what it is appropriate to share, so that we are not dumping our emotions on children but learning to share more of ourselves with them. This can help children accept their own fears rather than feel they have to

harden themselves against them. To feel fear, for instance, is to gain important information for self-protection, and to cut off from this process of learning leaves men insensitive and brutalized. Sometimes boys become bullies
because they are incapable of dealing with their inner anxieties.

Contact and Connection

Children learn from what we do and how we relate as fathers rather than
from what we say to them. It does little good to say to children that they
should do what we say, if they see us behaving quite differently in our
relationships. Traditionally children are left feeling inadequate or unworthy, for otherwise they believe their fathers would be keen to spend
more time with them. The fact that they get so little attention and that their
father seems more interested in the TV or the bottle seems to prove how
little value they have. Children often seek negative attention by behaving
badly or by drawing attention to themselves, because negative attention is
better than no attention at all. Relationships take *time* and *space* to build
and sustain, and so often as fathers we disappoint our children when we
promise something that we do not deliver. It is easy to feel that they do not
mind 'because they are only children' and we tell ourselves that we will
make it up to them later in some way. But they learn that we are not reli-
able and that we cannot be trusted. It would horrify us to realize that this is
what we teach, but often this is what our behaviour indicates.

As boys we were not taken seriously when we were children, so it is difficult to take our children seriously, even if we would wish otherwise. Fathers
think that if they spend 'quality' time with their children then this can make
up for whatever they have not done. But this is not a magical formula,
however important it is. It might be a way of sustaining a relationship which
is already firmly bonded, but if we have missed out on early contact then it
can take a great deal of time and attention to undo the distrust that has been
created. It is possible to change, but not simply through an act of will and
determination as we so often believe. Rather silences and difficulties will
remain and it will take time to restore a trust that has been broken. Fathers
with different class, 'race' and ethnic identities in the 1980s and 1990s want
to have more of a relationship with their children, even though the intensification of work in a period of economic crisis has made this hard to achieve.
This is a contradiction in the lives of many men these days and it cannot be
wished away with good intentions. Often they want to give more time but
they just do not have 'the time to give'. But this is also something that children can appreciate if it is carefully explained to them. They can appreciate
the time that is given, as long as attention is full.

Often we do not want to be confronted with the truth of what is going on,
especially by our children. But it is the youngest children who carry the
emotions *not* being expressed in the family. Children will put up with presents if this helps adults assuage their guilt, but they want contact and an

expression of interest that is so rarely forthcoming. Often as fathers we are trapped into our own emotional histories that we have barely acknowledged. Sometimes we will find ourselves reacting with a harsh and bitter tone which we might recognize and know from our own fathers. Sometimes this is a response we have embodied, for we have never learnt how to do the inner emotional work that might help us break the pattern. Though intellectually we want to respond differently to what we experienced with our fathers, we can find ourselves falling back into similar routines. This is what Freud (1961) crucially recognized, for we do not have the kind of control over our lives and relationships that a liberal theory encourages us to assume.

Unless we have learnt how to change our relationships with ourselves as men, it becomes hard to offer a different model to our children. Unless they see us making time and space for ourselves, and setting boundaries on the energies we give to work, they will find it hard to feel it is legitimate to have their own emotions, desires and needs. Unless they witness us taking ourselves seriously, rather than simply adapting to the demands of work, they will not learn how to take their own needs and desires seriously. Unless we can set firm boundaries with our children, as I have talked about it, so that we can respect our own time and space, they will find it hard to respect us and what we say.[9] Only when children witness how we reach out for love and support when we feel down, will it be easier for them to reach out when they feel sad and lonely. Only then will they learn not to keep their feelings to themselves, ashamed of sharing themselves and showing their vulnerability. This is the way we show self-respect and demonstrate that we have deeply held beliefs we are ready to defend. A sense of integrity often comes from deeply held beliefs, for it means we are ready to stand our ground. This is something that men, women and children all have to learn for themselves. It involves learning to *respect* our emotions as much as our ideas, our feelings as much as our beliefs.

As men learn to take time off work because children are sick and they are needed at home, they soon come into conflict with authorities at work. It seems to be one thing for women to make such demands but still quite another for men. Men are expected to have things 'organized' at home, so that it reflects upon their masculinity if they need to take time off. But it is only if we can make structural demands for a changed relationship between work and family that we will see men changing. As men recognize a need for closer contact with their children, they will begin to develop a different sense of what their lives mean. This is not a 'private' matter alone, but concerns the organization of production, schooling and health care in the larger society. The state does its best to sustain the notion that it is a 'private' matter. This is because it goes to the heart of the distinctions between 'private' and 'public' spheres that have organized dominant visions of modernity.[10]

As men gain a different vision of their lives which recognizes the needs for time with themselves, with partners, with work, with friends and with children, they will be forced to question a vision of male identity built around individual success and achievement. They will recognize there is more to life and to values than a democratic capitalist society easily allows. It is not simply a matter of balancing and prioritizing the demands made on men's time and attention in these different spheres of life. This is to sustain a conventional framework, all too familiar to middle class and working class men when they are responding to external demands. Rather there is a growing sense that men with diverse masculinities have to recover an inner relationship to self which allows them to *recognize* what particular nourishment they are getting from different relationships and activities. Often we do not think about our lives in this way because we find it hard to accept that a friendship might have exhausted itself or that we need a different direction in life. In our thirties and forties we drift, responding to external events, wondering where all the years have gone, rather than consciously shaping our lives. Possibly it is still just too threatening to recognize that our lives are limited and that we are also in a process towards death. As men we are particularly attached to notions of invincibility and myths that we will somehow live forever. But this also makes us strangely insensitive to ourselves.

As men we are allowed to be workers in the public sphere, and lovers and fathers in the private sphere of intimate relationships. Emotions, feelings and sexuality supposedly have no place within the world of work which is governed by an impersonal and objective notion of reason alone. Often we feel alienated and estranged at work, as Marx understood, but no longer believe that a transformation of work will be enough to bring self-realization and fulfilment. If there is a time to work there is also a time to play and make love. There is a time when we need to be with others but also a time when we need to be with ourselves. The sharp boundaries which have policed both public and private life within late modernity can no longer carry conviction as we approach the millennium. Often men feel trapped on a treadmill of work and home, especially in their mid thirties and their forties. They want something different and feel that there must be more to life than getting in the car to go to work and coming home too exhausted for contact or love. There is often a quiet desperation in men's lives, a sense that life is drifting away and that their dreams are not being realized.

Often as middle class heterosexual men we feel isolated and alone, though we do not want others to know we feel this way. We can find it hard to sustain male friendships that seem to break into a series of discrete events or social occasions. Somehow contemporary masculinities make it difficult to sustain connections, especially when we feel down or depressed. We are so used to proving that we can live on our own without the support of others that we constantly seem to drift into doing it and then find it hard to reach out towards others. Again it is important not to generalize and hard not to feel that I am talking too much out of my own middle class, Jewish, heterosexual experience. But even if there are crucial differences of class, 'race' and ethnicity, there is also a resonance with dominant masculinities that still so often set the terms. Often when we feel down or unhappy we become more controlling because at some level as men we feel more vulnerable to the rejections or putdowns of others. This can make it hard to relate differently, to reach out for the support of others when we most need to. But if we feel stuck it is difficult to reach out, especially to other men. In any case, as heterosexual middle class men we often think we know best what we need. This is part of a male superiority which needs questioning. It is not a helpful part of a revisioned manhood or the way to relate to women and children more equally.

Politics and Spirituality

Within an Enlightenment vision of modernity, politics and spirituality have been separated into distinct spheres. Politics has largely to do with the organization of power within the public sphere and little to do with how we are to live just lives within unjust and unequal societies. Within a liberal moral culture we learn that it is always possible for us as individuals to treat others with respect and justice, for it has to do with the manner of personal relationships. We learn that spirituality has very little to do with the ways we live our everyday lives but is a private and individual concern. It has to do with our beliefs as individuals.

This duality is reflected in a pervasive distinction between the inner and the outer. We learn to accept that as individuals we can do very little to change the world we live in, for as individuals we remain relatively powerless. This is echoed in traditional forms of psychoanalytic theory which often accept that we cannot change the outer world for it is 'given', and in any case individuals have different opinions about it, but we can change our attitudes towards it. There is less focus upon the ways we might change how we relate *in the present*, for these changes are taken to be 'superficial' if we have not dealt with the inner psychic early childhood forces which manifest themselves. So it is that we learn to do 'inner work' that in Freud's terms helps us to accept the 'reality principle' for what it is. The movement towards maturity for Freud is a movement from 'pleasure' to 'reality', from being governed by a pleasure principle towards accepting a reality that we have evaded or failed to fully acknowledge. In part this later Freudian inheritance sustains a Kantian distinction between 'inner' and 'outer', though Kant (1959) argues that we only have an inner relationship with reason that is the source of our freedom and autonomy. Though Freud enriches our vision of the inner life, the 'outer' so often remains a projection.

But this not a personal quest alone, for we cannot know who we are unless we also know where we come from. Growing in confidence and clarity is not a personal matter alone, for it involves recognizing our own histories and traditions and the ambivalent messages they have left us with. Within modernity we learn to put aside our class, gender, sexual and ethnic backgrounds, for these, as I have argued, are deemed to be forms of unfreedom that have to be transcended in our growth towards individuality, autonomy and freedom. But feminism, ecology and sexual politics have set issues of equality, freedom and individuality in a broader framework. They have made many women aware, for instance, of ways they have grown up to evaluate their experience in the dominant masculine terms of patriarchy. In order to find their own diverse voices they have had to distance themselves from the powerful influence of men and masculinities, learning to value their own experience. This is also something that gay men and lesbians have had to do for themselves, for they have had to learn to take pride in sexualities that were conventionally devalued and debased. This takes a particular kind of courage, to recognize the *integrity* of differences.

Though postmodern theories have helped to reinstate the different voices of the marginalized, who had felt that they had to prove their adequacy as human beings in the universal terms of the rational self, they have also made it hard to recognize the integrity of particular cultural traditions. If we cannot wish away who we are or where we have come from, then we have to accept and learn from our own individual and collective histories and traditions. We have to discover inner strength to work through what this has meant for us, recognizing for instance that a woman who has grown up within an orthodox Jewish or a Catholic tradition might find it harder to relate in any helpful way to what her tradition had to offer, because she carries so much anger at being rendered invisible for so long. At the same time it can be hard to question the patriarchal assumptions of these traditions without feeling that you are somehow betraying them.[11] It takes courage to face our hidden histories, and this cannot be forced but has to happen in its own time. It is a step that people have to take for themselves and others cannot take for them. They can give guidance and support.

If black men and women have to come to terms with a history of slavery and oppression without at the same time being overwhelmed by it, so Jews have to come to terms with the Holocaust. These become inescapable moments that cannot be wished away, though we might wish desperately that they had not taken place. It is in this sense that we have to come to terms with history. We cannot simply treat it as an intellectual construction of ever changing meanings, because we are still hurt by it and carry its sufferings into our own generations. Somehow coming to face ourselves involves learning *how to face* some of this history. But black people and Jewish people have also learnt they have to disentangle themselves from the images and representations that a dominant white Christian culture has prepared for them, for too often we learn to see ourselves through the eyes of the dominant culture.[12] We learn to feel ashamed and even despise aspects of ourselves and our histories as we do our best to make ourselves 'acceptable' in the eyes of others. Often marginalized groups find it hard to communicate and share with each other, for they can feel they are inevitably competing for the attentions of those who have power and authority. It is also that people often do not want to be reminded of the poverty they have struggled with. It is easier, but not just, to identify with the powerful when this is an option.

Similarly we cannot sidestep what patriarchy has done to women, gay men and lesbians over 2000 years and is still doing. But this should not mean that we feel ashamed of ourselves as heterosexual men, even if we feel shame for what has been done in our name. It is a history that we have to learn if we are to disentangle ourselves from its effects. We still very much inherit the arrogance and superiority of a late modernity that has been largely cast in the image of dominant white heterosexual men. But if this is not to leave heterosexual men feeling bad about themselves, tightening a screw that already makes men feel bad, then it should stimulate men into revisioning their inherited masculinities, working out different ways of relating both to themselves and to others. Though masculinities are tied up with relationships of power and dominance, they should not be exclusively identified with these relationships. It is important for men to recognize that they *can change* and that we do not have to relate in the ways we saw our fathers relate, or in ways that we were related to when we were children. But we have to take responsibility to break the cycle ourselves, for others will not do it for us.

We have to learn to disentangle what we want to celebrate and pass on to our children in the ways men can be with each other. We do not have to forsake the present in order to return to some lost notions of masculinity in the past. We face different issues in the present and many of them concern how we can be ourselves as men while learning how to have more open, honest and equal relationships with our partners and children. There are no easy models that we can conform to, but there is a lot that we can learn from diverse traditions that we also have to question. As we recognize the very different traditions of masculinity we have inherited, we can also face the relationships of power that have separated men and created hierarchies between them, as well as between men and women, parents and children. As we learn to change ourselves, so we *begin* to transform these traditions and relationships. We can learn from the past but we also have to be aware of what issues we face in the present.

Men are learning in many different ways how to come to terms with their masculinities and draw love and support from each other as men. As we learn to challenge each other, we can also appreciate what others are going through, for we have often been in a similar emotional place ourselves. As we learn to avoid a moralism that undermined so much of the sexual politics of the 1970s and 1980s we can also learn from the past experiences of men and honour their attempts at change.[13] Sometimes we do not take the right path for us, and there are many different paths that men can explore. But as we learn to listen to our emotions and feelings we can begin to define what we want and need more clearly. We can also respect what women have been struggling with over many years in the women's movement. As men we can support these struggles while knowing that we have to find our own way to give expression to ourselves as men. As we recognize the inhumanities in the ways people have treated each other, we can resolve to create different relationships for ourselves. We learn to change ourselves as part of a larger process of change as we grow in our own authority and wisdom and in a determination to make the world a more humane and just place to live.

Notes

1 For some helpful introductions to creation based spirituality see, for instance, the writings of Mathew Fox, *Original Blessings* (1983). This work refigures the traditional relationship between Judaism and Christianity, taking the emphasis away from a theology of sin and salvation.

2 The Sufi tradition is introduced in a personal way through the experiences of Irena Tweedie in *The Chasm of Fire* (1988).

3 For an exploration of some of the tensions between postmodern writings and spiritual traditions that seek to acknowledge a reverence for the earth see, for instance, Charles Jenks, *The Post-modern Reader* (1992); and the feminist influences in Susan Griffin, *Made from this Earth* (1982).

4 An attempt to open up questions about ethics and values in relation to a postmodernism that has too easily been identified with an ethical relativism is *Principled Positions: Postmodernism and the Rediscovery of Value*, edited by Judith Squires (1993). See also Z. Bauman's recent works engaging with postmodern theory, *Postmodern Ethics* (1995) and *Life in Fragments* (1995).

5 For a sense of Simone Weil's spiritual writings that are in crucial ways inseparable from her developing politics see *Gravity and Grace* (1952). I have discussed the relationship between her materialism and her spirituality in the concluding chapter of L. Blum and V.J. Seidler, *A Truer Liberty: Simone Weil and Marxism* (1989).

6 For some discussion about how men have changed in relation to domestic work and childcare see, for instance, Lynne Segal, *Slow Motion: Changing Masculinities, Changing Men* (1990); R.W. Connell, *Masculinities* (1996); Jane C. Hood (ed.), *Men Work and Family* (1993); and Victor J. Seidler (ed.), *The Achilles' Heel Reader: Men, Sexual Politics and Socialism* (1991c).

7 For some reflections upon the difficulties of communicating within heterosexual relationships see Deborah Tannen, *You Just Don't Understand* (1991); Dale Spender, *Man-Made Language* (1980); and Deborah Cameron, *Feminism and Linguistic Theory* (1985). For more of a therapeutic sense of how some of the knots can be undone without minimizing the workings of gender relations of power see Virginia Satir, *Peoplemaking* (1989).

8 To understand some of the contradictions that different men face in the 1990s, wanting to be more involved with their children but feeling the intensity of demands at work and the fear of unemployment, see, for instance, Angela Philips, *The Trouble with Boys* (1993).

9 For a sense of how relations between parents and children can be more free and egalitarian while at the same time recognizing the need for parents to give clear boundaries see Alan Graubard, *Free the Children* (1972); and Boston Women's Health Book Collective, *Ourselves and our Children* (1978).

10 To rethink the relationships between the public and the private in the face of the challenges of feminism and sexual politics see, for instance, *Feminism Theorizes the Political*, edited by J. Butler and J. Scott (1995); *Feminism/Postmodernism*, edited by Linda Nicholson (1990); Ann Phillips, *Democracy and Difference* (1993); and Carole Pateman, *The Sexual Contract* (1988) and *The Disorder of Women* (1990).

11 Feminist theology has helped bring into question the patriarchal assumptions of the dominant religious traditions. It has helped to open up a fundamental questioning that is still very much in process in relation to the possibilities of a more free and egalitarian spirituality. See, for instance, Mary Daly, *Beyond God the Father* (1973); Judith Plaskow, *Standing again at Sinai* (1990); Lucy Goodison, *Moving Heaven and Earth* (1992); Rosemary Ruether, *New Women, New Earth* (1995); and Elaine Pagels, *The Gnostic Gospels* (1982).

12 For a sense of the rewriting of black history and culture so that it begins to disentangle itself from the eyes of colonialism see, for instance, Martin Bernal, *Black Athena* (1987); and Paul Gilroy, *Black Atlantic* (1994). For some of the work that helps to make visible a Jewish culture and tradition so long marginalized within modernity and silenced by the Shoa see Richard Cohen, *Elevations: The Height of the Good in Rosenzweig and Levinas* (1994). I have approached some of these issues in the concluding chapter of *The Moral Limits of Modernity: Love, Inequality and Oppression* (1991b).

13 As we open up a broken conversation between different generations of men with diverse experiences and sexualities, it is important to recognize how men have struggled in the past. As we learn to acknowledge differences we can also respect our own struggles. See, for instance, *Telling Sexual Stories*, edited by Ken Plummer (1994); K. Porter and J. Weeks, *Between the Acts* (1990); *Growing Up Before Stonewall*, edited by P. Nardi, D. Sanders and J. Marmor (1994); M. Kimmel and T. Mosmiller, *Against the Tide: Pro-Feminist Men in the United States 1776–1990* (1992); and Victor J. Seidler, *Recreating Sexual Politics: Men, Feminism and Politics* (1991a).

References

Altman, Dennis (1982) *The Homosexualization of America*. New York: St Martin's Press.

Aries, Philip (1965) *Centuries of Childhood*. Harmondsworth: Penguin.

Aries, Philip (1974) *Western Attitudes towards Death*. Baltimore: Johns Hopkins University Press.

Armstrong, D. (1983) *Political Anatomy of the Body*. Cambridge: Cambridge University Press.

Armstrong, K. (1986) *Paul*. London: Fontana.

Askew, S. and Ross, C. (1986) *Boys Don't Cry: Boys and Sexism in Education*. Milton Keynes: Open University Press.

Bakan, David (1958) *Sigmund Freud and the Jewish Mystical Tradition*. New York: Schocken.

Baudrillard, J. (1995) *Symbolic Exchange and Death*. London: Sage.

Bauman, Zygmunt (1991) *Modernity and the Holocaust*. Cambridge: Polity.

Bauman, Zygmunt (1993) *Modernity and Ambivalence*. Cambridge: Polity.

Bauman, Zygmunt (1994) *Intimations of Postmodernity*. London: Routledge.

Bauman, Zygmunt (1995) *Life in Fragments: Essays in Postmodern Moralities*. Oxford: Blackwell.

Bauman, Zygmunt (1995) *Postmodern Ethics*. Cambridge: Polity.

Bell, D. and Valentine, G. (eds) (1995) *Mapping Desire: Geographies of Sexuality*. London: Routledge.

Benhabib, S. (1992) *Situating the Self*. Cambridge: Polity.

Benjamin, J. (1990) *Bonds of Love*. London: Virago.

Berghahn, M. (1988) *Continental Britons*. London: Berg.

Berlin, Isaiah (1981) *Against the Current*. Oxford: Oxford University Press.

Berman, M. (1981) *The Reenchantment of the World*. Ithaca: Cornell University Press.

Berman, M. (1982) *All That Is Solid Melts into Air*. London: Verso.

Bernal, M. (1987) *Black Athena*. London: Free Association Books.

Bernheimer, C. and Kahane, C. (1985) *In Dora's Case: Freud–Hysteria–Feminism*. London: Virago.

Bernstein, B. (1971) *Class, Codes and Control*, vol. 1. London: RKP.

Bettelheim, B. (1964) *The Empty Fortress*. New York: Free Press.

Bettelheim, B. (1975) *The Uses of Enchantment: The Meaning and Importance of Fairy Tales*. New York: Vintage.

Blasius, M. and Phelan, S. (eds) (1995) *We Are Everywhere*. London: Routledge.

Blum, L. (1980) *Friendship, Altruism and Morality*. London: Routledge.

Blum, L. and Seidler, V.J. (1989) *A Truer Liberty: Simone Weil and Marxism*. New York: Routledge.

Boadella, D. (ed.) (1976) *In the Wake of Reich*. London: Coventure.

Boadella, D. (1987) *Lifestream*. London Routledge.

Bock, G. and James, S. (ed.) (1992) *Beyond Equality and Difference*. London: Routledge.

Bordo, S. (1993) *Unbearable Weight: Feminism, Western Culture and the Body*. Berkeley, CA: University of California Press.

Boston Women's Health Book Collective (1978) *Ourselves and Our Children*. New York: Random House.

Boyarin, D. (1993) *Carnal Israel: Reading Sex in Talmudic Culture*. Berkeley, CA: University of California Press.

Boyarin, D. (1994) *A Radical Jew: Paul and the Politics of Identity*. Berkeley, CA: University of California Press.

Braidotti, R. (1991) *Patterns of Dissonance*. Cambridge: Polity.

Brittan, A. (1989) *Masculinity and Power*. Oxford: Blackwell.

Brod, H. and Kaufman, M. (1995) *Theorising Masculinities*. Newbury Park, CA: Sage.

Brown, P. (1989) *The Body and Society: Men, Women and Sexual Renunciation in Early Christianity*. London: Faber.

Butler, J. (1990) *Gender Trouble*. New York: Routledge.

Butler, J. and Scott, J. (eds) (1995) *Feminism Theorizes the Political*. New York: Routledge.

Cameron, D. (1985) *Feminism and Linguistic Theory*. London: Macmillan.

Campbell, B. (1994) *Goliath*. London: Virago.

Caplan, Pat (ed.) (1987) *The Cultural Construction of Sexuality*. London: Tavistock.

Capra, F. (1975) *The Turning Point*. London: Wildwood House.

Capra, F. (1988) *Uncommon Wisdom*. London: Wildwood House.

Carpenter, Edward (1906) *Love's Coming of Age*. London: George Allen and Unwin.

Carpenter Edward (1990) *Collected Writings*. London: Gay Men's Press.

Cartledge, S. and Ryan, J. (1983) *Sex and Love*. London: The Women's Press.

Cavell, S. (1979) *The Claims of Reason*. Oxford: Oxford University Press.

Cavell, S. (1995) *Philosophical Passages*. Oxford: Blackwell.

Chapman, R. and Rutherford, J. (1988) *Male Order: Unwrapping Masculinity*. London: Lawrence and Wishart.

Chesler, P. (1978) *About Men*. London: The Women's Press.

Chodorow, Nancy (1978) *The Reproduction of Mothering*. Berkeley, CA: University of California Press.

Chodorow, Nancy (1992) *Feminism and Psychoanalysis*. Cambridge: Polity.

Clarke, D. (ed.) (1991) *Marriage, Domestic Life and Social Change*. London: Routledge.

Cockburn, C. (1983) *Brothers: Male Dominance and Technical Change*. London: Pluto.

Cockburn, C. (1985) *Machinery of Dominance: Women, Men and Technological Knowledge*. London: Pluto.

Cohen, R. (1994) *Elevations: The Height of the Good in Rosenzweig and Levinas*. Chicago: University of Chicago Press.

Connell, R.W. (1987) *Gender and Power*. Cambridge: Polity.

Connell, R.W. (1996) *Masculinities*. Cambridge: Polity.

Cooper, Howard (1990) *Forms of Prayer: Days of Awe*. London: RSGB.

Corneau, G. (1991) *Absent Fathers, Lost Sons*. Boston: Shambala.

Cosgrove, S. (1976) *The Spirit and the Valley*. London: Virago.

Daly, Mary (1968) *The Church and the Second Sex*. New York: Harper and Row.

Daly, Mary (1973) *Beyond God the Father*. Boston: Beacon Books.

Daly, Mary (1984) *Pure Lust*. London: The Women's Press.

Davis, D. Brion (1989) *The Problem of Slavery in Western Culture*. Oxford: Oxford University Press.

Dennison, G. (1971) *The Lives of Children*. New York: Vintage.

Dinnerstein, D. (1976) *The Rocking of the Cradle and the Ruling of the World*. London: Souvenir Press.

Durkheim, E. (1961) *The Elementary Forms of Religious Life*. London: Allen and Unwin.

Dychwald, Ken (1978) *Bodymind*. London: Wildwood House.

Easlea, Brian (1981) *Science and Sexual Oppression*. London: Weidenfeld.

Easlea, Brian (1983) *Fathering the Unthinkable*. London: Pluto Press.

Edwards, Tim (1994) *Erotics and Politics*. London: Routledge.

Ehrenreich, B. (1983) *The Hearts of Men*. London: Pluto Press.

Ehrenreich, B. and English, D. (1989) *For Her Own Good*. London: Pluto Press.

Eichenbaum, L. and Orbach, S. (1983) *Understanding Women*. Harmondsworth: Penguin.

Eichenbaum, L. and Orbach, S. (1984) *What do Women Want?* London: Fontana.

Erickson, Erik (1950) *Childhood and Society*. New York: Norton.

Ernst, S. and Goodison, L. (1981) *In Our Own Hands*. London: The Women's Press.

Faderman, L. (1976) *Surpassing the Love of Men*. London: Junction Books.

Fagan, J. and Shepherd, I. (eds) (1972) *Gestalt Therapy Now*. Harmondsworth: Penguin.

Faludi, Susan (1992) *Backlash: The Undeclared War against American Women*. New York: Crown.

Fanon, Franz (1970) *Black Skin, White Mask*. London: Pluto.
Farrell, W. (1974) *The Liberated Man: Beyond Masculinity – Freeing Men and Their Relation-ships with Women*. New York: Random House.
Farrell, W. (1986) *The Myth of Male Power*. New York: Simon and Shuster.
Fernbach, D. (1981) *The Spiral Path*. London: Gay Men's Press.
Finch, J. (1989) *Family Obligations and Social Change*. Cambridge: Polity.
Foucault, Michel (1971) *Madness and Civilization*. London: Tavistock.
Foucault, Michel (1977) *Discipline and Punish: The Birth of the Prison*. New York: Pantheon.
Foucault, Michel (1980) *A History of Sexuality*, vol. 1. New York: Vintage.
Foucault, Michel (1985) *The Use of Pleasure*. Harmondsworth: Penguin.
Foucault, Michel (1986) *The Care of the Self*. Harmondsworth: Penguin.
Foucault, Michel (1988) 'Technologies of the Self', in L. Martin, H. Gutman and P. Hutton (eds) *Technologies of the Self*. London: Tavistock.
Foucault, Michel (1990) *The Care of the Self*. Harmondsworth: Penguin.
Fox, Mathew (1983) *Original Blessing*. Sante Fe: Bears.
French, Sean (ed.) (1992) *Fatherhood*. London: Virago.
Freud, Sigmund (1922) *Introductory Lectures on Psychoanalysis*. London: Allen and Unwin.
Freud, Sigmund (1953) *Three Essays on the Theory of Sexuality* (1905). Standard Edition, vol. 7. London: Hogarth.
Freud, Sigmund (1961) *Civilization and its Discontents*. New York: Norton.
Freud, Sigmund (1977) 'Three Essays on the Theory of Sexuality', in *Sexuality*. Harmonds-worth: Penguin.
Friedman, J. and Lasch, S. (eds) (1990) *Modernity and Identity*. Cambridge: Polity.
Fromm, Erich (1942) *The Fear of Freedom*. London: Routledge.
Fromm, Erich (1942) *To Have or to Be*. London: Abacus.
Frosh, S. (1995) *Sexual Difference: Masculinity and Psychoanalysis*. London: Routledge.
Frosh, S. and Elliot, A. (eds) (1995) *Psychoanalysis in Context*. London: Routledge.
Fuss, D. (1989) *Essentially Speaking*. New York: Routledge.
Fuss, D. (ed.) (1992) *Inside/Out*. New York: Routledge.
Gane, M. (1991a) *Baudrillard: Critical and Fatal Theory*. London: Routledge.
Gane, M. (1991b) *Baudrillard's Bestiary*. London: Routledge.
Gane, M. (1993) *Baudrillard Love*. London: Routledge.
Gay, Peter (1988) *Freud: A Life in Our Time*. London: Dent.
Giddens, A. (1991) *Modernity and Self-Identity*. Cambridge: Polity.
Giddens, A. (1993) *The Transformation of Intimacy*. Cambridge: Polity.
Gilligan, Carol (1982) *In a Different Voice: Psychological Theory and Women's Development*. Cambridge, MA: Harvard University Press.
Gilroy, Paul (1994) *Black Atlantic*. London: Verso.
Goodison, Lucy (1992) *Moving Heaven and Earth*, London: The Women's Press.
Goss, Edward (1949) *Father and Son: A Study of Two Temperaments*. Harmondsworth: Penguin.
Graubard, Alan (1972) *Free the Children*. New York: Vintage.
Griffin, Susan (1979) *Rape: The Power of Consciousness*. San Francisco: Harper & Row.
Griffin, Susan (1980) *Pornography and Silence*. London: The Women's Press.
Griffin, Susan (1981) *Women and Nature*. London: The Women's Press.
Griffin, Susan (1982) *Made from this Earth*. London: The Women's Press.
Grimshaw, Jean (1986) *Feminist Philosophers*. Brighton: Harvester.
Grosz, Elizabeth (1994) *Volatile Bodies: Towards a Corporeal Feminism*. Bloomington, IN: Indiana University Press.
Handelman, Susan (1991) *Fragments of Redemption*. Bloomington, IN: Indiana University Press.
Hanscombe, G. and Humphries, M. (eds) (1986) *Heterosexuality*. London: Gay Men's Press.
Hart, Kitty (1981) *Return to Auschwitz*. London: Sidgwick and Jackson.
Harwood, A.C. (1979) *The Way of a Child*. London: Rudolf Steiner.
Hearn, J. (1992) *Men in the Public Eye*. London: Routledge.
Hearn, J. and Morgan, D. (1990) *Men, Masculinities and Social Theory*. London: Unwin Hyman.

Heckman, Susan (1995) *Moral Voices, Moral Selves*. New York: Routledge.

Hillman, James (1975) *Revisioning Psychology*. New York: Harper and Row.

Hillman, James (1993) *One Hundred Years of Psychoanalysis and Still the World Is No Better*. London: Harper Collins.

Hite, Shere (1990) *The Hite Report on Male Sexuality*. London: Optima.

Hochschild, Arlie (1989) *The Second Shift: Working Parents and the Revolution at Home*. New York: Viking.

Hood, Jane (ed.) (1993) *Men, Work and Family*. Newbury Park, CA: Sage.

hooks, bell (1981) *Ain't I a Woman? Black Women and Feminism*. Boston: South End Press.

hooks, bell (1984) *Feminist Theory: From the Margin to the Center*. Boston: South End Press.

hooks, bell (1989) *Talking back: Thinking Feminist, Thinking Black*. Boston: South End Press.

hooks, bell (1992) *Black Looks: Race, Representation*. Boston: South End Press.

Horkheimer, Max (1972) *Critical Theory: Selected Essays*. New York: Seabury.

Hoyland, John (ed.) (1992) *Fathers and Sons*. London: Serpent's Tail.

Humphries, M. and Metcalf, A. (1985) *The Sexuality of Men*. London: Pluto Press.

Illich, Ivan (1976) *Limits to Medicine: Medical Nemesis*. New York: Pantheon.

Irigaray, Luce (1985) *This Sex Which Is Not One*. Ithaca, NY: Cornell University Press.

Irigaray, Luce (1994) *Je, Tu, Nous: Towards a Culture of Difference*. London: Routledge.

Jackson, David and Salisbury, Jonathan (1996) *Challenging Macho Values*. Brighton: Falmer Press.

Jagger, Alison (1983) *Feminist Politics and Human Nature*. Brighton: Harvester.

Jardine, A. and Smith, P. (eds) (1987) *Men in Feminism*. New York: Methuen.

Jay, Martin (1973) *The Dialectical Imagination*. London: Heinemann.

Jenks, Charles (1992) *The Post-Modern Reader*. London: Academy.

Jung, Carl (1956) *Symbols of Transformation*. London: Routledge.

Jung, Carl (1964) *Man and His Symbols*. London: Aldus Books.

Jung, Carl (1971) *Psychological Types, Collected Works*, vol. 6. London: Routledge.

Jung, Carl (1983) *Memories, Dreams and Reflections*. London: Fontana.

Jung, Carl (1986) *Aspects of the Feminine*. London: Routledge.

Kafka, Franz (1954) *Letter to My Father*. New York: Schocken.

Kaplan, Louise (1978) *Oneness and Separateness: From Infancy to Individual*. New York: Simon and Schuster.

Kant, Immanuel (1959) *Foundations of the Metaphysics of Morals*, trans. Leo White Beck. New York: Bobbs-Merrill.

Kant, Immanuel (1960) *Education*. Ann Arbor: University of Michigan Press.

Kaufman, M. (1993) *Cracking the Armor: Power, Pain and the Lives of Men*. Toronto: Viking.

Keen, Sam (1991) *Fire in the Belly: On Being a Man*. New York: Bantam.

Keith, M. and Pile, S. (1993) *Place and the Politics of Identity*. London: Routledge.

Keller, E. Fox (1984) *Reflections on Gender and Science*. New Haven, CT: Yale University Press.

Kellerman, Stanley (1975) *Your Body Speaks Its Mind*. New York: Simon and Schuster.

Kellerman, Stanley (1979) *Living Your Dying*. New York: Random House.

Kellerman, Stanley (1986) *Somatic Reality*. Berkeley, CA: Center Press.

Kimmell, M. (1987) *Changing Men*. Newbury Park, CA: Sage.

Kimmel, M. and Mosmiller, T. (1992) *Against the Tide: Pro-Feminist Men in the United States 1776–1990*. Boston: Beacon.

Kitzinger, Sheila (1967) *The Experience of Childbirth*. Harmondsworth: Penguin.

Kohlberg, Lawrence (1981) *Essays on Moral Development*. New York: Harper and Row.

Kubler-Ross, E. (1970) *On Death and Dying*. London: Tavistock.

Laing, R.D. (1960) *The Divided Self*. London: Tavistock.

Laing, R.D. (1961) *Self and Others*. London: Tavistock.

Laqueur, Thomas (1990) *Making Sex: Body and Gender from the Greeks to Freud*. Cambridge, MA: Harvard University Press.

Larrabee, Mary J. (ed.) (1993) *An Ethic of Care*. New York: Routledge.

Leboyer, F. (1977) *Birth without Violence*. London: Fontana.

Lees, Sue (1993) *Sugar and Spice*. Harmondsworth: Penguin.
Levine, Linda and Barbach, Lonnie (1983) *The Intimate Man*. New York: Doubleday.
Levine, Steven (1987) *Healing into Life and Death*. Bristol: Gateway.
Lowen, Alexander (1963) *Bioenergetics*. Harmondsworth: Penguin.
Lyndon, Neil (1992) *No More Sex Wars*. London: Sinclair Stevenson.
Lyotard, J.-F. (1984) *The Postmodern Condition: A Report on Knowledge*. Manchester: Manchester University Press.
Mac An Ghail, M. (1994) *The Making of Men*. Milton Keynes: Open University Press.
Malcolm, Norman (1986) *Nothing is Hidden*. Oxford: Blackwell.
Mangan, J.A. and Walvin, J. (eds) (1987) *Manliness and Morality: Middle Class Masculinity in Britain and America 1800–1940*. Manchester: Manchester University Press.
Mannoni, O. (1991) *Freud*. New York: Random House.
McCormack, M. and Strathern, M. (1980) *Nature, Culture, Gender*. Cambridge: Cambridge University Press.
Merchant, C. (1980) *The Death of Nature: Women, Ecology and the Scientific Revolution*. San Francisco: Harper and Row.
Miedzian, Myriam (1992) *Boys Will Be Boys*. London: Virago.
Mill, J.S. (1964) *Utilitarianism, Liberty and Representative Government*. London: Dent.
Miller, Alice (1981) *The Drama of the Gifted Child*. Faber: London.
Miller, Alice (1983) *For Your Own Good: Hidden Cruelty in Childrearing and the Roots of Violence*. Faber: London.
Miller, Alice (1984) *Thou Shalt Not Be Aware: Society's Betrayal of the Child*. New York: Farrar, Strauss and Giroux.
Miller, J. Baker (1976) *Towards a New Psychology of Women*. Harmondsworth: Penguin.
Miller, Stuart (1983) *Men and Friendship*. London: Gateway.
Minow, Martha (1990) *Making All the Difference*. Cambridge, MA: Harvard University Press.
Mitchell, Juliet (1971) *Psychoanalysis and Feminism*. Harmondsworth: Penguin.
Mitscherlich, A. (1970) *Society without Fathers*. New York: Schocken.
Mitscherlich, A. *The Difficulties of Mourning*. New York: Schocken.
Montagu, Ashley (1971) *Touching*. New York: Harper & Row.
Morgan, David (1991) *Discovering Men: Sociology and Masculinities*. London: Routledge.
Morrison, Blake (1994) *When Did You Last See Your Father?* London: Penguin.
Murdoch, Iris (1970) *The Sovereignty of Good*. London: Routledge.
Murdoch, Iris (1992) *Metaphysics as a Guide to Morals*. London: Chatto and Windus.
Nardi, P. (ed.) (1992) *Men's Friendships*. Newbury Park, CA: Sage.
Nardi, P., Sanders, David and Marmor, Judd (eds) (1994) *Growing Up before Stonewall*. London: Routledge.
National Lesbian and Gay Survey (1992) *What a Lesbian Looks Like*. London: Routledge.
Nicholson, L. (ed.) (1990) *Feminism/Postmodernism*. New York: Routledge.
Nietzsche, F. (1974) *The Gay Science*. New York: Random House, Vintage.
Nietzsche, F. (1983) *Untimely Meditations*. Cambridge: Cambridge University Press.
Nussbaum, Martha (1986) *The Fragility of Goodness*. Cambridge: Cambridge University Press.
Nussbaum, Martha (1995) *The Therapy of Desire*. Princeton: Princeton University Press.
Odent, M. (1985) *Entering the World*. Harmondsworth: Penguin.
Odent, M. (1984) *Birth Reborn*. London: Souvenir Press.
Osherson, Samuel (1987) *Finding Our Fathers*. New York: Fawcett.
Owen, Ursula (ed.) (1984) *Fathers and Daughters*. London: Virago.
Pagels, Elaine (1982) *The Gnostic Gospels*. Harmondsworth: Penguin.
Panichas, George A. (1977) *The Simone Weil Reader*. New York: David McKay.
Pateman, Carol (1988) *The Sexual Contract*. Cambridge: Polity.
Pateman, Carol (1990) *The Disorder of Women*. Cambridge: Polity.
Perls, Fritz (1971) *Gestalt Therapy Verbatim*. New York: Bantam.
Perls, Fritz (1972) *In and Out the Garbage Pail*. New York: Bantam.
Philips, Angela (1993) *The Trouble with Boys*. London: Pandora Press.
Philips, Ann (1993) *Democracy and Difference*. Cambridge: Polity.

Pile, S. and Thrift, N. (ed.) (1996) *Mapping the Subject: Geographies of Cultural Transformation*. London: Routledge.

Plant, Sadie (1992) *The Most Radical Gesture*. London: Routledge.

Plaskow, Judith (1990) *Standing again at Sinai*. New York: HarperCollins.

Pleck, J. (1981) *The Myth of Masculinity*. Cambridge: MIT Press.

Plummer, Ken (1994) *Telling Sexual Stories*. London: Routledge.

Poole, R. (1991) *Morality and Modernity*. London: Routledge.

Porter, D. (ed.) (1993) *Between Men and Feminism*. London: Routledge.

Porter, K. and Weeks, J. (1990) *Between the Acts*. London: Routledge.

Probyn, E. (1993) *Sexing the Self*. London: Routledge.

Ramazanoglu, C. (1989) *Feminism and the Contradictions of Oppression*. London: Routledge.

Ramazanoglu, C. (ed.) (1995) *Up Against Foucault*. London: Routledge.

Rattansi, A. and Westwood, S. (1994) *Racism, Modernity and Identity*. Cambridge: Polity.

Reich, W. (1970) *The Mass Psychology of Fascism*. Harmondsworth: Penguin.

Reich, W. (1972) *Sex-Pol: Essays 1929–1934*. New York: Vintage.

Reich, W. (1974) *The Function of the Orgasm*. Harmondsworth: Penguin.

Rieff, P. (1965) *Freud: The Mind of the Moralist*. London: Methuen.

Rimpoche, S. (1995) *The Tibetan Book of Living and Dying*. London: Rider.

Robert, Marthe (1977) *Freude: From Oedipus to Moses*. London: Routledge.

Robert, Marthe (1982) *As Lonely as Franz Kafka*. New York: Harcourt Brace Jovanovich.

Roberts, Helen (ed.) (1981) *Doing Feminist Research*. London: Routledge.

Rojek, C. and Turner, B. (1994) *Forget Baudrillard*. London: Routledge.

Roper, M. and Tosh, J. (eds) (1991) *Manful Assertions: Masculinities in Britain since 1800*. London: Routledge.

Rousseau, Jean Jacques (1964) *Discourse on the Sciences and Arts in the First and Second Discourses*, ed. Roger D. Masters. New York: St Martin's Press.

Rousseau, Jean Jacques (1979) *Emile or On Education*, ed. and trans. Allan Bloom. New York: Basic Books.

Rowbotham, Sheila (1973) *Woman's Consciousness, Man's World*. Harmondsworth: Penguin.

Rowbotham, Sheila (1976) *Socialism and the New Life: Edward Carpenter and Havelock Ellis*. London: Pluto Press.

Rowbotham, Sheila (1983) *Dreams and Dilemmas*. London: Virago.

Rubin, Lilian (1983) *Intimate Strangers*. London: Fontana.

Ruddick, Sara (1990) *Maternal Thinking: Towards a Politics of Peace*. London: The Women's Press.

Ruether, R. Radford (ed.) (1974) *Religion and Sexism: Images of Women in the Jewish and Christian Tradition*. New York: Simon and Schuster.

Ruether, R. Radford (1983) *Sexism and God-Talk: Towards a Feminist Theology*. Boston: Beacon Press.

Ruether, R. Radford (1995) *New Women, New Earth: Sexist Ideologies and Human Liberation*. Boston: Beacon Press.

Rutherford, J. (ed.) (1990) *Identity: Community, Culture and Difference*. London: Lawrence and Wishart.

Sabo, Donald and Gordon, D. F. (eds) (1995) *Men's Health and Illness*. London: Sage.

Sachs, Jonathan (1990) *Crisis and Covenant: Jewish Thought after the Holocaust*. Manchester: Manchester University Press.

Samuels, Andrew (1986) *Jung and the Post-Jungians*. London: Routledge.

Samuels, Andrew (1995) *The Political Psyche*. London: Routledge.

Satir, Virginia (1989) *Peoplemaking*. London: Souvenir.

Sayers, Janet (1991) *Mothering Psychoanalysis*. Harmondsworth: Penguin.

Segal, Lynne (1983) *What Is To Be Done about the Family*. Harmondsworth: Penguin.

Segal, Lynne (1987) *Is the Future Female?* London: Virago.

Segal, Lynne (1990) *Slow Motion: Changing Masculinities, Changing Men*. London: Virago.

Seidler, Victor J. (1986) *Kant, Respect and Injustice: The Limits of Liberal Moral Theory*. London: Routledge.

Seidler, Victor J. (1989) *Rediscovering Masculinity: Reason, Language and Sexuality*. London: Routledge.

Seidler, Victor J. (1991a) *Recreating Sexual Politics: Men, Feminism and Politics*. London: Routledge.

Seidler, Victor J. (1991b) *The Moral Limits of Modernity*. London: Macmillan.

Seidler, Victor J. (ed.) (1991c) *The Achilles' Heel Reader: Men, Sexual Politics and Socialism*. London: Routledge.

Seidler, Victor J. (ed.) (1992) *Men, Sex and Relationships*. London: Routledge.

Seidler, Victor J. (1994) *Unreasonable Men: Masculinity and Social Theory*. London: Routledge.

Seidler, Victor J. (1995) *Recovering the Self: Morality and Social Theory*. London: Routledge.

Seidman, S. (1992) *Embattled Eros*. New York: Routledge.

Sennett, R. (1980) *The Fall of Public Man*. Cambridge: Cambridge University Press.

Sennett, R. (1981) *Authority*. New York: Vintage Books.

Sennett, R. and Cobb, J. (1973) *The Hidden Injuries of Class*. New York: Vintage.

Shalaf, Myron (1985) *Fury on Earth: A Biography of Wilhelm Reich*. London: Macmillan.

Sharpe, Sue (1976) *Just Like a Girl*. Harmondsworth: Penguin.

Sharpe, Sue (1994) *Fathers and Daughters*. London: Routledge.

Skynner, R. (1976) *One Flesh: Separate Persons*. London: Constable.

Skynner, R. (1991) *Institutes and How To Survive Them*, ed. John R. Schlapobersky. London: Routledge.

Skynner, R. and Cleese, J. (1983) *Families and How to Survive Them*. London: Methuen.

Smart, B. (1993) *Postmodernism*. London: Routledge.

Solomon, K. and Levy, N. (ed.) (1982) *Men in Transition: Theory and Therapy*. New York: Plenum.

Spellman, E. (1990) *Inessential Women*. London: The Women's Press.

Spender, Dale (1980) *Man-Made Language*. London: Routledge.

Squires, Judith (ed.) (1993) *Principled Positions: Postmodernism and the Rediscovery of Value*. London: Lawrence and Wishart.

Stacey, Judith (1980) *Brave New Families*. New York: Basic Books.

Staples, Robert (1989) *Black Masculinity*. San Francisco: Black Scholar Press.

Steedman, C. (1995) *Landscape for a Good Woman*. London: Virago.

Stern, K. (1986) *The Flight from Women*. Minnesota: Paragon House.

Stevens, R. (1994) *Jung*. Harmondsworth: Penguin.

Stoller, R.J. (1968) *Sex and Gender: On the Development of Masculinity and Femininity*. New York: Science House.

Stoltenberg, John (1980) *Refusing to be a Man*. London: Fontana.

Tannen, D. (1991) *You Just Don't Understand*. London: Virago.

Taylor, Charles (1978) *Hegel*. Cambridge: Cambridge University Press.

Taylor, Charles (1990) *Sources of the Self*. Cambridge, MA: Harvard University Press.

Thewelait, Klaus (1989) *Male Fantasies*. Cambridge: Polity.

Thomas, David (1993) *Not Guilty: In Defence of the Modern Man*. London: Weidenfeld & Nicholson.

Thorne, Barrie (1993) *Gender Play: Girls and Boys in School*. New Brunswick, NY: Rutgers University Press.

Tolson, A. (1977) *The Limits of Masculinity*. London: Tavistock.

Treblicot, J. (1984) *Mothering: Essays in Feminist Theory*. Totowa, NJ: Rowan and Allenheld.

Turner, Bryan (1992) *Regulating Bodies*. London: Routledge.

Tweedie, Irena (1988) *The Chasm of Fire*. Shaftesbury: Element Books.

Walzer, M. (1983) *Spheres of Justice*. New York: Basic Books.

Walzer, M. (1989) *The Company of Critics*. New York: Basic Books.

Wandor, M. (ed.) (1972) *The Body Politic: Women's Liberation in Britain 1969–1972*. London: First Stage.

Ward, Dina (1992) *Memorial Candles: Children of the Holocaust*. London: Routledge.

Warner, Marina (1985) *Alone of all her Sex*. London: Pan Macmillan.

Weber, Max (1930) *The Protestant Ethic and the Spirit of Capitalism*. London: Allen and Unwin.

Weber, Max (1967) *The Sociology of Religion*. London: Methuen.

Weeks, Jeffrey (1977) *Coming Out: Homosexual Politics in Britain*. London: Quartet.

Weeks, Jeffrey (1985) *Sexuality and its Discontents*. London: Routledge.

Weeks, Jeffrey (1986) *Sexuality*. London: Horwood/Tavistock.

Weeks, Jeffrey (1996) *Inventing Moralities*. Cambridge: Polity.

Weil, Simone (1952) *Gravity and Grace*. London: Routledge.

Weil, Simone (1962) 'Human Personality', in Richard Kees (ed.), *Selected Essays 1934–43*. Oxford: Oxford University Press.

Weil, Simone (1965) *Seventy Letters*. Oxford: Oxford University Press.

Weil, Simone (1988) *The Need for Roots*, trans. A.F. Dills. London: Routledge.

Wheelock, Jane (1990) *Husbands at Home: The Domestic Economy in a Post-Industrial Society*. London: Routledge.

Whitford, M. (1991) *Luce Irigaray: Philosophy in the Feminine*. London: Routledge.

Whitford, M. and Lennon, K. (eds) (1994) *Knowing the Difference*. London: Routledge.

Wicks, Francis (1977) *The Inner World of Childhood*. London: Coventure.

Williams, Bernard (1973) *Problems of the Self*. Cambridge: Cambridge University Press,

Williams, Bernard (1981) *Moral Luck*. Cambridge: Cambridge University Press.

Williams, Eric (1964) *Capitalism and Slavery*. London: André Deutsch.

Winnicott, D. (1974) *Playing and Reality*. Harmondsworth: Penguin.

Wittgenstein, L. (1958) *Philosophical Investigations*. Oxford: Blackwell.

Wittgenstein, L. (1975) *On Certainty*. Oxford: Blackwell.

Wittgenstein, L. (1980) *Culture and Value*, trans. Peter Winch. Oxford: Blackwell.

Young, Iris Marion (1990) Justice and the Politics of Difference. Princeton: Princeton University Press.

Zilbergeld, Bernie (1980) *Male Sexuality*. New York: Bantam Books.

Index

abandonment, 49, 67–8, 71–2, 139, 156, 157
acceptance of masculinity, 16
Achilles' Heel (journal), 3, 4, 5, 18
aggression, 19–20, 24
AIDS, 29–30
anger, 7, 24, 43–4, 147, 151, 156, 189, 203
    of boys, 64, 136, 148, 154, 155
    of fathers, 83, 153–4
    fear and, 127–31
anima, 21, 43, 191
animal nature, 35, 39, 45, 71, 119
anti-sexist men's movement, 5, 6, 18, 177
appreciation of partner, 205–7
approval seeking, 26, 45, 76, 166
archetypes, 46
ashes work, 21, 56, 122–3, 131, 147
Astor, David, 74–5
authority, 114, 127
    of father, 35–6, 65–6, 82–3, 89–94, 140, 141
    respect and, 115–18, 142–3

babies, 79–80, 105–6, 110–11, 144, 145
barmitzvah, 108
Baudrillard, J., 21
beliefs, 103
Bettelheim, B., 55
biological difference, 104
birth, 79–80, 105–6
blame, 132, 171, 180, 202–4
Bly, Robert, 23, 108, 170, 177
    Iron John 6–7, 12, 16, 24, 28, 30n, 44, 55,
        74, 119, 125, 140–1, 201, 207
    competitive relationships, 173, 174
    fathers, 7, 62–3, 65, 86–7, 100–1, 107
    feminine, 41, 103, 191
    feminism, 9, 19, 39–40, 51, 62, 122, 150,
        194–5
    gay men, 25, 27–8
    grief, 161
    loss of father, 158
    myths, 54, 55–6
    warriors, 20–1, 122, 191–2
    wildness, 45–6, 104
boarding school, 49–50, 71–2, 136, 137,
    138–41, 147
body, 212
    emotional life of, 188–90
    as machine, 98, 186, 210

men and, 186–8, 193, 197
mind and, 156, 179, 184–6
bonding, 100, 105–8, 192
boundaries, 110, 114, 116, 117
boys, 5, 96–7, 201
    at boarding school, 49–50, 71–2, 136, 137,
    138–41
    feelings of, 60, 63–4, 65, 70–1, 135, 138,
    165–9, 172, 175
    mothers and, 69–73, 86, 87, 89, 197
Bush, George, 192

Callow, Simon, 29–30
caring, 126, 127, 147
change, 24, 221
childhood, 123, 141, 169, 171–2
childishness, 34–5, 36, 44–5
children, 84–5
    emotions of, 124–6
    giving time to, 112–14
    involvement with, 8, 206–7, 216–19
    irrationality of, 141–2, 146
    listening to, 141–3
    losing contact with, 149
    parents and, 84–5
    relationships with, 100, 105–7, 116, 144,
    214
        see also fathers, relationships with sons;
        daughters
    sharing feelings with, 115–16, 125, 126–7,
    217
    see also babies; boys
Christianity, 88, 95, 184, 188, 211
class
    fathers and, 90–2
    intimacy and, 109
'coming out', 25–6
communicaion, 181
    contact and, 128, 144–6
competition, 173, 174, 175–8
compromise, 26
conformism, 20
confusion about masculinity, 6, 23, 39, 103,
    201
Connell, R. W., 4
consciousness-raising groups, 5, 18, 58, 112,
    175, 177
consumerism, 28–9, 91, 130, 179

contact, 192, 216–19
  and communication, 128, 144–6
  fear of, 9, 24
  need for, 61, 63, 65
  physical, 185, 187, 193
control, 129–30, 135, 148, 154
  love and, 131–3
  power and, 197–9
  sexuality and, 185–6, 193–5
Cooper, Howard, 42

Daly, Terry, 22
denial, 6, 65, 66–9
  of emotions, 43–7, 50, 55, 66–9, 76–7, 81–2,
    121–4, 167
  experience and, 120–4
  of needs, 46, 50, 57, 98, 200
dependency, 44–7
difference, 28, 50–1, 104, 168
  integrity and, 94–7, 212–13, 220
  see also gender differences
disconnectedness, 32, 33, 150–1
disdain, 181
dominant masculinity, 3, 7, 11, 16, 38, 90,
    119, 152n, 173
  language and, 12
  Protestant moral culture and, 5, 44, 130
  reason and, 11, 38, 45, 197
dreams, 34, 35
drumming, 192

ecology, 38, 209, 211
emotional lives, 11, 98–9, 119–20, 129, 149,
    200
  bones, 188–90
  families and, 81–5
  feminism and, 131, 150–1, 182
  myths and, 53–5
emotional needs, 17, 89, 98–9, 130, 192
  communication of, 128
  denial of, 46, 50, 57, 98, 200
  and dependency, 44–7
  discounting, 63, 64
  recognition of, 166, 176
  as weakness, 38, 44, 171, 179
emotional work, 5, 46–7, 148–9, 151
emotions, 9–10, 11, 42, 151, 153–60
  acknowledging, 129, 130, 146–9, 151, 167,
    201–2
  control of, 131–3, 135
  denial of, 43–7, 50, 55, 66–9, 76–7, 81–2,
    121–4, 160–4, 167
  power and, 51–3
  reason and, 35, 41, 90, 110, 151, 156, 198
  as weakness, 5, 17, 66, 71, 83, 93, 120, 121,
    129, 137–8, 181, 190

  see also feelings
empowerment, 209–11
equality, 15, 18, 52, 206–7, 220
ethics, power and, 201–2
expectations, 80, 163, 166, 168
experience, 5, 16, 36, 113, 119–34, 200
  devaluing, 189, 194, 197, 198–9
  externalisation of, 45
  language and, 136–9
  levels of, 153–7
  reason and, 53
  subjectivity of, 36, 39, 188
expression of emotions, 146–9

fairytales, 54–5
families, 81–5, 108–9, 117
Fanon, Franz, 37
fantasies, 34, 35
fathers
  authority of, 35–6, 655–6, 82–3, 89–94, 140,
    141
  daughters and, 11, 87–8
  relationships with, 1–2, 7, 62, 63, 83, 107,
    161–2
  sons and, 63–6, 73, 85, 86–7, 99, 100–1
fear, 20–3, 24, 28, 33, 126, 138, 139
  anger and, 127–31
  of intimacy, 9, 33, 46, 173, 176, 185–6
  of rejection, 17, 33, 51, 80, 148, 172–5
feelings, 153–64
  about fathers, 63–4, 65–6, 67–8
  sharing with children, 115–16, 125, 126–7,
    217
  see also emotions
feminine aspect, 9, 21, 38, 41–4, 75, 103, 165,
    190–1
feminism, 3–4, 61, 93, 117, 158, 180, 194–5
  backlash against, 18, 19, 51, 22, 23, 41
  and ecology, 38
  and emotional lives, 131, 150–1, 182
  and gender differences, 6, 86, 87
  and masculinism, 21–2
  men's responses to, 6–7, 13–14, 17–20, 30n,
    39–40, 51, 100–1, 103, 111
  sexuality and, 185
Foucault, M., 34, 67, 193–4, 195–6n
Frankfurt School, 89, 90
freedom, 13, 121, 212, 220
Freud, Sigmund, 74, 155, 161
  emotions, 55, 67, 123, 129–30, 163, 165
  importance of fathers, 73
  individuality, 67, 76
  reality, 121, 157, 219
  sexuality, 43, 72, 190
  unconscious, 139
friendships, 61, 173, 218

gay liberation movement, 25, 26
gay men, 25, 27–30, 97
gender differences, 6, 93, 94–5, 97, 100, 104, 120, 206–7
  feminism and, 6, 86, 87
Goodison, Lucy, 46
grief, 123, 157–60, 161
guilt, 17, 170–2

happiness, 170–2, 179
histories *see* past
homophobia, 9, 25, 27, 31n, 165, 174
hurts *see* wounds

identity, 79–80, 153, 191, 199–200, 211–12
  postmodern, 32–4
  sexual, 25–30
  see also male identities
illness, 98, 186
independence, 46, 49, 50, 71, 73, 145, 175
  initiation and, 89–90
initiation, 7, 9–11, 19, 86–102, 104–5, 189
  intimacy and, 108–11
  memory and, 79–81
inner child, 34–5, 165–7, 169, 171
inner selves, 110, 133, 137, 201–2
integrity, 217
  of difference, 94–7, 220
intimacy, 178–82
  fear of, 9, 33, 46, 173, 176, 185–6
  initiation and, 108–11
Iron John (Bly) *see* Bly, Robert
isolation, 124–7, 174, 206, 218

Judaism, 95–6
Jung, Carl, 21, 42, 43, 107, 190–1

Kafka, Franz, 89–90
Kant, I., 36, 39, 67, 121, 184
knowledge, 36, 54, 67

language, 12, 79, 109, 110–11, 151
  children and, 143
  communication and, 144–6
  controlling, 135–6
  and experience, 136–9
  of myth, 55–8
learning, 79, 82, 112–13
listening, 114–15, 141–3
  and appreciating, 204–7
loss, 44
  of father, 67–9, 87, 158–9
  see also separation
lost childhood, 167–70
love, 26, 73–7, 109, 110, 112, 126, 145, 172, 182
  and control, 131–3

earning, 166
  and sex, 179–80
Lyndon, Neil, 51

macho man, 40, 49, 103
male identities, 25, 98, 161, 181, 185, 214
manhood, 62
  power and, 23–5
  transition to, 8, 9, 19, 25, 54, 86, 96–7, 99, 108, 109–10, 189–90
marginalization, 220
masculine and feminine aspects, 41–4
masculinism, 22
masculinities
  re-definition of, 25
  see also dominant masculinity; traditional masculinity
men's liberation, 2–3, 18, 195, 201
middle class families, 81–2, 108–9, 117
midrash, 96
mind, and body, 179, 184–6
modernity, 12, 32, 33, 54, 93, 94–7, 119
  and reason, 1, 34–7, 39, 53, 94, 110, 156, 210
morality, 100, 117
mothers, and sons, 69–73, 86, 87, 89, 197
mourning, 163
mythopoetic men's movement, 7, 8, 19
myths, 19, 34, 37, 141
  emotional life and, 53–5
  language, and, 55–8
  nature and, 37–40

naive men, 40, 103
National Coalition of Free Men (NCFM), 23
nature, 197–8, 202, 211
  myth and, 37–40
  see also animal nature
needs *see* emotional needs
'new lad' culture, 10
'new man' 8, 22

O'Hagan, Sean, 10
oppression, 61, 97
  of women, 99, 104, 201

past, 21, 122, 131, 146, 155, 200, 210, 220
patriarchy, 16, 17–18, 57, 77n, 220–1
personal, 3–5
pleasure, 170–2
political, 4–5
politics, and spirituality, 219–22
postmodernity, 10, 93, 96, 212–13
  feminism in, 4
  identities and, 32–4
  masculinity and, 11–13

power, 128, 155–6
  control and, 197–9
  emotion and, 51–3
  ethics and, 201–2
  manhood and, 23–5
power relations, 3, 6, 17, 22, 57, 97, 131, 175
  in the family, 85, 86, 87, 180–1, 214–15
private/public realm, 51–2, 86–9, 98, 209, 218
Promise Keepers, 7, 59n
Protestant moral culture, 16, 42, 45, 99, 137, 209–10
  dominant masculinity and, 5, 130
psychic hole, 99
psychoanalysis, 162–3, 189, 219
psychotherapy, 5, 53, 67, 68, 79, 150, 162, 168, 170–1

reality, 121–2, 123, 157, 219
reason, 54, 93, 129, 153–5, 184–5,
  children and, 141–2
  emotions and, 35, 41, 90, 110, 151, 156, 197, 198
  masculinity and, 11, 38, 41, 45, 52
  modernity and, 1, 34–7, 39, 53, 94–5, 110, 121, 210
Recreating Sexual Politics (Seidler), 6, 45, 55
Reich, Wilhelm, 188–9
rejection, 64
  fear of, 17, 33, 51, 80, 148, 172–5
relationships, 92, 165–83
  see also children, relationships with; fathers, relationships with; women, relationships with
repression, 67
resentment, 61, 110, 210–11
  towards feminism, 16, 17, 20, 22, 51, 52
respect, 66, 93, 115–18, 142–3
responsibility, 132, 171, 202–4
rules for children, 116

Sachs, Jonathan, 95–6
Segal, Lynne, 4
self, 27, 29, 80, 157, 218
  aspects of, 41–8
  initiation and, 98–101
  inner relationship to, 170, 172, 218
self-control, 35, 41-2, 90
self-esteem, 206
self-rejection, 17–18, 197, 199, 209–11
self-sufficiency, 46, 47, 60, 73, 127, 215
separation, 73–7, 105–8
sexual politics, 26, 220
sexual relationships, 24, 110
sexuality, 16–17, 23, 179–80, 184–5

Christianity, 88, 184, 209
  control and, 185–6, 193–5
  Freud and, 43, 72, 190
shame, 83, 139–41
sharing feelings, 28, 44, 58, 88–9, 99, 121, 126, 147, 150, 176–8, 191
  as boys, 53, 83
  with children, 115–16, 125, 126–7, 215, 217
Sherman, Martin, 29
Shirley Valentine (film), 125–6
Skynner, Robin, 8, 116
slavery, 95
spiritual values, 54
spirituality, 54, 200, 210, 211–13
  politics and, 219–22
spontaneity, 45–6, 138, 170
storytelling, 57
style, 10, 12
superiority, 140, 189, 203, 209, 211
  feelings of, 23, 181
support, 16, 46, 57, 110, 181, 183n, 187, 200
suppression of emotions, 156, 160–4, 168, 170, 189

theoretical, 4
time, 113–14, 145, 171
touch, 187
traditional masculinity, 7, 8, 194
  gayness and, 25, 26
trust, 132, 144

unconscious, 43, 139
Unreasonable Men (Seidler), 16, 90, 141

Vietnam War, 23, 56
violence, 5–6, 15
vitality, loss of, 20
vulnerability, ,42, ,128–9, 137, 150
  acceptance of, 201, 206
  fear of, 33
  sharing, 99, 121, 126, 176, 181, 191

war, and affirmation of masculinity, 8, 43
warriors, 20–1, 56, 58, 67, 122, 176, 191–2
weakness, 190–3
  emotions as, 5, 17, 66, 71, 83, 93, 121, 129, 137–8, 181, 190
Weber, Max, 29, 94
Weil, Simone, 79, 180, 213
Westernization, 37
Wheeler, John, 23
wildman movement, 104, 147, 175
wildness, 45, 47, 56, 104, 147
Wittgenstein, Ludwig, 12, 137, 213

women, 100, 202–3
  fathers and, 88
  oppression of, 99, 104, 201
  reason and, 92, 93, 94–5
  relationships with, 22–3, 24, 25, 62–3,
      130–2, 150, 175–7, 182, 203, 205–6,
      214–15
    emotional work in, 46–7, 86, 99, 132,
      136, 149
    ending of, 180, 204
    giving time to, 113
    superiority within, 189, 203

resentment of, 51–2
sexuality of, 185, 190
subjective experience of, 36, 39
women's movement, 2–3, 15
  see also feminism
work, 51–2, 170, 174, 176–7, 203, 214, 218
  as addiction, 129
  ethic of, 8, 161, 170
  fathers at, 90–1, 97, 161
working class families, 109, 117
wounds, 60–78, 83, 147